W9-AOS-577

The Compleat
I Hate to Cook Book

OTHER BOOKS BY PEG BRACKEN

The I Hate to Cook Book

The I Hate to Housekeep Book

I Try to Behave Myself

Appendix to The I Hate to Cook Book

I Didn't Come Here to Argue

But I Wouldn't Have Missed It for the World!

The I Hate to Cook Almanack

A Window Over the Sink

PEG BRACKEN

The Compleat
I HATE TO COOK
B O O K

DRAWINGS BY HILARY KNIGHT

Harcourt Brace Jovanovich, Publishers

SAN DIEGO   NEW YORK   LONDON

Library of Congress Cataloging-in-Publication Data
Bracken, Peg.
The compleat I hate to cook book.
Includes index.
1. Cookery.   I. Title.   II. Title: I hate to cook
book.
TX740.B627   1986   641.5   86-9990
ISBN 0-15-120480-2

Designed by Margaret M. Wagner
Printed in the United States of America
First edition
ABCDE

Table of Contents

Introduction to the Introduction

When they informed me that twenty-five years have elapsed since *The I Hate to Cook Book* appeared, I was astonished. Only think! Twenty-five long years, some longer than others. Well, some of them shorter than others too, come to think of it. But anyway, twenty-five of them, all kinds, and it just goes to show what can happen when you're not paying attention.

And then when they told me they wanted to publish the definitive *I Hate to Cook Book*, putting together in one big volume the recipes from various other books of mine that touched on cooking or not cooking, I was—well, the word is nonplussed. First, I wondered Why? Or, even, how come?

After all, a great deal of water has gone over the dam since 1961, and a great deal of dishwater down the drain. Think of all that's happened in those two and a half decades! The Moon Walk and the microwave oven. The Chinese political about-face and the electric wok. The liberated woman and the house-husband and the computerized barbecue. The word processor and the food processor, fiber optics and the transplanted heart and the fast-frozen bagel, as well as the croissantwich, your choice of tuna, lox, or ham salad. And all the international disasters, not to mention the domestic ones, like the time I got sea-sick trying to do Cherries Jubilee for fourteen people on a fast-moving boat. Oh, they were fully packed years, all right, and rich with change.

But on further reflection I found myself wondering if the culinary scene itself had really changed so much. And had the people who hate to cook? I knew I hadn't. My standard position in regard to cooking is still on the sofa with my feet up, around 5:30 P.M., thinking about it but not very hard. Dinner will be ready, dear, as soon as I decide what we're having.

In truth, there are two kinds of people in this world: the ones who don't cook out of and have *never* cooked out of *The I Hate to Cook Book*, and the other kind.

The first kind subdivides still further into two types, Type One comprising those admirable and, to me, incredible people who enjoy messing about with melon-ballers and fondue pots and filo dough, people who actually sift before measuring. They faithfully follow their Cooking Establishment gurus, and they cook splendidly, and they are very happy. Type Two began cooking in the sixties' and early seventies' communes, doing soya cutlets and veggie cupcakes and organically grown brown rice. (When their kids finally left home they headed for McDonald's and were last seen with a Big Mac in each hand and a double order of fries, not a bean sprout in sight.)

The second group—the *I Hate To Cook* people—consists mainly of those who find other things more interesting and less fattening, and so they do it as seldom as possible. Today there is an Annual Culinary Olympics, with hundreds of cooks from 44 countries ardently competing. But we who hate to cook have had our own Olympics for years, seeing who can get out of the kitchen the fastest and stay out the longest. And our children, who have grown up eating out of the *I Hate to Cook Book*, are basically of the same persuasion. Indeed, there have been some near-tragic instances of grown girls and boys leaving home for school or a job who actually stole their mothers' copies, the mothers in question having moved meanwhile to some godforsaken hole where the book was not readily available.

But now they may take heart, and so may everyone who is faced for perhaps the first time with a kitchen that's supposed to be cooked in. For here it is again—and not only the original book, containing those good things like Stayabed Stew and Sweepsteak (the mere mention of which brings sentimental tears to the eyes of twenty-and-thirty-year-olds now—why, that's Mother's Home Cooking!) but the cream of the recipes from my other books dealing mainly with food. Virtually nothing has been changed, because surprisingly enough it didn't need to be. (Where a recipe says 'shred half a cabbage', you'd use your food processor today, if you have one; otherwise you'd just go ahead and shred it.) And little has been added, except for one glorious and simple asparagus recipe that will make you Queen of the May every time you serve it, which will undoubtedly be often.

So here it is, with my earnest best wishes.
Who says you can't have it all?

—PEG BRACKEN

Introduction

Some women, it is said, like to cook.

This book is not for them.

This book is for those of us who hate to, who have learned, through hard experience, that some activities become no less painful through repetition: childbearing, paying taxes, cooking. This book is for those of us who want to fold our big dishwater hands around a dry Martini instead of a wet flounder, come the end of a long day.

When you hate to cook, life is full of jolts: for instance, those ubiquitous full-color double-page spreads picturing what to serve on those little evenings when you want to take it easy. You're flabbergasted. You wouldn't cook that much food for a combination Thanksgiving dinner and Irish wake. (Equally discouraging is the way the china always matches the food. You wonder what you're doing wrong, because whether you're serving fried oysters or baked beans, your plates always have the same old blue rims.)

And you're flattened by articles that begin "Of course you know that basil and tomatoes are soulmates, but *did* you know . . ." They can stop right there, because the fact is you didn't know any such thing. It is a still sadder fact that, having been told, you won't remember. When you hate to cook, your mind doesn't retain items of this nature.

Oh, you keep on buying cookbooks, the way a homely woman buys hat after hat in the vain hope that this one will do it. And, heaven knows, the choice is wide, from the *haute cuisine* cookbook that is so *haute* it requires a pressurized kitchen, through Aunt Em's Down-on-the-Farm Cookery Book, all the way to the exotic little foreign recipe book, which is the last thing you want when you hate to cook. Not only are there pleasanter ways to shorten your life, but, more important, your husband won't take you out for chop suey if he knows he can get good chop suey at home.

Finally, and worst of all, there are the big fat cookbooks that tell you everything about everything. For one thing, they contain too many recipes. Just look at all the things you can do with a chop, and aren't about to! What you want is just one little old dependable thing you can do with a chop besides fry it, that's all.

Also, they're always telling you what any dunderhead would know. "Place dough in pan to rise and cover with a clean cloth," they say. What did they *think* you'd cover it with?

This terrible explicitness also leads them to say, "Pour mixture into 2½ qt. saucepan." Well, when you hate to cook, you've no idea what size your saucepans are, except big, middle sized, and little. Indeed, the less attention called to your cooking equipment the better. You buy the minimum, grudgingly, and you use it till it falls apart.

But perhaps the most depressing thing about those big fat cookbooks is that you have to have one. Maybe your mother-in-law gives you a bushel of peppers or a pumpkin, and you must make piccalilli or a pumpkin pie. Well, there's nothing to do but look it up in your big fat cookbook, that's all. But you certainly can train yourself not to look at anything else.

Now, about this book: its genesis was a luncheon with several good friends, all of whom hate to cook but have to. At that time, we were all unusually bored with what we had been cooking and, therefore, eating. For variety's sake, we decided to pool our ignorance, tell each other our shabby little secrets, and toss into the pot the recipes we swear by instead of at.

I am well aware that to skilled and ardent cooks my innocent pride in these recipes will resemble that of the little man who showed up at the Patent Office last year with his new invention, designed for talking across great distances, which he had named "the telephone."

But honesty must out. If these recipes are helpful to even a few, I will consider my efforts well spent.

Then there was another factor. I've noticed that some misconceptions are being disseminated by new or newish cookbooks.

To take only one, consider those odd little books that keep pairing Cooking with Sex. For instance, how to cook him a Sunday morning breakfast that will make him propose. Then they go into such things as broiled curried orange slices.

Now we who hate to cook wouldn't dream of cooking Sunday

morning breakfast for a man until he *has* proposed. Preferably in writing. Even then, it will be good old-fashioned bacon and eggs.

Indeed, this whole tie-up of food and sex has been overdone. They don't have all that much to do with each other. Through the years, we who hate to cook find that there's usually a nice man around somewhere whether we are in one of our noncooking periods or in one of our totally noncooking periods.

(Though it's possible that cooking and sex have something to do with each other in rather an inverse way. I know a man who blissfully insists that his wife make her own kind of blackberry jam every summer, the kind, he says, that you pour on the toast. You see?)

These recipes have not been tested by experts. That is why they are valuable. Experts in their sunny spotless test kitchens can make anything taste good. But even *we* can make these taste good.

Their exact origins are misty. Some of them, to be sure, were off-the-cuff inventions of women who hate to cook and whose motivating idea was to get in and out of that kitchen fast. But most of them were copied from batter-spattered file cards belonging to people who had copied them from other batter-spattered file cards, because a good recipe travels as far, and fast, as a good joke. So, in most cases, it is impossible to credit the prime source, although the prime source was probably a good cook who liked to.

Bless her, and bow low. We who hate to cook have a respect bordering on awe for the Good Cooks Who Like to Cook—those brave, energetic, imaginative people who can, and do, cook a prime rib and a Yorkshire pudding in a one-oven stove, for instance, and who are not frightened by rotisseries. But we've little to say to them, really, except, "Invite us over often, please." And stay away from our husbands.

And, if you hate to cook, expect no actual magic here, no Escoffier creations you can build in five minutes or even ten. But you might well find some recipes you'll like—to use the word loosely—to make now and again. Perhaps you'll even find some you will take to your heart. At the very least, you should find a hands-across-the-pantry feeling, coming right through the ink. It is always nice to know you are not alone.

1. Counter Attack

PADDLING THROUGH THE COMBAT ZONE

"Take it one more round."
—ROD McKUEN

When you hate to cook, you mustn't blame yourself too much for getting ripped off at the grocer's more often than most people do. You must remind yourself that there are other areas in which you are more canny, and try to think what they are.

The fact is, eating well but cheaply is a luxury you're not prepared to pay for, in terms of either time or attention—a fuzzy-minded attitude you probably inherited from some fuzzy-minded ancestors. (Unfortunately, one must choose one's ancestors when one is hardly old enough to choose anything very intelligently.)

Also, there is no real cure for your basic impatience with comparison shopping and calculator shopping, both of which should be done in order to get the most out of food money.

Now certainly you ought to buy the weekend and midweek advertised Specials at several stores, if several stores are nearby.

But so often the Special is corned beef, when you just finished some. Or paper towels, which you bought a dozen rolls of yesterday, in an excess of domestic zeal, and you haven't room for any more. Even if you did, you don't feel like spending another penny right now on paper towels.

As for shopping with a calculator, it's just about necessary, unless you can tell instantaneously whether an 11-ounce box of cookies for ninety-eight cents is a better buy than a pound of the same cookies for a dollar-five.

Someday, perhaps, we'll have standard, clearly labeled boxes. Until then, reluctant cooks (and therefore reluctant shoppers) would rather pay the extra coppers for the cookies than work it out. Also, they sometimes feel: If it matters that much to you, you shouldn't be buying cookies anyway.

In this chapter, therefore, we'll try to stay out of the foggier areas.

Several truths shine bright as the major planets, such as the fact that a plastic lemon costs astronomically more per squirt than a bottle of reconstituted lemon juice. Nearly anyone can remember this and switch to bottled goods, unless he owns a plastic-lemon factory.

And let's look at some other facts, equally unarguable:

One 5-pound chicken is a better buy than two 2½-pound chickens, because of the more favorable meat-to-bone ratio.

Powdered milk is cheaper and works fine in your cooking. It makes a good frothy milk punch, too—milk, egg, sugar, whisky, beaten with an electric mixer.

Instant coffee costs least to drink. If you don't like it, regular coffee is next cheapest if you make it in one-cup filters, one per customer. This way people aren't drinking coffee just to drain the pot.

The grocer's or supermarket's own brand of food (or grog) is usually good, and usually cheaper than most nationally advertised brands. I think it often comes out of the same pot (or vat).

Fresh strawberry time* is the best time to eat frozen strawberries, or at any rate to buy them for your freezer if you have one. Prices are often cut then, to make room for the new season's pack.

Small boxes of anything usually cost more than large ones per ounce of food. And most things come a bit cheaper by the case.

But right here we run head on into a real problem of any one who hates to cook. I refer to those occasional will-o'-the-wisp compulsions to act housewifely—*i.e.*, take advantage of Good Buys. And this can lead to a freezer compartment or a pantryful of food that you never feel like cooking. (These housewifely compulsions generally melt away the minute you get the Good Buys home.)

---

* Or fresh asparagus time or bean time and so on.

Point One, therefore, is to buy in quantity only what you like and automatically use, most of the time. I mean staples, like ketchup and coffee, not Fringe Foods like asparagus and shrimp.

Of course, these are personal matters, and one man's Fringe Food is another man's staple. But whatever your Fringe Foods are, if you buy them in quantity they'll probably prove to be an extravagance without being any fun, and that's the worst kind.

Point Two, closely related, is to have some general notion of how long things keep.

Canned and deep-frozen foods are regarded by most of us as immortal, although they are not. The chances are that you will outlive them, because you'll get tired of looking at them.

On the whole, canned food has better staying power than deep-frozen. If they are good sound cans, no dents or leaks, and if you keep them at about 70°F, they'll be good for about three years.* This assumes, however, that you got them newly hatched, when in reality they might have been on the grocer's or wholesaler's shelves for months. That's something to consider.

To keep deep-frozen foods their maximum length of time, you need a fine rapport between your own deep-freezer (if you have one) and the grocer's. Each should be at 0°F. You can check your own with a freezer thermometer, and if it's wrong have it repaired. But you can't always see the grocer's thermometer, and he won't always tell you. If these things matter greatly to you, you may have to change grocers, though my own tendency is not to worry too much over a degree or two among friends.

Assuming then, that the temperature situation is well in hand, it might be well to look at some facts about storing things, on the chance that a few will stick.

These deep-frozen foods won't necessarily poison you after the time limit, though the fish might, but they won't taste very good.

FROZEN FOODS YOU'D BETTER EAT WITHIN 12 MONTHS
| Most meat | Vegetables |
| Fruit | |

FROZEN FOODS YOU'D BETTER EAT WITHIN 6 MONTHS
| Pork | Fish |
| Poultry | Cheese |

FROZEN FOODS YOU'D BETTER EAT WITHIN 2 OR 3 MONTHS
| Cured pork sausage | Hamburgers |
| Bacon | Cooked Foods |

* Though pickles and sauerkraut may die in a year.

Clearly, it would be smart to date the frozen foods the minute they come home, but one seldom does.

Then there's the matter of mixes.

When you buy something ready-mixed or prepared, you're buying labor, of course, which is why it costs more. It is often a good bargain, too, if you like the product.

On the other hand, it seems silly to buy the seasoned flour you shake and bake your chicken in: Or, when you buy crumbed fish— and crumbing fish is easy to do—you may be buying about as much bread as fish. And it isn't very hard to add raisins to cereal or water to your own pancake flour, and it's usually cheaper.

Next, we come to the matter of premiums.

Some people enjoy getting anything short of a poke in the eye if they get it for nothing, or think they do. And—few things being free in this world—if it pleases you to think you found one, there's certainly no reason to pass it up.

For instance, if all you were looking for was a dry mop to rearrange the dust with, and you find one as cheap as the rest that's attached to an ABSOLUTELY FREE inferior plastic alarm clock, this is a little bonus. So you might as well take it along, because some days you don't want to get up anyway.

But one should be careful not to let the tail wag the dog, not to get a mop solely because an inferior flashlight comes with it, or a jar of jam because it's in one of those dandy reusable containers.

THINGS TO BEWARE OF

I believe the Irritant Quotient, or I.Q., of the reluctant cook is higher than most people's, and this can lead to unnecessary trouble.

For instance, from a standing start, she can get sicker quicker than most people do hearing a little jingle like "Nothing says lovin' like something from the oven." Or when an ad tries to sell her Sex when all she wants at the moment is Orange Juice, she'll sometimes make a violent mental note never to buy that brand.

However, this can be cutting off her own nose. The product may be perfectly all right, and even a good buy. It is the advertising agency, usually, and not the manufacturer that puts the Freud into the food. The manufacturers go along with it because they are basically good simple food people who are over-impressed by the ad-men.

So you must shut your eyes and often your ears to these things and simply consider the taste, the size, and the price.

Then there is the matter of the new packaging. Sometimes you'd rather like to know why the manufacturer changed the old one. Did the other fellows change theirs, and he's only following suit? Or did he, perhaps, put a thicker bottom on the bottle so that it holds only 6 ounces now instead of 7½, though it's priced the same?

(In a recent inquiry, a food packer explained, in some of the most enchantingly backside-to reasoning since *Alice in Wonderland*, that he lessened the quantity so that the customer wouldn't have to pay a higher price.)

When something like this comes to your attention, you can register a negative vote by buying something else. It probably won't change anything immediately, but it will make you feel better.

There is also the heavy thumb gambit. Sometimes you might try making an informal check, yourself, to see whether the prepacked ten pounds of potatoes weighs ten pounds or nine and a half.

And the check-out counter presents pitfalls. Grocers used to train their cashiers to put the fresh tomatoes in the bottom of the bag, then drop in the canned pineapple from a considerable height.

They don't do this so much any more. But now some grocers, the rascals, teach the help to throw in the price of an extra item once in a while on a long list where it probably won't be noticed. If it *is* noticed, it's an Oops, sorry about that. (When you read about the handsome sums grocers lose annually to shoplifters, you marvel that more grocers don't do it. Still, we teach our children that they mustn't cheat just because Johnny does.)

In any case, it's a good idea for the customer to count purchases, periodically, and even total them herself if she can add that far. Not often, just once in a while. This will help keep the boys on the straight-and-narrow, and the customer solvent.

Speaking of lists, supermarkets rather count on your not making one, for few people do, in this day of the impulse buy.

Preoccupied cooks are exceptionally listless and therefore impulse prone. They face an additional hazard—that of buying something twice or three times. I once ended up with three little jars of fenugreek—I needed some for a recipe I was supposed to try but kept postponing. Each time I'd make a new resolve to try the recipe, I'd buy another jar of it, because I knew I wasn't the sort of person who kept exotic things like fenugreek around the house.

It's a good idea, therefore, for the person who hates to cook to stand and stare at her own food shelves and spice cupboard now and then, to make sure of what she has or hasn't.

Though she'll probably never be a list-maker, she may find the following Mental Crutch helpful for making a list in her head as she drives or strolls along:

One—Run	Eight—Gate	Fifteen—Lifting
Two—Zoo	Nine—Wine	Sixteen—Licking
Three—Tree	Ten—Den	Seventeen—Leavening
Four—Door	Eleven—Football team	Eighteen—Waiting
Five—Alive	Twelve—Delve	Nineteen—Pining
Six—Stick	Thirteen—Hurting	Twenty—Horn of Plenty
Seven—Heaven	Fourteen—Courting	

Assume, then, that you need (1) Butter (2) Baking Chocolate (3) Nutmeg. . . . You tie Run vividly to Butter in your mind: you're splashing through yellow puddles of it, running over tall buttery mountains. Then, when you want to remember the first thing on your list, you think One, and your mind steps neatly from One to Run to Butter. Or it should. And so you proceed, chocolate-coating the animals at the zoo, and so on up to twenty, if you like, and lots of luck.

I've stressed the list here because—mental or written—it is still the main weapon in the customer's small armory. And heaven knows we need something. It's unsettling to find you've spent the price of a good record or a new shirt on food you didn't know you needed till you saw it. (The unwilling cook would rather run amok in a clothes shop or a bookshop than a supermarket.)

Yet never have products looked so appealing, nor food people found us so embarrassingly predictable.

For instance, they know we hate to stoop. They've found that we're twice as apt to reach for things at see level as we are at knee level.

They know we'll often buy four of something marked four for a dollar, when we wouldn't buy it individually for 25 cents.

They've learned that we flock sheep-like when they heap things high and cluttered somewhere, without reducing the price of the items at all.

They've found also—and this surprised me—that quantities of things appeal to us far more than one or two. That is, if there are fifty identical cans of Jean's Beans on the shelf, we don't say to ourselves, "My, there's a lot of Jean's Beans left—I guess nobody likes them very much." No, we reach for a couple. But if there are only two cans of Jean's Beans there, we will probably reach for something else.

It is interesting to ponder why we react like this, or anyway you might get ten seconds or so out of it, on a dull morning.

2. Good Cooksmanship

OR HOW TO TALK A GOOD FIGHT

Now once in a while you'll find yourself in a position where you have to talk about cooking. This is usually a sitting-down position with other ladies hemming you in so you can't get away.

Actually, your cooking is a personal thing, like your sex life, and it shouldn't be the subject of general conversation. But women who love to cook often love to talk about it, too, and if you're going to make any sort of show, there are several points to keep in mind.

For instance, words.

Never say "fry" if you don't mean "deep-fat fry." You can say

> "sauté"
> "brown in butter"
> "sizzle in butter"

or you may go all the way and say "cook it *à la pôele*," which is a French phrase meaning "stew in butter at such a low temperature that the object is cooked before it starts to brown." But "fry" means the way you would cook doughnuts, if you ever did, which you don't, because you can buy perfectly lovely doughnuts all made.

(The boys behind the counter at Joe's Café aren't aware of these distinctions, of course, and if you ask them to sauté you an egg, or cook one *à la pôele*, there's no telling what sort of an *oeuf* you'd get. But you are not down at Joe's Café.)

Similarly, if you can possibly avoid it, don't say "onions." Say "shallots," even though you wouldn't know one if you saw one. This gives standing to a recipe that otherwise wouldn't have much. You're on safe territory if anyone calls you on the shallot business, too, because shallot also means a small green onion, as well as some distant and exotic relative of the onion family, so don't worry a bit.

Another one is "cooking sherry." Just say "sherry." Actually, cooking sherry is quite satisfactory for your modest purposes in most hot cooked entrées. It is cheaper to use, too, because you don't nip as you cook, and, moreover, it saves you on salt. But I'm warning you, the cooking experts will raise their eyebrows. And while we're at it, you might glance over the following greatly abbreviated list:

NAUGHTY WORDS	GOOD WORDS
crisp	crispy
hot	piping hot
cold	chilled
put in the oven	pop in the oven
it tastes good with . . .	it's a good foil for . . .
light brown	golden
top with bacon	garnish with crispy bacon curls

This brings us to another related department, and it is a good thing it does. You've no idea how hard it is to organize a cookbook, with all the different things in it. Next time, I'm going to write a Western with just a horse and a hero.

However, the department we now find ourselves in is FANCY GARNISHES, and those mad gay touches that are yours alone. These are the things you see in cookbooks and magazines that have you thinking, "Now that's a bright idea; I ought to *do* that," but you never remember to.

Well, here they are again. I must emphasize, though, that things that seem mad and gay to us who hate to cook are probably pretty routine to the people who love to. You see, when you hate to cook, you are singularly unobservant where cooking and food are concerned. You're also easily impressed; and if you ever do anything so foreign to your nature as floating a lemon slice on soup, you talk about it for weeks afterward.

Well, a lemon slice isn't the only thing you can float on soup.

There's popcorn. Plain popcorn or cheese popcorn. It looks pretty and it's easier than croutons.

Then there are chopped walnuts, pecans, or toasted almonds, any one of which is good on cream of chicken or celery soup.

There's also chopped raw celery or green pepper or green onion tops for any sort of soup that needs some additional crispness.

Then there are fancy garnishes in general.

For instance, with any sort of melon you can serve a bowl of chopped crystallized ginger or powdered ginger.

You can garnish nearly any meat, hot or cold, with chutneyed peach halves. You brush the fresh or canned peach halves with melted butter, put them in a 350°F oven for 10 minutes, then fill the halves with chutney and heat them *another* 5 minutes.

And to garnish fish, you can dip small bunches of white seedless grapes first in lemon juice or egg white and then in granulated sugar, dry them on a rack, and scatter them around the serving dish.

Then, if you've bought some frozen chicken pies, you can stud their tops thickly with almonds (blanched but not toasted, because that'll happen while the pies bake) before you put the pies in the oven.

Should you ever be so foolish as to make cream-cheese balls for a canapé, you may stick thin pretzel sticks into them instead of toothpicks. That way the whole thing gets eaten, and you don't have your ash trays overflowing with toothpicks. (This works just as well, of course, with cubed processed cheese.)

This is as good a place as any to digress briefly into the gay mad aspects of the *container* department, or, what you serve things *in*. For instance, the clever hostess often serves her crackers in a brandy glass! This would seem to leave her the cracker barrel to serve her brandy in, but then a lively party is probably what she's after.

You may use tall beer glasses for your parfaits, too. Or middle-sized brandy glasses. Or ordinary water goblets. The only thing to be careful of here is to make sure you have a fine complete glassware service, containing parfait glasses you *could* have used. Otherwise you just look terribly valiant.

Then there are napkin rings. The ordinary person puts napkins in them, but the clever hostess has bottoms put in hers and uses them for cigarette cups. Or instead of serving a liqueur in her elongated liqueur glasses, she puts one or two little flowers in them, like hyacinths or pansies, and puts them between each pair of place settings, instead of having one floral centerpiece. This, of course, uses up her liqueur glasses, but we can assume that she's serving Irish Coffee.

However, this is far too big a field to cover in the small space available here. To sum up: When you are looking for something to put something in, think of an *unlikely* object to put it in—jam in the eggcups, flowers in the chamberpot, bats in the bird cage—and then *do* it.

And so, back to food, and conversations about it. There are four handy words to remember: OF COURSE I ALWAYS . . . This is your lead-in for any of those little touches you want to get across. Never cry, "Girls! I tried the oddest thing the other day, and it tasted just marvelous! What I did was . . ." No, you understate it, you throw it away, with "Of course, I always mix my dry mustard with white wine" and if you're among people who'll believe anything, you can substitute champagne for white wine, for this is highly regarded in certain circles I don't belong to.

The big thing is to remember those four little words, OF COURSE I ALWAYS . . .

. . . add a quarter of a cup of sesame seeds to my sage-onion chicken stuffing

. . . drop a couple of chocolate bits into my demitasse for a good mocha taste

. . . dip fish and chops in biscuit mix or pancake flour before I fry them

. . . brush steaks or chops with soy sauce before I broil them

. . . add some tarragon to my scrambled eggs

. . . add a little marjoram to the garlic in my garlic bread

. . . add a little chervil to my ordinary biscuit mix

. . . add a little brandy to my pumpkin pie

. . . put a little grated orange peel in my cranberry sauce

. . . blend chopped parsley and a dash of lemon juice with butter and put a dollop of it on broiled steaks

. . . put a little red wine in my onion soup

. . . fatigue my lettuce

This last, incidentally, is a nice gambit in conversations of this sort, because chances are good that someone will ask you what it means. It means to toss your salad greens with just a drop or two of oil—so that each leaf gets a microscopically thin coating—*before* you add your salad dressing. For some reason, it makes the greenery crisper.

Now, there is one more thing we must consider in this chapter: THE SPECIALTY.

These days it is important to have a specialty, because you never can tell on what bright sunny morning you may wake up and discover that you are a celebrity. Perhaps you were the eleven-billionth person to go over the Golden Gate Bridge, or maybe you had ten children in two years, all quintuplets.

No matter. The reporters will arrive, and the second thing they'll ask you for, after your measurements, is your Kitchen Specialty. You owe it to yourself and to your public to have something on tap besides tuna sandwiches.

". . . Miss Sugar Belle, 37-22-35, star of the current hit, Holler Down a Rain Barrel, *writer, producer, and star of her own TV show, author of the current bestseller* Wheee for Me!, *wife of handsome TV tenor Vic Ricotta, and mother of four strapping teenage boys, was interviewed in the rambling oak-beamed sewing room of her rambling oak-beamed farmhouse.*

'Yes, I always design and make my own clothes,' she told this reporter, 'as well as breeding Bedlingtons and doing all the electrical repairs around the place.'

'But when you're as busy as you are, Miss Belle,' we asked, 'how do you find time to keep that big good-looking husband of yours happy?'

Sugar Belle twinkled that famous Sugar Belle twinkle, got up, and moved out to the rambling oak-beamed kitchen.

'Why, honey child,' she said, 'I just whomp him up a batch of my little ole Cotton-pickin' Jam Tarts!' "

COTTON-PICKIN' JAM TARTS

4½ oz. cream cheese	1 cup flour
¼ lb. butter	jam or preserves

Sugar Belle melts her butter, blends it with the cheese, and stirs in the flour to make a nice smooth dough. Then she puts it in the freezing compartment for about an hour, until it's firm. Next, she nips little pieces off, about the size of golf balls, rolls them out, trims them into squares, and puts a teaspoon of jam on each. (If you wonder why Sugar Belle doesn't just roll the whole thing out and cut it into squares, it is because the dough is hard to handle that way.) Then she folds them into triangles, seals the edges with a floured fork, and bakes them on a greased baking sheet at 450°F until they're brown, which is from 10 to 15 minutes. And when she puts a big plateful of these in front of her husband, you just ought to see his face light up!

You see, the recipe for your specialty needn't be complicated. In fact, it had better not be, because there is always the off-chance that someday you might have to demonstrate. It just needs to be good and a little bit interesting, that's all. Any of the following four recipes would work out all right for you, too.

SUGAR BELLE'S RYE DROP CAKES

(And believe me, everybody in Sugar Belle's family gets up early for these.)

1 egg	1 cup rye flour
1 teaspoon baking soda	½ cup white flour
1 cup buttermilk	pinch of salt
	deep fat for frying

She beats that egg with enthusiasm. Then she mixes the baking soda with the buttermilk till it fizzes up. Deftly, she adds this to the egg, then sifts the flours and salt, and mixes everything together. Finally, she drops spoonfuls of it into hot fat—at doughnut (very high) temperature—and lets them bob around till they're brown. Then she serves them with butter and individual saucers of maple syrup to dunk them in.

When Sugar Belle is having some famous directors and writers and everybody over for an *intime* after-the-theater supper, she loves to serve:

SUGAR BELLE'S SOUR CREAM MUSHROOMS
4–5 Servings

4 cups mushrooms, thickly sliced	1 cup sour cream
3 tablespoons butter	salt, pepper

She sautés the mushrooms in a heavy pan. When they are *barely* tender, she adds the sour cream and cooks it very slowly, or else it might curdle up and embarrass her no end. When the sauce has thickened, she adds the salt and pepper and serves it on toast.

She has one more specialty, too, which she'll carry on about for hours if you let her. Says it's good by itself and tremendous with barbecued steak, chicken, or chops. She calls it her own:

HELLZAPOPPIN CHEESE RICE
6 Servings

4 cups rice, cooked	small pinch each of thyme and marjoram
4 eggs	
2 tablespoons minced onion	1 package chopped, cooked frozen spinach
1 tablespoon Worcestershire sauce	
1 teaspoon of salt	1 cup milk
1 pound grated sharp Cheddar	4 tablespoons melted butter

She beats the eggs till they're light. Then she adds the milk and all the seasonings. Finally, she folds in the cheese, spinach, and rice, and pours the whole works into a greased casserole. After she pours the melted butter over it, she sets it in a 375°F oven to bake for 35 minutes and she takes off her apron.

Understand now—you and Sugar Belle needn't actually *make* these things. Unless you are absolutely cornered, you merely need to *talk* about making them. For, while they're all good and easy, still it is more trouble to make them than not to make them; and my feelings will not be a bit hurt if you don't. I will understand.

3. Cooking if Alone

EATING WITH YOUR SHOES OFF

". . . In the middle of the woods
Lived the Yonghy-Bonghy-Bo. . . ."
—EDWARD LEAR

It is a barefooted fact that cooking and eating alone can be remarkably relaxing. There is no one to comment on the fact that it's meatloaf again or to interrupt with larger issues when you want to talk about smaller ones, and vice versa.

Not that it is completely clear sailing, even so. One of the reefs that you can strike when you hate to cook, is that some of the best things are big.

For instance, an important thing to know about cooking for yourself is how to cook a Prime Rib for one person. You can then have a couple of slabs of lovely juicy rosy-rare roast beef whenever you like, without wallowing in leftover meat, or paying too much for one slice of it in a restaurant.

We'll come to that in a minute, after we look at the problem itself—the problem of cooking to stay alive when there's no one there to see, and you can accordingly get by with anything.

The problem hasn't really been solved by several recent books on the subject, which tell you how to make Pickled-Beet-and-Macaroni Salad for One, or Ox Tongue with Raisin Sauce for One, and that sort of thing. These books don't get to the heart of it. Their authors, who obviously like to cook, have no idea what people who don't are willing to put up with, in exchange for the sheer joy of not cooking. The minimal cooking done in these situations is truly breathtaking.

I know an elderly lady whose breakfast is whole-wheat toast, bacon, and coffee; whose lunch is a vitamin pill with a Metrecal chaser; and whose dinner is an 'Old-Fashioned' and something frozen. She's the healthiest elderly lady you ever saw, too, as I happen to know, because she is my mother.

What she relies on to make those frozen dishes extra-palatable is a remote-control box for her television set, to cut off the commercials. (She finds it impossible to eat with all those people whining about their underarm odor and their dandruff.)

I also know a man who lives alone—hates to cook—and never tires of frozen spinach soufflé, which is fortunate, because that's all he ever has for dinner at home besides a pan-fried chop or a steak. Sometimes he pours ready-mix cheese sauce on the soufflé. Not always.

And I know a girl who leans heavily on eggs. Hard-boiled. Soft-boiled. Scrambled. Or, in rare moments of culinary enterprise, in a Spanish omelette. She simmers, in butter, some onion, green pepper, and chopped fresh tomato (I believe that's where the Spanish comes in). Then she pours it over the omelette.

I asked her if she didn't get tired of eggs, and she cackled that she did, but they were still better than cooking.

—But enough of case histories, and back to the Prime Rib.

BACHELOR'S BEEF

(Or, How to cook a prime rib for one.)

Ask the butcher for 1 rib of beef. This will weigh around two and a half pounds.

It's important that you freeze it, because it must be roasted frozen. So wrap it in foil and do so. (You should have thought of this yesterday.)

An hour and a half before you want to eat, take it out, unwrap it, and rub it all over with garlic, if you like garlic, and then with a tablespoon of salad oil or olive oil.

Stand it on its side in a baking pan, propped against two scrubbed or peeled baking potatoes. Roast it at 400° for one hour and twenty-five minutes if you like it rare; 10 minutes more if you like it fairly well done. Let it stand 5 minutes before you slice it.

I did this one night when I had a guest. There was enough left over for good cold beef the next night and several sandwiches thereafter, which I consider a good bargain.

Other than the Prime Rib, meat is easy for the person who cooks and eats alone. The grilled or pan-fried steak (from T-bone to Minute), the chop, the ham slice, the sausage, and the hamburger take care of most situations when you're meat-minded.

Still, hamburger can pose a problem, as illustrated by the case of a friend of mine. Several months ago she bought and froze two pounds of ground chuck, thinking some day she'd make a meat loaf. But she could never remember to thaw it in time, and so she always had something else. At last reports, the frozen chopped steak was still there, and when she moves the next tenant will probably take it over with the apartment. (And he'd better read the information on pages 7–8.)

Three Ways with Hamburger

Certainly there are hundreds of hamburger variations, but the Plain or Classic is still best for day-in day-out wear. A good easy system is this:

> Mix lean ground round beef lightly with:
> a pinch of minced onion flakes
> 1 teaspoon beef bouillon, powdered, or a crumbled cube.

If you want to be positive your hamburger will be moist, add a teaspoon of water. Logically enough, this will see to it. But I don't know why it shouldn't be moist anyway if the meat is all right and you don't overcook it.

Shape this into a rather thick cake—1¾ inches—and put it in a very hot iron frying pan in which you've sprinkled some salt. No fat. Fry it at high heat, about five minutes per side, depending on how pink you like it in the middle.

The second way is to chop plenty of carrots, celery, and onion into the chopped meat before you shape it into a patty. This is minor health insurance for people who resist vegetables. Then cook it the same way.

The third way is:

POOR LONELY MAN'S POIVRADE

*(Which you will like if you like pepper, and pepper
steak, but won't if you don't. Pepper steak or Steak au Poivre is a
yes-and-no proposition.)*

Crush a tablespoonful of whole peppercorns with a blender or potato masher or wooden-spoon handle or pestle, whatever you have. Then roll the chopped-meat patty in it so it's thoroughly coated, and fry it in butter. When it is done, salt the patty, put a little more butter in the pan and a tablespoon of dry vermouth (or other dry white wine), mix it around, pour it over the patty, and eat it.

Before we get any farther into the pantry, let's list here some equipment you will probably enjoy having:

A rack or stand for books and newspapers—the sort that holds them open—in case you decide to dispense with the television set altogether and read, which you may do with never a by-your-leave. Indeed, one of the blessings of solitary dining is its engaging informality. I often think of my grandmother, one of whose pleasures it was, when alone, to take out her teeth and eat ice cream.

A good frozen-food knife with a strong serrated edge, preferably electric.

A good can-opener. Electric ones are fine if you can stand the noise.

A good supply of varied bottled cocktails or aperitifs, if you like one before dinner.

Vitamin pills. It's best to have your doctor's advice here. Otherwise you'll probably waste money on vitamins you don't need. Vitamins seem to come in and go out like the tides, and it's hard to remember which ones are passé and which are currently hot.

Now for some other mainstays besides meat.

As indicated earlier, the reluctant solo cook is rather a creature of habit, who tends to major in one—and only one—of several eating patterns.

1. The English Muffin (or soft roll) with Something on It
2. The Egg with Something under It
3. The Milk Shake with Something in It
4. The Soup with Something beside It
5. The Baked Potato with Something over It

That is, when the chips are down and the freezer contains mainly what you don't feel like thawing or eating, it will be one of these you revert to. So let us take a brief look at each one.

1. THE ENGLISH MUFFIN

For Muffin you may read Toast or Hamburger Bun or French Roll. In fact, you can read Open-Sandwich here and be perfectly correct. If you prefer a closed sandwich, you can put the other muffin half or bread slice on top. But there's no reason to unless you're going to put it in your pocket and take it somewhere, for it's only starchier and not so attractive.

The first step is the same: slice it with a sharp knife. When it's toasted, butter it, and (2) place something on it, whatever you can find that seems likely. Then (3) top it with something else, and (4) slide it under the broiler for a moment. Step 4 is often unnecessary, and is mainly employed to give the illusion of something hot. The combinations in the following list in which broiling really improves things are marked with a B.

Arrangements are endless, of course, and some are better than others. It depends on what is in one's rather erratically stocked pantry.

TOP:	shrimp	any smoked fish	
MIDDLE:	hard-boiled egg in mayonnaise	cream cheese or sour cream	
BOTTOM:	muffin or bread	muffin or bread	
TOP:	fried egg	slice of cheese (B)	
MIDDLE:	onion slice	fried egg	
BOTTOM:	muffin or bread	muffin or bread	
TOP:	sardines	scoop of Camembert (B)	
MIDDLE:	potato salad	cooked bacon, tomato	
BOTTOM:	muffin or bread	muffin or bread	
TOP:	cucumbers	slice of beef	
MIDDLE:	smoky-cheese spread	slice of onion	
BOTTOM:	muffin or bread	muffin or bread, spread with blue cheese	
TOP:	Parmesan cheese	cooked bacon	
MIDDLE:	tuna in mayonnaise	peanut butter	
BOTTOM:	muffin or bread	muffin or bread	
TOP:	canned pizza sauce (B)	jam	
MIDDLE:	onion slice	cream cheese	
BOTTOM:	muffin or bread	muffin or bread	
TOP:	cheese, cooked bacon (B)		
MIDDLE:	chutney		
BOTTOM:	muffin or bread		

Finally, in this department, a good curry-flavored spread. It takes chopping, but it goes far and keeps well, covered in the refrigerator.

CURRIED SPREAD

Mix together:

1 cup chopped ripe olives	½ cup mayonnaise
4 thinly sliced green onions	½ teaspoon salt
1½ cups grated cheese	½ teaspoon curry powder

Spread it on a toasted muffin half and broil it till the cheese melts. This is equally good, of course, on any kind of toasted bread or split roll.

2. THE EGG

If you automatically think Eggs when you're wondering what to eat, you should automatically think Big Eggs when you're at the supermarket. Little ones are no bargain, and I don't know why the hens bother to lay them. If a recipe calls for one egg, a small one can often spoil it. All the recipes written today assume that you're using large eggs.

The egg group is closely allied to the muffin group, as we have seen. Indeed, it is sometimes hard to say whether a dish is an egg on a muffin or a muffin under an egg.

Egg eaters have their comfortable habits, too: soft-boiled, hard-boiled, scrambled with diced ham or Spam. . . . And sometimes they branch out, putting a fried egg on a slice of fried corned beef. Or they spread anchovy paste on toast and put a poached egg on it. If they are quite rich, they buy Hollandaise to put on it. (They'd never make it.)

Another good egg arrangement is:

WOLFE EGGS

*(Which differ from chicken eggs in that they came out of a
Nero Wolfe mystery story.)*

Fry 2 pieces of bread on both sides in plenty of butter, then spread them with liver paté. (You could use deviled ham, but it was liver paté in the book.) Either fry gently or poach 2 eggs, one for each slice of bread. Place them on the bread, sprinkle generously with Parmesan cheese, and slide them under the broiler for just a minute.

3. THE MILK SHAKE

The very term Milk Shake implies that you have a blender,* which is devoutly to be hoped, when you hate to cook and live alone. Though you'll use it only for a milk shake and, at rare intervals, crumbs or soups, it is well worth having. When you are healthy, it saves you time and effort, and when you are sick, alone, it can practically save your life. When you have the flu, for example, a milk shake with an egg and brandy can be edible or drinkable when little else is.

A big point about the milk shake is that it's hard to make a bad one. Though proportions are basically

1 cup milk
1 average scoop of ice cream
2 tablespoons syrup or 1 teaspoon flavoring

you can vary them according to what you have. It will be thicker or thinner or fruitier or not so fruity but still good.

When you count heavily on milk shakes and haven't too much ice-cream storage space, vanilla is the best kind to keep on hand, because it combines well with so many things:

frozen or canned fruit
rum, brandy, whisky (or rum or brandy
    flavoring)
instant coffee
sliced bananas
thawed frozen fruit-juice concentrates
fruit, chocolate, or caramel syrup

And that is only a start. Add sugar if it seems to need it, or an egg if you want extra nourishment.

4. THE SOUP

Soup devotees have an easy time of it. Usually they prefer the dehydrated and then the canned, in that order. Or they mix a couple of cans in the blender. But the selection all around is limitless, and they haven't a problem. With a roll or crackers, and fruit or a bakery fruit pie, they consider themselves fed.

5. THE BAKED POTATO

People who depend subconsciously on baked potatoes sometimes depend, as well, on an aluminum nail to bake one quickly. This cuts the

* of which more in Chapter 21.

time in half, and the baking from inside out seems to improve the potato.

Then they butter, salt, and pepper it and eat it.

For a special occasion, they might use it as a base for something else—cheese sauce or canned chicken à la king or creamed canned tuna. But not often.

Or, in a burst of unprecedented kitchen activity, they can simmer ¼ pound of fresh mushrooms in about 3 tablespoons of butter, add half a cupful of sour cream, simmer it till it's hot, and pour it over the split baked potato. With a tall glass of wine or vegetable juice, this is a good dinner.

In addition to cleaving with fair consistency to one of the categories we just passed, the reluctant solo cook usually shows an unswerving loyalty to a small group of prepared pantry items, if they taste all right and are easy enough. Another person might start to twitch after the second night on Corn Chowder, with a probable third coming up. But not the people who hate to cook. It appeals to them—as Mt. Everest did to Mallory—because it is *there*.

Other things that can be steady and comforting friends, depending on your personal taste buds, are:

> canned corned beef with some Worcestershire sauce and chopped onion added. Fry it crisp. If you have any Swiss or Cheddar, grate a little on top and let it melt under the broiler;
> canned ravioli, with plenty of Parmesan;
> chili. Heat and serve plain or pour over the Classic Hamburger.

The list can go on and on, for everyone has favorites.

And while we're touching ever so delicately on seafood, a good swift recipe is

OLD STONY-LONESOME'S SEAFOOD NEWBURG

½ cup canned cream sauce
½ cup crabmeat
¼ cup cooked shrimps

Heat the cream sauce (to make it on your own, mix 1 tablespoon flour, 1 tablespoon butter, and ½ cup milk), then add 2 teaspoons sherry and the seafood. Bake it in a casserole for 20 minutes at 350°F with crumbs on top if you have some.

THE MATTER OF VEGETABLES

Getting enough vegetables is no problem if you like them. You munch raw carrots, turnips, celery, and so forth, and you don't mind making a meal of tiny canned French peas (drained and heated with lettuce and onion and butter).

But this happy attitude isn't shared by everyone. Like curly hair or a taste for opera, it's probably something you're born with. If you didn't happen to be, your solution is usually to throw out some old lettuce every couple of weeks (because you buy it even though you don't eat much of it, and it goes west with remarkable speed).

The average delicatessen isn't much help. Delicatessens usually specialize in the macaroni or potato sort of salad, which isn't what you need. Also, you could buy half a dozen cabbages for the price of a pound of their coleslaw. (See, incidentally, page 252.)

In this situation, if you customarily eat lunch out, you can make lunchtime Garden Produce Time, at a place where the soups and salads are good.

For home consumption, you can look into the dehydrated salad dressings, which are usually better than the bottled. If it is a good strong-flavored one, like Roquefort, you'll find you can taste hardly anything through it. You can also mix it with a package of the frozen mixed vegetables, cooked and chilled, and eat it till it's gone.

It is wise to keep big cans of vegetable juice around, and drink a glass now and again. Some brands taste quite all right, even without the vodka. If they don't, celery salt and Tabasco may help.

Another good approach to the vegetable is a can of concentrated beef consommé, chilled until it's jelled, then casually mixed with almost any salad vegetable or combination of them.

These could be:

> coarsely chopped tomato
> coarsely chopped avocado
> coarsely chopped cucumber
> thinly sliced zucchini squash
> watercress or parsley.

Put it all in a chilled bowl, with a lemon wedge on the side.

This is a good breakfast on a hot morning, by the way, and it is also handy to remember as a first course for dinner, should you be feeding a guest. It gives the impression that you eat better than you do, and that they are eating more than they are. It is a good put-off —the old British boardinghouse term for something that partially fills the stomach before the roast appears and thus makes the meat go farther.

THE MATTER OF DESSERTS

Desserts are fruit, or a bakery cake—or a frozen cake, or a bag of chocolate bars, or *marrons glacés* over some ice cream (and it is marvelous how much longer the marrons last when there is only you to eat them). In other words, you never make desserts, you buy them.

I read an article once about cooking for one that gave directions for an easy one-person mousse. You whip ½ cup of heavy cream, add ½ cup of crushed strawberries, with a little sugar, then freeze for three hours. But the reluctant cook sees—with that swift grasp of essentials that distinguishes her every move—that it would have a basically strawberries-in-ice-cream taste, and be more work. She might just as well buy some vanilla ice cream and pour the berries over it. Which is what she does.

THE MATTER OF SHOPPING

Recently, a man I know wanted to buy a compact car. When he exclaimed over the high price of one, the salesman shrugged and said, "Well, if you want economy, you gotta pay for it."

This is truly the case when the solo cook buys groceries. Even so, the Tiny Extravagant is cheaper in the long run than the Large Economy. When you shrewdly buy five pounds of potatoes at a resounding bargain price, you bask in the glow of it for weeks, while the potatoes sprout quietly away. So it's best to buy small amounts of everything except possibly the canned or dehydrated stand-bys you know you'll eat.

And you should not forget about dried foods when you're cooking, or not cooking, for yourself. Powdered milk is good to keep handy, unless you drink so much fresh milk that you can depend on yourself to have it around. The powdered kind makes good milk shakes and milk punches, too.

Dried fruit is handy—more dependable than fresh, cheaper than frozen, and has interesting possibilities. You can put plump dried prunes in a jar, cover with gin, and leave them for a week. (Be sure they're the plump ones, for the hard wrinkled kind will just sit there squinting at you, no matter how much gin they're in.) These are good with after-dinner coffee.

Frozen foods are fine, of course, though they're still not the entire answer. There is a limit of the number of TV dinners you can eat (and some people reach it with the first one).*

The best answer, I think, is to buy nothing from a feeling of duty (*I really should eat more carrots*) or economy (*I loathe Brussels sprouts but they're good value*). Instead, buy only what you truly like, and eat all of it at once. A package of whole asparagus, if you like it, with cheese in some form (or the All-Around Crumb Topping, page 123) is a satisfactory meal. Or chow mein. Or any of many others.

This brings us to the cheerful matter of balancing a couple of days instead of a couple of meals, which is the pleasantest way to operate by yourself.

Preparing those Basic 7† daily is an appalling thought if you're of the noncooking persuasion. You're not about to do it.

But you can come out the same doorway, approximately, by thinking big, in forty-eight-hour chunks. If one day is mainly meat and vegetables and the next is mainly fruit, cheese, and bread, you eat more of fewer things at one time. Which means fewer leftovers and less all-around preparation.

Clearly, the reluctant cook cooking for herself alone tends toward *la basse cuisine* instead of *la haute*. Still, there are many ways to run a railway, and this one has its advantages.

A minor point but still a plus, it gives scope to what Virginia Woolf called one's angularities—a possible predilection for apple pie and cheese for breakfast, or artichokes seven nights running, or dinner that's wholly shredded wheat. You simply go along, taking your own sweet way and your vitamin pills.

More important, eating to stay alive saves time and usually money that can be applied to activities closer to the heart.

---

* Frozen individual chicken or meat pies are more satisfactory. I know a lady—an accomplished cook she is—who adds sherry to a jar of chicken, creamed, and pours it over the tops of hot chicken pies, to hearten them a bit. This is a good solution for luncheon guests.

† 1. whole-grain cereal or bread
2. fats: butter, oil, et cetera
3. proteins: meat, fish, eggs, cheese
4. milk, one pint
5. a citrus fruit and another fruit
6. a leafy green or yellow vegetable
7. a sweet

4. Canapés and Heartburn Specials

OR WHO STARTED THIS BUSINESS?

It is an interesting fact that people who hate to cook love to talk and, in general, make merry. When the sun has set and the party starts to bounce, you want to be in there bouncing, too, not stuck all by yourself out in the kitchen, deep-fat frying small objects or wrapping oysters in bacon strips.

This is one of the many drawbacks to the Canapé. Most canapés take a certain amount of doing. Not only must you make them and remember to serve them, but you must also service them—refilling and reparsleying—because as time ticks by, those platefuls of appetizers tend to acquire that lived-in look, and by eight o'clock they look as though the guests had been walking through them barefoot.

Indeed, though I don't like to pick on something so much smaller than I am, it is hard to think of a kind word to say about the Canapé. If canapés are good, they are usually fattening; and they are also expensive, not only in themselves, but in the way they can skyrocket your liquor bill. The more solid the canapé base your guests lay, the more cocktails they can carry, and goodness knows when you'll get them into the dining room. Then, when you finally do, they're apt to be too full to eat much, which is the worst thing of all. When you hate to cook, it's more than flesh and blood can stand to go to all the trouble of cooking dinner only to have it merely pecked at.

Actually, the only possible excuse for canapés is when you are having a cocktail party pure and simple, with no dinner to follow. And, by the way, entertaining in this fashion makes a certain crafty sense. People sometimes become befuddled at cocktail parties, and later they may invite you for dinner when they only *owe* you for cocktails.

If, in addition to your canapés and cocktails, you have a large tureen of soup on the sideboard, with some cups and saucers around and a plate of crackers, your prospects become even brighter. Your women guests, especially, will appreciate you for this. They will probably see to it that their husbands consume enough soup to make it unnecessary to go home and cook dinner; and your bread may come back gloriously buttered.

And so to the canapés.

There are, as you know, some fifty or sixty thousand possibilities to pick from: open sandwiches, closed sandwiches, wee sausages in dozens of disguises, oysters ditto, cheese, puffs, cookies, crackers, and enough dunks and dips to float the *Queen Elizabeth*.

When you hate to cook, you rely heavily on shop-bought items, and quite rightly, too, because many of them are very good. A dish of peanuts is usually emptied faster than the plateful of bread rounds fancied up by loving hands at home.

But sometimes, life being what it is, and women being the way we are, you feel that you should make something *yourself*. After all, Ethel made that good cucumber-Roquefort thing or whatever it was, and you can't get Ethel's recipe because she's coming to your party. (Well, you could, but you'd feel sort of silly.)

So you look in your big fat cookbook and find so many complex-sounding affairs, which, as you taste them in your mind, don't sound worth the trouble, that you shut the book quickly. Then you can open *this* cookbook and find just a few: all carefully selected, made frequently by women who hate to cook as much as you do, and at least a couple of which may well set Ethel right back on her heels.

BETTY'S COCKTAIL COOKIES   *Makes about 40*

Mix together:

½ cup flour
2 tablespoons butter

1 jar processed bacon-cheese
or onion-cheese spread

Now shape it into a neat roll, wrap it in waxed paper, and refrigerate it. When it's firm, slice it as you would cookies, and bake them at 400°F for 10 minutes. (Don't bother to grease the pan.)

PARTY PEG'S CHEESE STICKS

pastry dough
Parmesan

Make your usual pastry recipe—or use the ready-mix kind—and roll 'er out as far as she'll go. Sprinkle a lot of Parmesan all over it, fold 'er over once, and roll 'er out again. Repeat this maneuver half a dozen times, using more Parmesan each time, of course. Then cut it in strips, sprinkle with paprika, if you like, and bake at 400°F for about 10 minutes.

CHEESE BALLS

(This is an every-girl-for-herself sort of thing.)

Combine a package of cream cheese with jars of any processed cheese spreads you like—onion-cheese, blue cheese, et cetera, plus any left-over odds and ends of cheese you have, grated. Then add sherry, grated onion, cream, Worcestershire, and/or whatever else you like, to taste.

Form it into *small* balls, somewhere between a golf ball and a tennis ball, roll them in crushed nuts, and wrap them individually in aluminum foil before you store them in the refrigerator.

These are not to hang on the Christmas tree, they are to bring forth, with crackers, for dropper-inners. Small balls are better than one big one, because they're gone before they get that gnawed-at look.

LITTLE ROUND CHINESE MEAT BALLS

You mix this together:

1½ pounds ground beef	1 tablespoon powdered
½ cup soy sauce	ginger
2 tablespoons water	1 crushed garlic clove

Then you make little balls, about an inch in diameter, put them in a roasting pan, and bake uncovered, for an hour, at 275°F. Serve them with 50 toothpicks, because it makes 50 meatballs.

ONION ROUNDS

Slice an onion as thin as humanly possible. Then cut thin slices of bread into rounds, using a cookie cutter, butter them, put an onion slice on each, sprinkle grated cheese on top, and heat them slowly under the broiler until the cheese bubbles.

The next three *hors d'oeuvres* are for those rare occasions when you feel you must be teddibly teddibly. The rest are for any time when you feel duty-bound.

CAVIAR

Serve it ice-cold in its little jar, surrounded by hot buttered Melba toast. Or plain Melba toast. Or, for purists, water crackers.

SHRIMP LEAVES

Simmer an artichoke in salted water, which also contains a cut garlic clove and a drop of olive oil, for 40 minutes. Cool it. Then carefully remove the best leaves. On the tender edible end of each leaf, put a drop of mayonnaise very slightly flavored with curry. Now put a wee shrimp on the wee dot, and arrange the leaves on a platter.

THE DIP

If you have a package of cream cheese in the house, you always have a dip in the house, because you can thin it a bit with milk, canned milk, or cream, and add:

salt	lemon juice
pepper	grated onion

and there you are. Just keep on tasting.

You can proceed from there, if you like, and add a little Worcestershire, or chopped anchovies or sardines.

If, in addition to the cream cheese, you have some sour cream in the house, and an avocado, these proportions work nicely:

FLORIDA DIP

1 large ripe avocado	dash of Tabasco, salt, pepper
small package of cream cheese	small can anchovies, diced (optional)
½ cup sour cream	2 tablespoons fresh lemon juice

Mash the avocado till it's lumpless, then blend in everything else.

Note: When you use a hollowed-out red cabbage to hold a dip, it looks rather festive, and there's no bowl to wash. On the other hand, when you use a bowl to hold a dip, there's no cabbage to hollow out. You may take your choice.

CLASSIC CALIFORNIA DIP

(In case someone hasn't heard.)

Combine a pint of sour cream with a package of onion-soup mix.

NEOCLASSIC CALIFORNIA DIP

Add onion-soup mix to a good big ripe mashed avocado, with 1 tablespoon of lemon juice.

OLIVE-OYSTER DIP

You start, of course, with your package of cream cheese. Cream it with mayonnaise until it's smooth and thick, then add a small jar of chopped-up smoked oysters and half a cupful of minced ripe olives, a bit of garlic salt, and a dash of lemon.

Another good thing to remember, in the canapé line, is stuffed eggs. They are easy, and they always get eaten up, which is important. Leftover canapés are difficult to cope with except by following our enduring Leftover Rule (p. 65).

OLIVE EGGS

Hardboil some eggs, devil the yolks with mayonnaise, mustard, sugar, vinegar, salt, pepper and put a small pimento-stuffed olive in each egg, too.

GUSSIED EGGS

Hardboil some eggs and cut them lengthwise in three wedges (which makes the eggs look fancier and go farther). Then, when you devil the yolks, add anchovy paste to taste, or chili sauce, or deviled ham. Or you can add curry to them and put a little caviar on top, which makes a very gussied egg indeed.

About that anchovy paste, incidentally. A tube of it will keep almost forever in your refrigerator. A friend of mine has one she's kept for six years (her husband can't stand anchovy paste), and it's still going strong.

HORSE-RADISH BREAD

Combine 2 tablespoons of horse-radish with 2 tablespoons of butter. Spread on thin-sliced bread rounds.

POTTED CHEESE

3 8-oz. packages sharp processed cheese
1 pound bacon, fried crisp, crumbled, drained
1 bunch green onions, diced small

Mix it all up and put it in a pretty oven-proof bowl, then bake it at 400°F for 20 minutes. Serve hot or cold, as you like, with crackers.

PORTED CHEESE

(No cooking at all.)

Grate or grind half a pound of any processed cheese, then mash it till it's smooth. Add 2 or 3 tablespoons of port wine, put in as many caraway seeds as you like—enough so they're noticeable, anyhow—then press it into a pretty jar you can serve from. Cover it tightly and store it in the refrigerator.

A Good Canapé to Know About:
THE MINIQUICHE

Make a rich pastry of:

> ¾ cup butter
> 6 oz cream cheese
> 2 cups sifted plain flour

Beat the butter with the cheese and gradually add the flour. Chill it. Then form it into big-marble size balls and press them into very small patty pans or a tartlet pan. Put a teaspoon of *deviled ham* in each. Or crumbled *bacon*.

Mince a middlesized *onion* and sauté it in 1 tablespoon of *butter*. Add ¼ cup grated *cheese* (Cheddar, Emmenthal, or Swiss), mix it up, and spoon a bit of it on top of the ham in those little pastry cups. Then make an uncooked custard; combine

> 1 large egg (or 2 medium)
> ¼ cup milk
> a little *more* grated cheese
> a touch of nutmeg
> a dash of pepper

and spoon it evenly into cups. Don't put in as much as you think you should; it will bubble up and run over. Now bake them at 450°F for 10 minutes, then reduce the temperature and bake for another 15 minutes, till the custard sets and the quiches are golden brown.

Not So Classy but Easier:
THE 4-WAY PIZZA

Get a frozen plain pizza. Score it lightly into 4 quarters. Put chopped ripe olives on one, crumbled fried sausage on the next, anchovies on the third, and sautéed mushrooms on the last. Bake according to directions and serve in squares or slivers.

The following two canapés are cheap, astoundingly good and make quantities.

TING LING'S PEANUT BUTTER CRISPS

A loaf of sliced white bread (slices preferably
    about ⅜" thick)
1 jar smooth peanut butter
equal amount of peanut oil
Fine breadcrumbs mixed with Italian
    seasoning

De-crust the bread and slice it in strips about ¾" wide by 2½" long.
Spread them on a big baking sheet and dry in a 250°F oven for an
hour or so, or till quite crisp. In a blender or with a hand-mixer, mix
the peanut butter and peanut oil. Dip each strip of bread in and out
of the mixture briskly, let drip for half an hour, then roll in the crumbs.
These keep well for a long time in a tightly closed tin.

GOLD NUGGETS

In the blender or food processor, combine:

1 pound processed mature Cheddar cheese
    cut in chunks
1 cube butter

Add

¼ pound flour

Mix it, drop it in half-dollar size bits on an ungreased baking sheet,
and stick a walnut half on each. Bake at 400°F for 6 minutes.

Finally:

FRENCH-FRIED POTATO SKINS

baking potatoes
vegetable oil
salt

Bake some big potatoes as usual, then cut them lengthwise in quarters
and scoop out the pulp. (What you do with it depends on how you
feel; maybe throw it out, maybe save it for potato cakes sometime.)
    Then heat some vegetable oil to 365°F and fry the skins till they
are golden-brown. About 2 minutes. Then drain them on brown paper
bags, salt them, and serve them forth.
    Good plain or with sour cream or apple sauce. They'll stay crisp
a good while, too, on a warm plate in a pre-heated 200°F oven.

And so we come to another well-known nonessential—the snack in the wee small hours.

There is no reason, of course, why anyone should eat anything at this time except for babies on the 2:00 a.m. feeding. Yet people do. After a full dinner and a football game or a movie or a committee meeting or practically any other sort of evening activity, people eat.

There are two kinds of late-snack invitations. One is the sort that a cheerful husband proffers the whole dance floor while the band plays "Good Night Ladies." "Lesh all come over t'our housh for shcrambled eggsh!" (His wife is the feverish-looking lady by the door, with the armful of coats. She knows there are five eggs in the refrigerator, every one of them spoken for.) These occasions are seldom outstandingly successful.

The second kind is the invitation you issue yourself because these things are a community habit and it's your turn. If you can't move out of the community, you should make the first move—as part of your community endeavor—and suggest that everyone stop eating so much. But until you get around to this, the following late-snack ideas may be helpful. They are all easy and they take very little last-minute doing.

First, and at the risk of belaboring a point, don't forget about Soup.

You can make it any time and keep it on simmer (or in a big covered casserole dish in a 200°F oven) until you get back from the festivities. Make either of the easy soups on p. 60 or combine a couple of canned soups. For instance:

> Onion Soup and Chicken Noodle
> Cream of Mushroom and Cream of Spinach
> Cream of Mushroom and Cream of Oyster
> Cream of Tomato and Cream of Celery

(Be sure to notice whether your soup is condensed or ready to serve. If it is condensed, dilute it according to directions before combining. You can combine a ready-to-serve soup with one which you diluted, yourself, very satisfactorily.)

With the soup, serve a big basket of cheese crackers, or a Left Bank French Loaf (p. 169). All in all, this is a reasonably painless production.

Then there are Hot Sandwiches.

You can assemble these some time during the day, and have coffee and water ready in your percolator. Then you need only to fry them or heat them at the last minute. For instance:

FRENCH-FRIED SANDWICHES

Cut the crusts off sandwich bread. Butter the slices as you ordinarily do, and use a little home-made mustard (equal parts dry mustard and flour, moistened with water or vinegar). Then combine:

> ham and Swiss cheese
> chicken and Swiss cheese
> beef and Swiss cheese
> et cetera

and chill the put-together sandwiches until you're back from the theater and ready to eat. Then, for 6 sandwiches, beat 3 eggs with half a cup of cream or evaporated milk. Dip the sandwiches in it and fry them in butter or deep fat.

PIZZA SANDWICHES

Spread one side each of 2 slices of bread with canned pizza sauce. For the filling, use a slice of salami, a slice of Cheddar or processed cheese (the processed will melt better), and a sprinkling of garlic. Pan-fry the sandwiches in butter.

STUFFED TUNA BUNS
6 Servings

Combine these items:

¼ lb yellow cheese, diced
3 hardboiled eggs, chopped
7 oz can tuna
½ cup mayonnaise

2 tablespoons each:
   green pepper, chopped
   onion, chopped
   stuffed olives, chopped
   sweet pickle, chopped

Then stuff it into 6 hot-dog or hamburger buns, wrap the buns in aluminum foil, and forget about them. Later, they just need heating in a 350°F oven for 30 minutes.

FRIDAY-NIGHT SANDWICH   *4 Servings*

(You can do the mixing ahead of time. Then you need only fry the bacon, assemble the sandwiches, and broil them. Don't cheat and leave out the caraway seed. It makes all the difference, and you will be glad that you were upright and true.)

Mix together in a bowl:

1 small can crabmeat
2 celery sticks, chopped fine
4 whole green onions,
    chopped

1 small can mushrooms
1 teaspoon caraway seeds
enough mayonnaise or sour
    cream to moisten

Then, make sure you have on hand:

4 slices bread
8 slices bacon

4 slices Cheddar cheese

When it's cooking time, fry and drain the bacon, and toast the bread on one side only. Spread the crabmeat mix on the untoasted side, cover with bacon, top with a slice of Cheddar. Heat under the broiler till the cheese melts.

RODEO SANDWICH   *4 Servings*

(This is the only sandwich here that can't be done too satisfactorily ahead of time. But it's quick to make anyway, and it has the additional virtue of calling for nothing you don't ordinarily have in the house.)

4 slices bacon
4 slices Cheddar cheese
4 slices onion

4 eggs
toast or French bread

Chop the bacon and fry it until it's crisp. (Scissors are handier than a knife for this.) Now drain off most of the fat and spread the bacon evenly around in the frying pan. Then break the 4 eggs—individually—into the pan so they stay individual. Break the yolks with a fork. Put a big slice of cheese on each egg, and a slice of onion on top of that, and cover the pan. When the onion slice is transparent and the cheese is melted, cut the whole works into 4 sections and serve it open on toast or a slab of French bread.

Now, once in a while you may need a supper-type dish which you can prepare entirely in advance . . . for a poker party, for instance. Men usually seem to feel that after all the strenuous wrist exercise involved in an evening of cards, they need hearty nourishment. In this case, try:

OLÉ

(Good with beer and French bread.)

1 pound ground beef	1 small can tomato sauce
1 large onion, grated	1 teaspoon chili powder
1 can sweetcorn	8 oz. noodles
1 can condensed cream of	salt, pepper
tomato soup	grated cheese

First, cook the noodles. While they cook, fry the meat and onion in a pan until the meat browns, then add everything else and simmer till it's well acquainted. In a big casserole dish, alternate layers of noodles with meat mix, then top it with the cheese. When you're ready, or your husband is, bake it at 350°F for 30 minutes.

And then, of course, there's always shcrambled eggsh.

5. Day-by-Day Entrées

OR THE ROCK PILE

Never doubt it, there's a long, long trail a-winding, when you hate to cook. And never compute the number of meals you have to cook and set before the shining little faces of your loved ones in the course of a lifetime. This only staggers the imagination and raises the blood pressure. The way to face the future is to take it as Alcoholics Anonymous does: one day at a time.

This chapter contains recipes for a fair number of everyday main dishes. Some of them aren't very exciting. In fact, some are pretty dull—just as a lot of recipes are in the other cookbooks, but the other cookbooks don't admit it. And some of the recipes in this chapter are so—well, so simple—that they'd have any *cordon bleu* chef pounding his head with his omelette pan.

The thing about these recipes is this: they're *here!* You don't have to ferret them out of your huge, jolly, encyclopædic cookbook. *And they'll get you through the month with a few to spare.*

After all, who needs more recipes than this? You already have your own standard routines: the steak-roast-and-chop bit, the frozen-TV-dinner bit, the doctored-up-canned-beans bit, not to mention your mother's favorite recipe for Carrot-Tapioca-Meat Loaf Surprise. And if somebody waves a dinner invitation, you leap like a trout to the fly. So, with these additional recipes, you're in.

Now, the points that are special about them are these:

1. They all taste good.

2. They are all easy to make.

3. Each has been approved by representative women who hate to cook, and not one calls for a *bouquet garni*.

4. Some do two jobs. They involve either meat, fish, or chicken plus a vegetable, so all you need is bread of some kind, or meat, fish, or chicken and a starch, so all you need is a vegetable.

5. Many can be made ahead. (Of course, you won't do this very often. When you hate to cook you keep postponing it. But once in a while, you wake up full of fire. This is the time when you can lump dinner right in with the other dirty work you do around the house in the morning, and get it *done*.)

6. There's hardly a recipe that can't be interrupted at least three-quarters of the way through, with no ill effects, and then finished shortly before dinner, AFTER YOU HAVE REHEATED IT TO THE POINT WHERE YOU LEFT IT.

It is important to look at recipes in this light. To make it easier, I think I will put STOP HERE* in recipes where it makes sense (which it doesn't if something takes only 5 minutes anyway).

What you do with it after you've stopped depends on what's in it and how long it will be before you start it again. I see no reason to refrigerate something entirely cooked (or a casserole that's mainly cooked meat, cooked rice, and cheese, for instance) if I'm going to reheat it in a few hours. I leave it on top of the stove. It's everyone's own decision, I think, and depends, too, on how full the refrigerator is.

7. Most of them are quick to make. Actually, you can't trust the word "quick" any more. Some cookbooks, when they say "quick," mean that you needn't grind your own flour. Others mean that you can pour a can of tomato soup over a veal chop and call it Scallopini.

We must face facts. If a recipe calls for eleven different chopped ingredients and cream sauce and a cheese-topped meringue, you don't call it "quick" if you hate to cook. On the other hand, that tomato

---

* I was going to use only the initials SH, but I found that it gave a strangely hushed and reverent feel to the page.

soup on the veal chop will taste remarkably like tomato soup on a veal chop, and you can't call it Scallopini.

One more troubling thing for cookbook writers is explaining how many people a recipe will serve. Actually, of course, who knows? It depends on the people and the menu. So I've pussy-footed by saying "servings," which means that four servings could serve four people once or two people twice or one high-school boy for an afternoon snack.

The really jet-propelled recipes in this book are in Chapter 15. But here we take a middle-of-the-road path. Thawing and/or cooking time isn't what bothers you most when you hate to cook; it's preparation time, which, in these recipes, is mercifully short. For instance:

SWEEP STEAK   4–6 Servings

(So-called because a couple of seasons ago this recipe swept the country.)

2 to 3 pounds round steak or pot roast
package of onion soup mix

Put the meat on a sheet of aluminum foil big enough to wrap it in. Sprinkle the onion-soup mix on top of it, fold the foil, airtight, around it, put it in a baking pan, and bake it at 300°F for 3 hours or 200°F for 9 hours, it really doesn't matter. You can open it up, if you like, an hour or so before it's done, and surround it with potatoes and carrots.

STAYABED STEW   5–6 Servings

(This is for those days when you're en negligée, en bed, with a murder story and a box of chocolates, or possibly a good case of flu.)

Mix these things up in a casserole dish that has a tight lid.

2 pounds stewing beef, cubed
1 can of little tiny peas*
½ cupful sliced carrots
2 chopped onions
½ teaspoon salt, dash of pepper

1 can cream of tomato soup thinned with ½ can water (or celery or mushroom soup thinned likewise)
1 big raw potato, sliced
piece of bay leaf*

Put the lid on and put the casserole in a 275°F oven. Now go back to bed. It will cook happily all by itself and be done in 5 hours.

* If you don't like this, leave it out.

Incidentally, a word here about herbs and seasonings. These recipes don't call for anything exotic that you buy a box of, use once, and never again. Curry powder, chili powder, basil, thyme, marjoram, and bay leaf are about as far out as we get. And if your family says, "What makes it taste so funny, Mommy?" whenever you use any herbs at all, you can omit them (although if you omit chili from chili or curry from curry, you don't have much left, and you'd really do better to skip the whole thing).

But as a rule, don't hesitate to cut the amount of a seasoning down, or leave it out, when it's one you know you don't like. This goes for green pepper, pimento, and all that sort of thing, too. (I mention this only because we ladies who hate to cook are easily intimidated by recipe books, and we wouldn't dream of substituting or omitting; we just walk past that particular recipe and never go back again.)

We must assert ourselves. I, by way of example, think rosemary is for remembrance, not for cooking, and the amount of rosemary I have omitted from various recipes would make your head swim. The dishes turned out quite all right, too.

YOUR BASIC MEAT MIX OR THE 4-WAY MEATLOAF

(Face it. The fastest food is raw food. Next comes the quick chop, steak, cutlet. Next the Meat Mix, frozen in small balls to thaw fast and used half a dozen ways. In fact, the family can eat meatloaf most of the time and never know it.)

Buy

   1 pound sausage meat
   3 pounds lean ground beef

preferably on sale but if it isn't, buy it anyway. (People who hate to cook hate to shop, so bargains are a matter of luck.) Now add:

½ cup milk	½ cup minced onion*
4 eggs	Salt, pepper & garlic salt or
4 slices bread, crumbled*	dry mustard, celery salt,
4 tablespoons parsley	marjoram, thyme, or a
2 tablespoons	bit of each
Worcestershire sauce	

* If you're too busy to crumble bread and/or mince onions, use 1 package stuffing mix and/or 1 package dried onion soup.

That's the MIX. Put ¼ of it in a loaf pan and bake at 350°F for about 50 minutes. Make the rest into one-inch meatballs and divide them into 3 separate packages, about equal size, to freeze.

Second week: STUFFED PEPPERS. Remove tops and seeds from four green peppers, simmer them for 5 minutes, then stuff them with the frozen meatballs right out of the freezer. Pour something wet over them—cheese sauce, tomato sauce, whathaveyou—and bake at 350°F for 45 minutes.

Third week: JUST PLAIN MEATBALLS. Take out another package, flour the meatballs frozen, and brown them in a frying pan. Put them in a casserole dish. Make gravy out of the pan drippings (or if you prefer a gravy mix, use that). Either way, add to it a ½ cup of sour cream, pour it over the meatballs, and bake them covered at 350°F for an hour.

Fourth week: STUFFED CABBAGE. Make a cream sauce using 1 tablespoon flour, 1 tablespoon butter, and ½ cup milk (or buy a package of cream sauce mix and make up according to directions). Now chop a small head of cabbage coarsely, cook it in boiling water for 5 minutes, and drain it. Grease a big casserole dish. On the bottom put a chopped raw tomato. Next, half the drained cabbage. Next, a package of frozen meatballs. Now add the rest of the cabbage, dot with butter, cover and bake for an hour at 350°F. *Before serving, heat the cream sauce, add a pinch of nutmeg and pour it over.*

Now, actually you needn't hold this down to 4 pounds of mix. If you have enough muscle and a big enough bowl, make more. Those meatballs could show up with pastry wrapped around them, for a variation of Cornish Pasties. Or layered with pasta, mozzarella, and tomato sauce for free-style lasagna . . .

A DEPENDABLE BEEF BURGUNDY

Cut 2 pounds of boneless lean round steak into 2-inch chunks, brown in a little oil, then pour on 8 fl oz red wine. Stir it around. Then add:

1½ teaspoons salt
¼ teaspoon pepper
1 teaspoon paprika
1 teaspoon marjoram

2 medium onions, sliced
½ lb fresh mushrooms
2 seeded green peppers, cut in rings

Cover and simmer it in an electric frying pan (or on a very low burner or in the oven at 250°F for 5 hours). Then take the meat and vegetables out of the broth and keep them warm somewhere. Skim as much fat as possible off the broth. Better still, if you've time, semi-freeze the broth so the solidified fat is easy to remove. Then boil it down to thicken it a bit, and if you want it thicker still, stir in a tablespoon of cornflour mixed to a smooth paste in cold water. *TO FREEZE:* Pour the whole works into a big casserole dish, or seven or eight little ones, wrap, and freeze. To serve it, eventually, reheat it in a 400°F oven for about 40 minutes for the large, 25 for small.

PEDRO'S SPECIAL   *3 Ample servings*

(Very easy: very good with beer; good even without it.)

1 pound ground beef
1 chopped onion
1 garlic clove, minced
1 can tomato sauce plus ⅓
    can tomato juice,
    consommé, or water
pinch of thyme

1 pound can butter beans or
    red kidney beans with
    liquid
2 tablespoons chili powder
1 can of sweetcorn
a bit of lettuce
more chopped onion

Brown together, in a little oil, the meat, onions, and garlic. Stir in the tomato sauce, thyme, and chili powder. Now dust off a good-sized casserole, grease it, and alternate layers of this mixture with layers of beans and corn, ending with corn. Bake it, covered, at 350°F for 45 minutes, and uncover it for the last 10. Before you serve it, strew some shredded lettuce and chopped raw onion on top, for that Olde-Tyme Mexicali look.

BEEF A LA KING   *4 Servings*

(Don't recoil from the odd-sounding combination of ingredients here, because it's actually very good. Just shut your eyes and go on opening those cans.)

All you do is mix up these things in the top of your double boiler:

1 can condensed chicken noodle soup,
    undiluted
1 can condensed cream of mushroom soup,
    undiluted
2 hardboiled eggs, sliced
¾ pound chipped beef (you can parboil* it
    first to make it a little less salty, but you
    don't have to)
½ green pepper, chopped
3 tablespoons chopped pimento
1 teaspoon minced onion
1 tablespoon Parmesan (if you have it)
1 small can mushrooms (if you have one)

Heat it all over hot water and serve it on practically anything.

ROSEMARY'S GREEN PEPPER STEW   *4 Servings*

(This is a good casserole for times when people straggle in at all hours. You can shut it off and reheat it again till the cows come home or the family does.)

1 pound lean ground beef	1 large green pepper cut in
1 teaspoon salt	rings
2 tablespoons mustard (plain	1 clove garlic, minced
or foreign)	1 can Mexican-style sweet corn
1 medium onion, cut in rings	½ cup chili sauce

Mix the first three things. In a large frying pan sauté the onion and green pepper rings, not much, just enough to break their spirit. Add the meat mixture, mess it about a bit, and cook till browned. Add garlic and corn and simmer for 15 minutes. Add chili sauce and mix lightly, re-cover, and simmer another 10.

* Parboil means to boil briefly in water.

SKID ROAD STROGANOFF   *4 Servings*

8 oz uncooked noodles
1 beef bouillon cube
1 garlic clove, minced
1 large onion, chopped
2 tablespoons cooking oil
1 pound ground beef
2 tablespoons flour

1 teaspoon salt
½ teaspoon paprika
About 6 oz mushrooms,
fresh or canned
1 can condensed cream of
     chicken soup, undiluted
1 cup plain yogurt
chopped parsley

Start cooking those noodles, first dropping a bouillon cube into the noodle water. Brown the garlic, onion, and beef in the oil. Add the flour, salt, paprika, and mushrooms, stir, and let it cook 5 minutes while you light a cigarette and stare sullenly at the sink. Then add the soup and simmer it—in other words, cook on low flame under boiling point—10 minutes. Now stir in the yogurt—keeping the heat low, so it won't curdle—and let it all heat through. To serve it, pile the noodles on a platter, pile the stroganoff mix on top of the noodles, and sprinkle chopped parsley around with a lavish hand.

Now, you noticed that chopped parsley in the Stroganoff we just passed? This is very important. You will notice a certain dependence, in this book, on PARSLEY (which you buy a bunch of, wash, shake, and stuff wet into a covered jam jar, and store in the refrigerator, where it will keep practically forever), and PARMESAN (which, if you were a purist, you'd buy a rocklike chunk of, and grate as you need it. Inasmuch as you're not, you buy it in bulk at an Italian delicatessen or in a box with holes in the top, at the grocer's), and PAPRIKA (which you buy an ordinary spice box of and keep handy on the kitchen stove).

The reason for these little garnishes is that even though you hate to cook, you don't always want this fact to show, as it so often does with a plateful of nude food. So you put light things on dark things (like Parmesan on spinach) and dark things on light things (like parsley on sole) and sprinkle paprika on practically everything within reach. Sometimes you end up with a dinner in which everything seems to be sprinkled with something, which gives a certain earnest look to the whole performance, but it still shows you're trying.

To repeat, the important thing is contrast.

GOOD SOYA SHORT RIBS   *4 Servings*

First, make the sauce—mix together:

1 cup tomato sauce
¾ cup water
2 tablespoons vinegar

4 tablespoons soy sauce
2 teaspoons sugar

Then put about 3 pounds of lean short ribs of beef (ask your butcher) in a plastic bag with a little flour and give them a good shake. Next put them in a heavy iron casserole with a tight-fitting lid. On top put plenty of sliced onions—2 good-sized ones, anyway—pour the sauce on top, close the lid, and bake for 3 hours at 300°F.

SWISS LOAF   *6–7 Servings*

(This is a somewhat interesting sort of a meat loaf.)

2 pounds ground beef
4½ oz Swiss cheese
2 beaten eggs
1 large chopped onion
1 large chopped green pepper
1 teaspoon salt

¼ teaspoon pepper
1 teaspoon celery salt
½ teaspoon paprika
2 cups milk
1 cup dry bread crumbs

Just mix these things together in the approximate order they're given, then press it all into one big greased loaf pan, or use two. Bake, uncovered, at 350°F for about an hour and a half, then yodel for the family.

CHILLY-NIGHT CHILI   *6–8 Servings*

(A good cheap classic chili recipe that's easy to remember because it's one of everything.)

1 pound ground beef
1 big onion, chopped
1 or 2 cans of red kidney
    beans, depending on
    how many you're
    feeding

1 can tomato soup, undiluted
½ teaspoon salt
1 tablespoon chili powder
    (then taste and add more
    if you like)
ripe olives, if they're handy

Brown the meat and the onion in a little butter and cook till the meat is brown—about 10 minutes. Add everything else, then let it simmer covered for half an hour.

Just a word here about what to serve *with* things. You may have noticed that many recipe books are full of suggestions. "With this," they'll say, "serve Curried Peaches, crisp hot cornsticks, and Angel Torte."

The reason they do this isn't just to be helpful. Between you and me, it is also to make that entrée recipe sound better. You can make meat loaf sound almost exciting if you talk long enough about Crusty Cheese Potatoes and Heart of Artichoke Salad and Fudge Cake, but you still haven't changed the basically pedestrian quality of the meat loaf. Furthermore, when you hate to cook, what you serve with something is what you happen to have around; and you wouldn't dream of cooking all those things for one meal anyway.

So this recipe book won't suggest accompanying dishes very often, except in cases where it is really hard to think of one, or when the entrée looks a bit pathetic and needs bolstering.

Now for the LAMB department. Lamb, when you hate to cook, usually consists of chops or a leg of. It was a great day for me when I discovered lamb shanks.

LOVELY LAMB SHANKS   *4–5 Servings*

4 lamb shanks, chopped*
1 peeled cut garlic clove
4 tablespoons flour
3 teaspoons paprika
1 teaspoon salt
½ teaspoon pepper
3 tablespoons fat
3 cups hot water
1½ cups raw rice

Shake your shanks, well rubbed with garlic, in a plastic bag containing the flour and seasonings. Brown them on each and every side in the hot fat. Add the water and the garlic clove—speared with a toothpick, so you can find it later—and simmer covered for an hour. Then add the rice, simmer, covered, for another half hour, and you're done.

LAMB SHANKS TRA-LA   *4–5 Servings*

(This has the easiest barbecue sauce you'll ever make, and it's very good too.)

1 large onion, sliced thinly
1 cup tomato ketchup
1 cup water
½ cup mint jelly
2 tablespoons lemon juice
4 lamb shanks, chopped*
flour, salt, pepper, to dredge meat in
3 tablespoons fat

* Make sure the butcher chops them. Otherwise, though they'll still taste good, they'll look rather like rolled-up trouser legs and be harder to eat.

Combine the first 5 ingredients and heat them until the jelly melts. Dredge the shanks in the flour, et cetera, and brown them in the fat in an iron pot or deep pan. Be sure you pour off the excess fat after they've browned. Then pour the sauce on, cover, and simmer—basting once in a while, if you happen to think of it—for an hour and a half.

(Lamb shanks are the lower parts of legs of lamb, which your butcher would cut, on request.—Ed.)

LAMB CHOPS MIGNON

You start with inch-thick lamb chops. Cut the bones out of them, then wrap a bacon strip around each and fasten it with a toothpick. Put a teaspoon each of Worcestershire sauce and ketchup on each chop, set them on a rack in the oven—with a drip pan beneath—and bake at 350°F for about 35 minutes, until the bacon is crisp.

This makes a pretty party platter, incidentally, with some fat tomato slices and parsley around the edge.

OLD FAITHFUL   *4 Servings*

4 medium-thick lamb or pork chops	1 large onion
1 cup raw rice	2 ripe tomatoes
1 can consommé or broth or bouillon (chicken is best)	½ green pepper, cut in rings
1 tiny pinch of marjoram	salt, pepper
1 tiny pinch of thyme	2 tablespoons of fat

Brown the chops in the fat in a pan. While they're browning, put the rice in the bottom of a greased casserole dish, and slice the vegetables. Next, lay the chops on the rice and top each one with slices of onion, tomato, and green pepper, salting and peppering a bit as you go. Pour the consommé in, add the marjoram and thyme, and let it fend for itself in a 350°F oven for an hour.

The Problem of Falling in Love. You often do, when you hate to cook, fall in love with one recipe which seems to have simply everything: it's fast, it's simple, and the whole family *likes* it. And so, like impetuous lovers since time began, you tend to overdo it. You find yourself serving the little gem three times a week, including Sunday breakfast. Your problems are solved. You're serene. Oh, you love that little recipe!

But no recipe can stand such an onslaught. After a while, it just doesn't taste as good as it did the first time. You begin to wonder what you ever saw in it. Presently, you stop making it. Eventually, it's lost in limbo, and that's the end of *that* love affair.

Two things are responsible for this all-too-common occurrence: first, you overdid it, and, second, you probably started to kick it around. You felt so safe with your own true love that you began taking it for granted, not exactly following the recipe, using vinegar instead of lemon juice, or canned mushrooms instead of fresh mushrooms (because you *had* some vinegar or canned mushrooms). Soon, without your being aware of it, the recipe has undergone a sea change, and become something rich and undoubtedly strange, all right, but not at all the same recipe you started with.

The moral is this: When you make proper contact with a recipe, *don't make it again for an entire month.* Keep it warm and cosy, the ace up your sleeve, in your card index or checked in your recipe book, while you try some more. Presently, you'll have several aces up your sleeve, which is a very delectable state of affairs indeed.

In the PORK and HAM department, we come to:

MAXIE'S FRANKS   *4–6 Servings*

(This is a fast, good frankfurter and sauerkraut routine.)

½ onion, chopped (or 2 tablespoons minced dried onion)	1 tablespoon brown sugar
	1 teaspoon prepared mustard
2 tablespoons cooking oil	1 large can sauerkraut
¾ cup ketchup	10 or 12 frankfurters or hot dogs
¾ cup water	

You make the sauce first. Sauté the onion in the oil until it's tender, then add the ketchup, water, sugar, and mustard, and bring to a boil. Now open the sauerkraut, drain it well, and put it in a big casserole. Arrange the frankfurters—slashed or split—on top, pour on the sauce, and bake, uncovered, at 350°F for 30 minutes.

DR. MARTIN'S MIX   *4–5 Servings*

(It takes about 7 minutes to put this together. Dr. Martin is a busy man.)

Crumble 1 to 1½ pounds of pork sausage meat into a pan and brown it. Pour off a little of the fat. Then add:

1 green pepper, chopped
2 green onions, chopped
2 or 3 celery sticks, chopped
1 can chicken consommé or
   bouillon

1 cup raw rice
1 tablespoon Worcestershire
   sauce
½ teaspoon salt

Dr. Martin then puts the lid on and lets it simmer at the lowest possible heat while he goes out and sets a fracture. When he comes back in about an hour, his dinner is ready.

PORK CHOPS AND SPUDS

Use the grater with the big holes to grate your potatoes for scalloping; it's much easier than slicing. Then prepare them in your habitual scallop fashion, whatever that may be. (If you don't have a habitual fashion, you might pour over them a can of condensed cream of mushroom soup slightly diluted with a third of a can of milk.) Lay the pork chops on top of the potatoes and put the casserole dish in a 350°F oven, uncovered. If you happen to think of it, turn the chops over in half an hour and salt and pepper them. You bake this for an hour all told.

And so to CHICKEN.

CHICKEN-RICE ROGER   *5–6 Servings*

2½ pound fryer (or enough
   frozen breasts or thighs,
   thawed)
¾ cup uncooked rice
salt, pepper
¼ cup broth

1 tablespoon grated onion (or
   half a garlic clove, minced)
2 chicken-bouillon cubes
   dissolved in 1¾ cups
   water
small can of mushrooms

Flour and then brown the chicken in a little oil. While it browns, put the rice, salt, and pepper in a greased casserole and sprinkle in the grated onion. Put in the mushrooms, juice and all. Arrange the chicken artfully on top, pour the bouillon over it, and dot with the butter. Cover it. Bake it at 350°F for an hour.

SATURDAY CHICKEN   *4–6 Servings*

1 disjointed fryer (or any 6 good-sized pieces
    of chicken)
1 can condensed cream of mushroom soup
1 cup cream (don't cheat and use milk; the
    cream makes a lot of difference)
salt and garlic salt
paprika
chopped parlsey

Take your chicken and salt and garlic salt it a bit, then paprika it
thoroughly. Next, spread it out, in one layer, in a shallow baking pan.
Dilute the soup with the cream, pour it over the chicken, and sprinkle
the chopped parsley prettily on top. Bake it, uncovered, at 350°F for
1½ hours.

Speaking of cooking, incidentally, and I believe we were, one of its
worst facets is grocery shopping. (See Chapter 1.) When you hate to
cook, a supermarket is an appalling place. You see so many things
that they all blur, and you finally end up with a glazed look and a
chop. So take this cookbook along when you go shopping. Then,
when you see a can of shrimp, for instance, it might ring a far-away
bell, and you can look in your little book to see what we'd do with
it, we women who hate to cook. We'd commit:

HURRY CURRY   *4–6 Servings*

½ teaspoon curry powder
1 large chopped onion
1 tablespoon butter
1 can condensed cream of
    shrimp or chicken soup

1 cup sour cream or yogurt
1 cup cooked shrimp
1 cup raw rice

Start the rice cooking. Then, in the top part of your double boiler,
simmer the onion and curry powder in the butter till the onion's tender
but not brown. Add the soup, set the pan over hot water, and stir till
it's smooth. Add the sour cream and the shrimp, and heat till it's hot
clear through. Serve over hot rice, with sprigs of parsley and a spatter
of paprika.

   (If you keep a jar of chutney in the refrigerator—it keeps practically
forever—you can serve it forth whenever you make a curry dish, and
you'll feel less guilty about skipping the chopped peanuts and onions
and all those other messy little odds and ends.)

Also, even simpler and cheaper, we'd make:

PORTLAND PILAFF
3–4 Servings

7 oz can shrimp
1 cup raw rice
4 tablespoons butter
a bit of chopped onion,
    green or otherwise

1 can chicken consommé
diluted with ½ can
water (or 2 chicken-
bouillon cubes dissolved
in 2 cups hot water)

Use a heavy ovenproof pan. Cook the rice in the butter till it's the color of a nice camel's-hair coat. Add the consommé and onion, cover the pan, and bake for 35 minutes at 325°F. Now take the drained shrimp, and pour the little rascals in. (If you can afford 2 cans, so much the better.) Bake for 10 more minutes.

CANCAN CASSEROLE
3–4 Servings

(This is about the easiest tuna casserole that ever happened, and it's quite good.)

Beat 2 eggs and add a small can of evaporated milk. Then add:

2 cans cream-style sweet corn
7 oz can tuna fish, broken a bit with a fork
1 green pepper, chopped
1 middle-sized onion, grated

Pour it all into a buttered casserole dish and bake it, uncovered, at 325°F for 1 hour.

TUNA-RICE CURRY
4 Servings

(Handy to know about, because you probably have on hand everything it calls for.)

2 teaspoons curry powder
2 cups cream sauce
1 cup cooked rice
3 hardboiled eggs, chopped
½ teaspoon salt

7 oz can tuna fish
1 onion, chopped
1 tablespoon parsley
2 tablespoons chopped green
    onion (for garnish)

Mix the tuna with eggs, cooked rice, onion, parsley, and salt. Stir the curry powder into the cream sauce, add it to the tuna mixture, and bake it all in a greased casserole at 325°F for an hour. Put the chopped onions on top of it before you serve it, and put a bowl of chutney on the table.

(It is good psychology when serving a casserole dish to use individual casseroles instead of one large one. They look more interesting, and, also, if they're not entirely eaten, you need have no compunction about throwing the leftovers out; see Leftover Rule, p. 65.)

SOLE SURVIVOR   *4 Servings*

(Except for plain fried fish, this is the easiest sole recipe I've run into. You can make it with halibut, too.)

4 sole fillets
1 cup cream sauce
1 small can shrimp

Lay out the fish effectively in a shallow greased baking dish. Bake the fish at 400°F for 20 minutes. Then reduce the heat to 300°F, pour the cream sauce (to which you have added the shrimp) over the fish, and bake it for another 15 minutes.

CELERY FISH STICKS   *4 Servings*

16 frozen fish sticks thawed
1 can condensed cream of
    celery soup
½ cup milk

1½ tablespoons chopped chives
    or green onion tops
1 tablespoon lemon juice
3 tablespoons grated Cheddar
    cheese
paprika

Put the fish sticks in a shallow buttered baking dish. Thin the celery soup with the milk, and measure out a cupful. (Save the rest for somebody's lunch or throw it out.) Add the chives, lemon juice, and cheese to the thinned soup, pour it over the fish sticks, and sprinkle with paprika. Bake it at 425°F for 20 minutes.

A GOOD SIMPLE FISH DISH   *4–6 Servings*

2 tablespoons butter, melted
Salt, pepper
1–2 pounds sole fillets
¼ cup dry vermouth

3 tablespoons minced herbs
    parsley, tarragon, chervil
½ cup fresh breadcrumbs
4 green onions, thin-sliced
    (including some of the
    green)

Melt the butter in a baking dish big enough to hold all the fish in a single layer. Then salt and pepper both sides of the fish. Dip them in the butter, both sides. Put the green onions and herbs in the pan, lay the fish out on it, and cover it neatly with the crumbs. Pour the vermouth over it all, dot with some more butter—2 oz should do it —and bake uncovered at 365°F till the crumbs are brown and the fish cooked . . . about 30 minutes.

A parenthetical note here. It is understood that when you hate to cook, you buy already-prepared foods as often as you can. You buy frozen things and ready-mix things, as well as pizza from the pizza man and chicken pies from the chicken-pie lady.

But let us amend that statement. Let us say, instead, that you buy these things as often as you dare, for here you usually run into a problem with the basic male. The average man doesn't care much for the frozen-food department, nor for the pizza man, nor for the chicken-pie lady. He wants to see you knead that bread and tote that bale, before you go down to the cellar to make the soap. This is known as Woman's Burden.

But sometimes you can get around it. Say, for instance, that you are serving some good dinner rolls that you bought and then merely put into the oven for a few minutes, as the directions said to. At dinner, you taste them critically. Then you say, "Darn it, I simply can't make decent rolls, and that's all there is to it!"

If you are lucky, and have been able to keep him out of the kitchen while you were removing the wrapping, he will probably say, "What's the matter with you? They taste fine."

Then you say, in a finicky sort of female voice, "I don't know— they just don't seem as *light* as they ought to, or something . . ." And the more stoutly he affirms that they're okay, the tighter the box you've got him in. Admittedly, this is underhanded, but, then, marriage is sometimes a rough game.

And don't worry one minute because it's a little more expensive to buy these things than to make them. Maybe you're a breadwinner yourself. Or maybe you do your own wallpapering, while that lady down the road, who so virtuously rolls her own noodles, pays vast sums to paper hangers. Maybe you make your own clothes, or sell Christmas cards at home, or maybe you're just nice to have around the house.

HOMEBODY BEANS

3–4 Servings

(This couldn't be better or simpler, except that you must be around to attend to it every 2 hours for 6 hours. Don't be afraid those already-cooked beans will cook to a pulp. For some mysterious reason, they don't.)

2 average-sized cans kidney (or baked) beans
½ pound bacon, the leaner the better
3 big raw tomatoes (or an equal quantity of
    drained canned tomatoes; raw are better)
2 raw onions, sliced

In a casserole dish, alternate layers of the beans, the thick-sliced tomatoes, and the onions till you run out. Bake at 300°F for 2 hours, uncovered.

Now cut the bacon in half (the short strips work better) and lay half of them on top. Put the casserole back in the oven, uncovered, for another 2 hours, by which time the bacon should be brown. Punch it down into the beans, and put the rest of your bacon strips on top. Bake it uncovered for another 2 hours, and you're done.

Or you can make:

BURGUNDY BEANS

4 Servings

2 15-oz cans butter beans
3 green onions
2 tomatoes, chopped
½ green pepper, chopped
½ pound ground beef
1 cup red wine

Just fry the onions and green pepper in a little oil until they're tender, then add the crumbled ground beef and brown it. Next, add the chopped tomatoes and the wine, and simmer it all for 5 minutes. Add the beans, pour it all into a casserole, and bake, uncovered, for 30 minutes in a 350°F oven.

Then there is always CHEESE.

Now cheese is something of a yes-and-no proposition. It isn't too trustworthy, because you have to concentrate on it; and when you hate to cook, you don't want to. After you've produced a curdled Welsh Rabbit or a Welsh Rabbit that resembles a sullen puddle of rubber cement, the tendency is to leave cheese severely alone.

However, cheese has the virtue of keeping nicely, so long as you haven't unwrapped it (or so long as it's grated and in a covered jar in your refrigerator; see Leftover chapter). And when there's a good half pound or so of cheese in your refrigerator, you always have a comfortable awareness that there's at least one supper on ice. (What that supper will probably be is soup and Grilled Cheese Sandwiches, and there's nothing the matter with that, either, particularly if you spread the bread with butter and a little dry mustard mixed with vinegar.)

Then there are these 2 recipes. Neither can make a fool of you, and they are both very good.

CHEESE AND WINE BAKE
4 Servings

6 to 8 slices stale or lightly
   toasted bread
½ cup chicken bouillon
½ pound Swiss cheese, grated
1 cup dry white wine
3 eggs

butter, garlic clove
½ teaspoon salt
1 teaspoon Worcestershire
   sauce
½ teaspoon mustard
½ teaspoon paprika
½ teaspoon pepper

Ready? Mince the garlic clove and cream it into enough butter to spread the bread with. Then spread it, and put the slices butter side down in a big shallow cake pan or casserole dish.

Beat up the eggs, and to them add the wine, the bouillon, all the seasonings, and the cheese. Pour this over the bread, and bake, *uncovered*, at 325°F for 30 minutes.

(This is a handy dish, incidentally, if you're going out somewhere, to a cocktail party, for instance, before dinner. Before you go, you can do everything up to pouring the mixture over the bread.)

CHEESE-RICE PUDDING
4 Servings

(A cross between a pudding and a soufflé. If you like, you can serve it with mushroom sauce—some of the canned varieties aren't bad—or creamed tuna, or you can top it with a few bacon strips.)

1 cup rice
4 eggs
2 cups milk

2 tablespoons melted butter
¼ pound grated sharp
   Cheddar cheese
½ teaspoon salt

Cook the rice, without salt. Then separate the eggs. Beat the yolks slightly, add the milk, butter, cheese, salt, and cooked rice. Beat those egg whites now till they're very stiff. Fold them into the egg yolk-milk business. Pour it into a greased baking dish and bake at 350°F uncovered, for 25 minutes.

Finally, let us—all of us ladies who hate to cook—give a thought to SOUP.

A hearty soup, that is. A satisfying soup. A soup that—with bread or crackers, carrot strips, and a dessert made by somebody else—will fill up the family. Here are 3 good ones.

HEIDELBERG SOUP   *3–4 Servings*

2 cans potato soup or Vichyssoise
5 slices bacon, chopped
4 slices salami, slivered
12 green onions, chopped, including some of
    the green
black pepper
parsley

While the soup heats, fry the chopped bacon, drain it, and pour off all but one tablespoon of fat. In it, fry the salami and the onions. Add them, plus the bacon you just cooked, to the soup. Parsley it up, and serve.

BISQUE QUICK   *6 Servings*

2 cans tomato soup, condensed
½ can pea soup, condensed
1 can chicken consommé or bouillon
1 cup thick cream
7 oz can crab meat, shrimp or lobster
¾ cup sherry

Heat everything but the wine in the top of your double boiler. Just before you serve it, add the sherry.

LIBERAL POTTAGE   *8–10 Servings*

(Divers elements all stewing together.)

Put a pound of lentils in an extra big saucepan with 4¾ pints of water. Bring it to a boil, turn off the heat, and let it stand for 2 hours. Now fry

6 big chopped onions
2 garlic cloves
1 pound lamb meat (shoulder, neck,
    whathaveyou)

for 15 minutes and put it in a deep casserole. Drain the lentils (but save the water) and add them, along with

a green pepper, seeded and chopped
a 15 oz can stewed tomatoes
several stalks celery, chopped
4 chopped carrots

Stir it up and add some lentil-liquid, just enough to cover everything. Salt and pepper to taste, then cover and bake in a slow, slow oven, about 250°F—for 2 hours. Longer won't hurt; just check once in a while for dryness and add more juice if it needs it.

6. The Leftover

Some women can keep a leftover going like an eight-day clock. Their Sunday's roast becomes Monday's hash, which becomes Tuesday's Stuffed Peppers, which eventually turn up as Shepherd's Pie, and so on, until it disappears or Daddy does. These people will even warm up stale cake and serve it with some sort of sauce, as some sort of a pudding.

But when you hate to cook, you don't do this. You just go around thinking you ought to. So, much as you dislike that little glass jar half full of Chicken à la King, you don't throw it away, because that would be wasteful. Anyway, you read somewhere that you can put spoonfuls of it into tiny three-cornered pastry affairs and serve them hot, as hors d'oeuvres.

Actually, you know, deep down, that you never will. You also know you won't eat it yourself for lunch tomorrow because you won't feel like it, and you know it won't fit into tomorrow night's dinner, which is going to be liver and bacon, and you know you can't palm it off on Junior (kept piping hot in his little school lunch thermos)

62

because he wouldn't even touch it last night when it was new. You know how Junior is about pimentos.

But still you can't quite bring yourself to dispose of it! So you put it in the refrigerator, and there it stays, moving slowly toward the rear as it is displaced by other little glass jars half full of leftover ham loaf and other things. And there it remains until refrigerator-cleaning day, at which time you gather it up together with its little fur-bearing friends, and, with a great lightening of spirit, throw it away.

Do you know the really basic trouble here? It is your guilt complex. This is the thing you have to lick. And it isn't easy. We live in a cooking-happy age. You watch your friends re-doing their kitchens and hoarding their pennies for glamorous cooking equipment and new cookbooks called *Eggplant Comes to the Party* or *Let's Waltz into the Kitchen*, and presently you begin to feel un-American.

Indeed, it is the cookbooks you already have that are to blame for your bad conscience and, hence, for your leftover problems. For instance, consider that two thirds of a cupful of leftover corn. They'll tell you to use it as base for something they call Scrumptious Stuffed Tomatoes. Mix some breadcrumbs and chopped celery with the corn and season it well, they'll say, with a fine vague wave of the hand, and then stuff this into your hollowed-out tomatoes and bake them.

Now, ideas like this are all very well for the lady who likes to cook. This is a challenge to her creative imagination. Furthermore, she'll know *how* to season it well (coriander? chervil?) and while the result may not be precisely Scrumptious, it will probably be reasonably okay.

However, if you hate to cook, you'll do better to skip the corn gambit and simply slice those nice red tomatoes into thick chunks and spread them prettily on some nice green parsley or watercress and sprinkle them with salt and pepper and chopped chives and serve them straight. Because you're not about to use much creative imagination on that stuffing, inasmuch as the whole idea didn't send you very far to begin with; and your Scrumptious Stuffed Tomatoes are going to taste like tomatoes stuffed with corn.

Then there is another thing these cookbooks do. They seem to consider *everything* a leftover, which you must do something with.

For instance, cake. This is like telling you what to do with your leftover whisky. Cake isn't a leftover. Cake is cake, and it is either eaten or it isn't eaten; and if the family didn't go for that Mocha Icing, you give the rest of the cake to the neighbor or to the lady downstairs before it gets stale. (Maybe *she'll* make something out of it, but you won't have to eat it. Maybe she'll even throw it away, but if so, you won't know about it, so it won't hurt. Like what happened to that twenty-second batch of nameless kittens you finally had to take to the city pound, there are some things you don't exactly want to know.) And certainly you don't want to let the cake get stale so you can make a Stale-Cake Pudding for the family. They're the ones who left so much of it the first time, remember?

Or cheese. Cookbooks will tell you what to do with your leftover cheese. But cheese isn't a leftover; it's a staple. If you'll grate those odd bits and put them in a covered jar in your refrigerator, *toward the front*, you may remember to sprinkle it on things, sometimes, and use it for grilled cheese sandwiches. (Don't believe what they tell you about wrapping cheese in a cloth dipped in wine to keep it fresh, because this doesn't work; it just wastes the wine. Vinegar, used the same way, is somewhat more satisfactory, but it is still an awful nuisance.) The only thing that really works is cling wrap.

And eggs! Most recipe books show tremendous concern about the egg white, if you didn't use the white, or the yolk, if you didn't use the egg yolk. There are four thousand things you can make and do with an egg white or an egg yolk, all of which call for more cooking and usually result in more leftovers, which is what you were trying to get away from in the first place. More about this in the Dessert chapter—see pages 192–93.

The one thing they don't mention is giving the egg yolk or the egg white to the dog. It's very good for his complexion, and for cats' complexions, too. What did that egg cost? No more than a dime, probably, and half of that is a nickel which would be cheap for a beauty treatment at twice the price.

Right here we've come to the heart of the matter. Your leftovers were never very expensive to start with. Does the chocolate soufflé get left over? Or the choice red out-of-season strawberries? No. It's that dreary little mess of mixed vegetables, which isn't worth shucks. You have to reason these things out.

Just one more word about the leftover before we get down to where the work is. Home Ec-sperts and other people with diplomas in Advanced Cream Sauce have gone so far as to rename leftovers "Plan-overs." They actually want you to cook up a lot more of something than you'll need, and then keep it around to ring exciting changes on, as they put it, through the weeks to come.

It's true that certain people like certain things better the next day. Scalloped potatoes, when they're fried in butter. Or potato salad. Or baked beans. Every family has its little ways. And it's perfectly true that leftover Spanish Rice or Meat Loaf makes an adequate stuffing for Baked Stuffed Green Peppers, if you get around to doing it before the Spanish Rice or Meat Loaf starts looking disconsolate.

But when you hate to cook, don't ever fall into the Plan-over Trap. You'll end up hating yourself, too, as you think of that great pile of Something which you'll have to plough through before you can once again face the world clear-eyed and empty-handed.

The drill is this: Cut down the recipe, if you need to, so that there is only enough for the meal you're faced with. Then buy, as the French do, in small niggling quantities. How has a lady profited if she gains two avocados for eighty cents instead of one for fifty cents if she doesn't need the second one and so lets it rot away?

And the motto to paint on your refrigerator door is this:

WHEN IN DOUBT, THROW IT OUT.

Just remember: if vegetables have been cooked twice, there aren't enough vitamins left in them to sneeze at. Furthermore, if your refrigerator is jam-packed with little jars, it will have to work too hard to keep things cold. Presently its arteries will harden, and you will have to pay for a service call—the price of which would more than buy a lovely dinner out for you and your husband, with deferential waiters and soft music.

Finally, and possibly most important, all those leftovers are hard on the family's morale when they open the refrigerator door. Wondering what's for dinner, they begin to get a pretty grim idea, and presently they begin to wonder what's with Mother. The inside of her refrigerator doesn't look like the insides of the refrigerators they see in the magazine pictures, and Mother loses face.

Actually, the only sort of leftover you need to concern yourself with is meat. It takes more character than most of us have—even those of us who hate to cook—to throw out two or three pounds of cooked beef, lamb, ham, pork, or turkey. So let us consider the meat problem.

Before you do a thing with that great sullen chunk of protein, ask yourself a few questions:

Have you incorporated it into a dish of scalloped potatoes, with plenty of cheese on top?

Have you augmented it with a few slices of Swiss cheese from the delicatessen and served it forth as a Toasted Club Sandwich, in neat triangles surrounding a mound of coleslaw?

Have you re-presented it as an honest cold meat platter, with deviled eggs in the middle? It's easy to forget the obvious.

And have you ground up a chunk of it with pickles and onions and celery and added some mayonnaise, as a spread for after-school sandwiches?

If you can truthfully answer yes to the foregoing, then buckle down. You are about to start cooking.

This is a good recipe you can make out of *any* leftover meat.

LET 'ER BUCK   *4 Servings*

1 loaf French bread, cut in
    half lengthwise
1 jar mild-flavored processed
    cheese spread
sliced or chopped leftover
    meat

2 small cans mushrooms
1 teaspoon marjoram
4 chopped green onions
1½ cans tomato purée
4 tablespoons olive oil (or
    other salad oil)

Spread out a big piece of aluminum foil, cupping the edges so the juice won't run over, in a shallow baking tray. Place the 2 halves of bread on it, cut side up. Then, working coolly and efficiently, spread the next 5 ingredients, in the order listed, on the bread. Be sure you spread the cheese right to the edge, all over, because this keeps the bread from getting soggy. Then spoon the tomato sauce on top and, finally, drizzle the oil over the works. Put it in a 325°F oven for 20 minutes.

The following is a good recipe to keep frozen for that wee-small hours snack mentioned previously. Or for any number of other unspecified occasions when you have to produce FOOD.

THE NEITZEL GRINDER*

Take small loaves of French bread, or cut big loaves into 10-inch chunks. Cut them in half the long way. Brush both cut sides with garlicky olive oil; you might keep a cut garlic clove marinating in a bottle of olive oil for situations like this.

What you put on them depends on what is on hand. The last one is always different from the first one, because (as you will have noticed) ingredients never run out simultaneously. Arrange, sandwich-style, Mozzarella Cheese, Anchovy Fillets, sliced Luncheon Meat or Salami. Or maybe it's Edam or Swiss Cheese, stuffed Olives, Pimentos, Ham, or Liverwurst, or Sardines, or plain sliced cold Beef—whatever is there. The important thing is no mayonnaise if you're going to freeze them. If you're not going to freeze them, heat them for about 15 minutes at 350°F. If frozen they take about half an hour at the same

* The Grinder is also known as the Submarine, the Hoagie, the Hero, the Po' Boy, the Torpedo, the Rocket, the Cuban, and the Bomber.

temperature. A nice touch is to insert a few fresh tomato slices when people are ready to eat.

And here are some things besides hash, stuffed peppers, and shepherd's pie that you can make out of LEFTOVER ROAST BEEF.

HUSHKABOBS

(So-called because the family isn't supposed to know it's just that old Sunday roast still following them around.)

You need a barbecue skewer per person.
You also need:

> inch-size beef cubes, 5 per person
> large mushroom caps, canned or otherwise
>   (or green pepper strips)
> small whole onions
> quartered greenish tomatoes

First you make a marinade by mixing:

¼ cup cheap red wine	1 cut garlic clove
¼ cup olive oil	pinch of thyme and marjoram

Let the beef cubes sit in this for 3 or 4 hours, and stir them occasionally. Then string them on skewers, alternating with the vegetables, which you also brush with the marinade before cooking.

If it's barbecue season and you have one, barbecue them. If not, broil them.

In either case, cook them fast, close to the heat. You cooked that meat once, you know. All it has to do now is brown.

BEEF ENCORE

(Known in some circles as Eiffel Trifle.)

leftover roast beef, sliced	1 tablespoon flour
1 cut garlic clove	½ teaspoon paprika
2 onions, thinly sliced	½ cup white wine
1 tablespoon butter	1 cup beef consommé
	1 teaspoon good wine vinegar

First, melt the butter in a frying pan, then sizzle the cut garlic clove in it for 2 minutes and remove it *immediately*. Put the onions where the garlic used to be, and sprinkle the flour over them. Stir until it is light brown, add the wine and consommé and cook very slowly for

15 minutes. Add the meat and paprika. Don't let the sauce boil now. Simmer just long enough to heat the meat through—about 5 minutes. Just before you serve it, add the wine vinegar.

And here are three things to do with LEFTOVER ROAST LAMB.

GOOD LEFTOVER LAMB SANDWICHES

(With soup, there's supper.)

Grind up about a pound of your leftover lamb and add 3 tablespoons of grated Parmesan cheese. Add some mayonnaise to make a good smooth spread, and add some prepared mustard and horseradish, too, according to your taste. Then spread it on thin-sliced buttered wholemeal or rye bread. Serve with lettuce.

INDONESIAN CURRY   *4 Servings*

(This is a mild curry which came from Indonesia via San Francisco.)

5 tablespoons butter	1 cup water
1 chopped onion	1 lb diced leftover lamb
2 apples, peeled and chopped	4 tablespoons flour
2 cans beef consommé	2 teaspoons curry powder
juice of 1 lemon	1½ cups rice

Sauté the onion and the apple together in a deep pan until they're tender, using 2 tablespoons of the butter. Then add the rest of the butter, and sift the flour and curry powder in, too. Stir all this until it's comfortably integrated. Then add the consommé and the water, lemon juice, and cubed lamb. Simmer it all from half an hour to an hour, while the rice cooks.

This gives you a nice little breather. You may now put your feet up and have a cocktail, or else you may dirty up a lot of little dishes with

chopped peanuts	sliced bananas
chopped green onions	grated orange rind
chopped almonds	grilled, chopped bacon
toasted coconut	raisins
diced cucumber	chutney

to serve as side dishes with your curry. Take your choice.

LAMB PEPPERS

6 Servings

(You can use leftover veal for this, too.)

Cut the stem ends of 6 pretty green peppers and take the seeds out, then parboil the peppers 5 minutes, or till they're barely tender. Now mix together:

1 cup finely chopped lamb
½ cup breadcrumbs
½ cup chicken consommé or
    bouillon

1 large tomato, chopped
½ teaspoon salt
½ teaspoon garlic salt
1 teaspoon vinegar

Stuff this into the peppers and bake them in a 350°F oven for 15 minutes, in a greased pan.

NOW! Two Good Things, to Go with Leftover Beef or Lamb (or indeed Ham!)

JET-SET NOODLES

Cook 8 oz egg noodles the way the package says to. Meanwhile, combine:

8 oz cottage cheese
1 cup sour cream
½ teaspoon salt
⅛ teaspoon pepper
2 snipped chives or chopped green onion stalks
1 tablespoon butter

Put it all together, mix it, and pour it into a goodsized casserole. Dot it with butter and bake for 40 minutes at 325°F. If you'd like the noodles a little browner-looking, put it under the hot broiler a minute or so before you serve it.

RICE SHIMMELFENNER

3 tablespoons butter
2 medium onions
1 cup raw rice

1 can consommé
1 teaspoon each rosemary &
    marjoram (or other herbs)

Melt the butter in a frying pan, sauté the chopped onions for 5 minutes, add the rice and stir till it's a lovely beige. Then add the consommé plus enough water to total about 3 cups of liquid. Add the herbs and simmer for 40 minutes more.

Now let us assume you're about to grapple with a HAM, or what's left of one. Nothing looks bigger. On the other hand, there are many things you can do with it—ham loaf, ham croquettes, ham-and-egg pie, et cetera—recipes for which you can find in your big fat cookbook. Here are 3 you probably can't.

HAM-BEAN SUPPER   *6 Servings*

1 lb diced ham
2 large cans kidney beans
3 tablespoons olive oil
4 small onions, sliced
½ teaspoon salt

½ teaspoon sugar
dash of cayenne
½ green pepper, chopped
3 good-sized tomatoes, sliced
1 tablespoon grated Parmesan

First cook the onions in the oil till they're light brown. Add the green pepper, cayenne, sugar, salt, and the drained beans (and throw the juice away). Toss all this for 3 or 4 minutes in the pan. Then spread all the diced ham in the bottom of an ungreased casserole, cover it with the bean mixture, spread the sliced tomatoes on top of *that*, and sprinkle the Parmesan on top of everything. Bake it, uncovered, for 30 minutes at 350°F.

JUDY O'GRADY'S HAM   *6 Servings*

First, cook 12 oz of noodles till they're tender. Next, grind up:

½ pound leftover ham
½ pound sharp Cheddar

1 green pepper

Then add to it:

1 teaspoon horseradish
½ teaspoon salt
1 can condensed cream of
    mushroom, chicken, or
    celery soup thinned
    with ¼ cup milk

Whistling cheerily, you may now mix everything together, including the noodles, and bake it, covered, in a buttered casserole at 350°F for 40 minutes. Then remove the cover, sprinkle some crumbs on top, dot with butter, and brown it under the broiler.

THE COLONEL'S LADY'S HAM   *5–6 Servings*

½ pound ham, cut in strips
2 tablespoons butter
1 chopped onion
2 teaspoons flour

1 cup sour cream or yogurt
¾ cup mushrooms
1 cup raw rice

Start cooking the rice to serve it on. Then sauté the ham strips and onion in the butter till the onion is tender. Sprinkle the flour over it, stir it in, make sure the heat's low, then gradually stir in the sour cream and the mushrooms. Stir this conscientiously for a few minutes while it all thickens, and that's it.

For more ideas for what to do with even older ham see Chapter 23 —Shutting The Garden Gate.
    Then there is always LEFTOVER PORK.
    Remember, it's very nice sliced cold, served with cold applesauce. You can also make:

GUNG HO

(This is so simple it's embarrassing; but everyone likes it, including little children, which is a big point.)

You cut the leftover pork in strips, removing as much fat as you can. If you saved some of the good brown pan drippings, add a little water—say ¼ cup—stir it up and heat, then add enough chicken consommé or bouillon to make a reasonable amount of sauce. (If you didn't save any drippings, the consommé alone is all right.) You now add the pork strips to this and heat them in it, then pour it all over cooked, hot, drained Chinese noodles. Top with chopped green onions and serve with soy sauce.

SUB GUM YUK

3–4 Servings

First you take a can of chow mein noodles and put three quarters of it in a bowl. Set the rest aside for toppings later. Now mix up with the noodles you put in the bowl:

1 can condensed cream of
    mushroom soup
¼ cup water
1 cup diced leftover pork
1 cup sliced celery

½ chopped onion
½ teaspoon salt, pepper
2 teaspoons soy sauce or
    sherry
¼ cup chopped cashews or
    walnuts

Put this into a buttered casserole dish, top with the rest of the noodles, and if you have any more nuts around, in addition to that ¼ cupful, put them on top of the noodles. Bake, uncovered, at 350°F for 30 minutes. (This is very good, incidentally, made with a 7 oz can of tuna instead of leftover pork.)

LEFTOVER CHICKEN: Who ever has any leftover chicken? I never have any to speak of, and neither does anyone else I know—just a leftover drumstick once in a while, and what you do with that is eat it.

LEFTOVER TURKEY is, of course, a bird of a different feather. The following 4 recipes are good because they don't make the starry-eyed assumption that you have a lot of gravy and stuffing left over.

TURKEY DIVAN

5–6 Servings

6 good-sized slices of turkey
1 can condensed cream of chicken soup
    (thinned slightly with 2 tablespoons
    sherry and a little cream)
1 package frozen broccoli, cooked
grated Parmesan cheese

Put about one fourth of the soup mixture in a buttered casserole. Put the broccoli in, cover it with slices of turkey meat, and pour on the rest of the sauce. Sprinkle the Parmesan generously on top and bake at 350°F uncovered, for about 20 minutes.

SOUR CREAM TURKEY CURRY   *6 Servings*

1½ lbs cooked turkey meat,
   chopped
2 tablespoons butter
2 teaspoons curry powder

1 chopped onion
1 can chicken broth
2 tablespoons flour
1 cup sour cream

Melt the butter in a double boiler, and add the curry powder and chopped onion. Cook for about 5 minutes. Then stir in the flour and the chicken broth, stirring till it's a smooth sauce. Then add the turkey and the sour cream. Keep it hot (have the water barely simmering so the sour cream won't curdle) while you cook some rice to serve it on. Actually one should have done this first but one doesn't always think to.

ATSA MY TURKEY!   *6 Servings*

First, cook and drain 8 oz of fettuccini or plain egg noodles. Then simmer over low heat for 5 minutes:

   1½ lbs chopped cooked turkey
   ½ cup condensed chicken broth
   ½ cup dry white wine

Add the noodles to the turkey now, along with:

¼ cup milk
6 tablespoons diced
   Mozzarella cheese
6 tablespoons grated
   Parmesan cheese

2 teaspoons butter
1 teaspoon salt
¼ teaspoon pepper

Cook it over very low heat, stirring frequently, for 10 minutes. (Or use the double boiler.)

TURKEY TETRAZZINI
5–6 Servings

(This isn't exactly effortless, because you have to make that cream sauce; but if you ever have company the day after Thanksgiving, you'll thank me for it.)

½ pound spaghetti
¼ pound fresh mushrooms
5 tablespoons butter
⅓ cup flour
2 cups turkey broth or
    chicken consommé

1 cup light cream
2 tablespoons sherry
1 lb diced turkey
½ cup grated Parmesan
salt
pepper

First, you cook the spaghetti the way the package tells you to. Now slice the mushrooms and sauté them in a bit of the butter till they're light brown.

Then you make the cream sauce: blend the rest of the butter with the flour in the top of a double boiler, add the turkey broth, and cook it, stirring, till it's smooth and thick. Add the cream, salt, pepper, and sherry.

Now divide the sauce in half. In one half put the turkey meat, and in the other half put the mushrooms and cooked spaghetti. (At this point you may wonder why you ever started this, but actually you're nearly out of the woods.)

Put the spaghetti-mushroom half in a greased casserole and make a hole in it. Into the hole pour the turkey half. Top it with the Parmesan, and bake, uncovered, at 400°F for 20 minutes.

And next time, for heaven's sake, get a *little* turkey!

Should you feel the need to use up brown, splotchy bananas which the kids won't touch, make:

AUNT HENRY'S EASY BANANA JAM

(Good on toast or ice cream.)

6 very ripe bananas mashed   juice of 6 lemons

Now add a cup of sugar to every cup of the banana-juice mixture and set it on low heat. Cook it for about an hour, stirring frequently. If it starts turning pink, don't be upset; it depends on what kind of bananas they are. Maybe it will, maybe it won't. Anyway, skim off the froth as the jam cooks. Then refrigerate it if you're going to eat it pretty soon, as you probably will. Or pour it into sterilized jars and seal it with paraffin.

7. The Regional or Foreign Specialty

I GUESS YOU ALWAYS LOSE A LITTLE IN THE TRANSLATION

"Animals will expend energy to introduce variability into an otherwise constant or consistent situation even when there is no extrinsic reward."
—BERNARD BERENSON and GARY A. STEINER

An element of cookmanship occasionally confuses the kitchen picture, the way béarnaise complicates a steak. And it isn't easy to make any sort of showing, especially if you don't want to very much or very often.

However, when you do, it's likely that you'll have the best luck with the Regional or Foreign Specialty, though even here it isn't plain sailing. Indeed, the specialty poses an interesting problem, alive with pros and cons. Let's consider first its disadvantages.

For one, any dish tends to lose some of its charm when you get it home, away from the sound of the temple bells or the cable cars (just as a pretty little wet rock you find at the beach isn't quite so pretty dry on your kitchen window sill). When you've gone to the trouble of making it, only to find those important intangibles missing, something within you dies.

Nor is it roses all the way for the guest. If you're serving your *pissaladière* after the manner of the Niçoise to people who haven't been where you've been, all they will taste is the *pissaladière*. If they are treated, into the bargain, to a full description of that off-the-beaten-track restaurant where you discovered it—that tiny, picturesque place where they spoke only Diners' Club—they are going to feel that the evening is longer than it actually is.

In addition, some regional or foreign specialties are better than others, depending on the region. Indeed, you would suspect certain recipes from certain regions of having been ridden out of there, on a rail. I'd like to have seen the Scots haggis leaving town.

On the other hand, some are good and also surprisingly easy to make. For instance, I used to regard with simple awe those people who had the temerity to make Scotch Shortbread. Then I found that it's only slightly simpler than a peanut-butter sandwich.

This holds true for a number of well-known dishes. If you can't make Alfredo's Fettuccine, for another example, you're in real trouble. And such a plus factor mustn't be minimized by the reluctant cook.

Therefore, given this advantage, a slight Otherwhere aura can be another. Maui Banana Bread, for example, spreads some *aloha* around, while Mrs. Womack's Banana Bread does not, although the recipes happen to be identical. (Mr. and Mrs. Womack once visited Hawaii and had a very nice time, too.) Similarly, a Croque Monsieur has it all over a grilled cheese sandwich.

One important thing: if you are going to specialize in a regional specialty, it is wise to choose one from a region other than your own. As a general rule the further away your specialty came from, the better.* And in this fast-frozen jet age, ingredients for most things are generally available, at least for our modest purposes here.

And so, listed alphabetically, are some regional or foreign dishes that taste quite all right and are easy to make—no pitfalls or sudden sauces.

Some are classics, although here and there a few nonessentials have been omitted (the same way editors cut chunks out of Sir Walter Scott without hurting him much).

---

* Should someone indicate an uncalled-for familiarity with the dish anyway, you can say casually, "This is rather an interesting version of Chlodnik, don't you think," which implies that you're familiar with other versions.

ANTIPASTO

A first course of antipasto is easy and attractive, as well as helpful if you don't think the roast will quite stretch. You can serve it in the living room, too, passing out individual plates and forks, then the platter. This will alert the guests that they're on the last drink.

On a large platter, arrange several or all of these:

curried deviled eggs
thin-sliced Italian salami or any good ham
    from the delicatessen
crescents of cantaloupe or honeydew melon
best-grade sardines
black olives
artichoke hearts, marinated in vinegar-and-oil
    dressing
cherry tomatoes
radishes
tuna (sprinkled with lemon juice and pepper)
mild Italian peppers

BOILED BEEF VIENNESE

*(Boiled beef sounds flat as a matzo, which is too bad,
because it's quite good, especially with horseradish. So perhaps
you'd better call it Tafelspitz.)*

2 pounds beef chuck and 2 or 3 beef bones
1 teaspoon salt
3 peppercorns
a carrot and a celery stalk and 2 small onions
handful of parsley tied in a cheesecloth bag

Put everything in a casserole dish with water to cover. After it comes to the boil, lower it to simmer, and simmer it covered about 3 hours (or bake in a 275°F oven), STOP HERE. Then reheat it, slice the beef, and eat it, with plain horseradish, or with horseradish mixed to taste with whipped cream and lemon juice.

(If you cool and skim the fat, then strain the broth and season it with some pepper, salt, and nutmeg, it's a good soup for another time.)

It was in Brittany, at an inn with the improbable name Ty Chupen Gwenn, that I encountered this good simple apple recipe to serve with pork or chicken.

CHERCHEZ LES POMMES

First, in a big iron frying pan, put an inch of water, ¾ cup sugar, ¼ cup cider vinegar, 1 tablespoon butter, and stir. Let it come slowly to a boil. Now peel and quarter 4 or 5 of the tartest, juiciest apples available. Reduce the heat so the liquid simmers, and put the apples in. Turn them with care occasionally. Cook till the liquid is absorbed and the apples look a bit glazed.

CROQUE MONSIEUR

(Croquer means "to munch," so this would seem to be a simple directive.)

16 slices good bread (not the squeezable kind)
16 slices of Swiss cheese
8 slices ham, boiled or baked, so long as it's
    good
butter

Actually, this is a sandwich within a sandwich. Put a slice of ham between 2 slices of cheese, then a slice of buttered bread on either side. Fry it gently in butter. (You could French-toast it instead and they won't take away your chef's apron. First dip it in egg and milk beaten together, *then* fry it in butter.)

DANISH ALMOND SHEET   *Makes 2–2½ dozen*

Rich easy cookies you bake in one big piece.

½ pound butter
¾ cup sugar
¼ pound chopped almonds

2 beaten eggs
2 cups flour
granulated sugar (to sprinkle
    on top)

Melt the butter, then add everything else except the topping sugar, mix it, and cool it a bit.

Now put it in the middle of a baking sheet and press it out gently but fervently, in the hope that it will cover the whole thing. It may, then again it may not. In any case, sprinkle it with sugar, and bake it for about 12 minutes at 375°F till it's golden-brown. Cut it in squares, rectangles, or rhomboids.

EDDY'S OYSTER LOAVES

6 Servings

(Eddy was a San Franciscan who owned a bar and made small oyster loaves for his married male customers to take home to their wives. These were pacifiers. But Eddy is dead now, and Mother must pacify herself. This is good for a special lunch. I also know a family who has it traditionally as Christmas Eve supper.)

3 dozen fresh oysters
3 small loaves French bread
½ teaspoon garlic powder
¼ cup melted butter
milk

First, almost split the loaves lengthwise, leaving a hinge. Scoop out the soft middle and save the crumbs. Then add a half-teaspoonful of garlic powder (not salt) to 2 tablespoons of melted butter, and brush the cavities.

Next, drain the oysters and save the liquid. Sauté them in the rest of the butter till the edges curl—about 5 minutes. Put the oysters into the loaves, mix the crumbs you saved with the oyster liquid you saved, and add them, too. Shut up the loaves now. STOP HERE.

Then wrap them in cheesecloth dipped in milk, twisting the ends and tucking them under the loaf. Bake them on a baking sheet for half an hour at 350°F. Cut them in half before you serve them.

FETTUCCINE ALFREDO

4 Servings

(Two things are important here: 1) to use Parmesan cheese you grated yourself, and 2) to toss the noodles vigorously, with controlled abandon, so that each and every millimeter of every one is covered with the butter and cheese.)

½ pound broad egg noodles
½ pound butter
½ pound Parmesan

Cook the noodles till they're tender—about 10 minutes. Drain them well. Put them in a hot bowl, add butter cut in chunks (melted butter would give it a non-Alfredo flavor) and add the grated cheese. Then mix.

HIGH-RISE YORKSHIRE PUD

(No one knows who started the unfounded rumor that Yorkshire Pudding is risky or in any way a test of cooksmanship. These individual puds can be easily made by anyone who is bright enough to blow her nose.)

Set the oven at 450°F. Grease 6 custard cups or patty pans with vegetable shortening (not oil) including the outside of the cup rims. Set them on a baking sheet. In a bowl, dump

> 1 cup unsifted flour
> ½ teaspoon salt
> 2 eggs (just break them over the bowl and
>   drop them in so they're staring at you
>   with their big yellow eyes)
> 1 cup milk

Beat this with an eggbeater till it's just mixed—about 15 seconds. Now fill the cups half full and set the baking sheet in the 450°F oven. Let them bake for 25 minutes. Then, without opening the oven, lower the temperature to 400°F and bake for another 30–35 minutes in all. That's it. You will have 6 splendid individual Yorkshire Puddings so golden brown and exuberantly puffed-up that it's almost embarrassing.

IRISH SODA BREAD

(This is a big easy crusty faintly sweet loaf (you cut it in wedges), comforting as a turf fire in a thatched cottage. It is handy when you're out of bread.)

> 2 cups flour
> ½ teaspoon baking soda
> 1½ teaspoons baking
>   powder
> ½ teaspoon salt
> 1 tablespoon sugar
> 4 tablespoons shortening
> ½ cup raisins or currants

> ¾ cup sour milk (add a
>   tablespoon of vinegar to
>   milk and let it set 5
>   minutes)
> 1 tablespoon caraway seeds

Sift the dry ingredients, cut in the shortening, add the raisins and caraway seeds. Add the milk, knead it all a moment, shape it into a round loaf about ¾-inch thick, and put it in a greased pan. Bake 30 minutes at 375°F.

ITALIAN CHOP SUEY   *6 Servings*

(or Chinese Macaroni)

2 medium onions
2 green peppers
5 stalks of celery
1½ pounds ground round

1 can tomato paste
¼ cup soy sauce
1 pound small shell
  macaroni

Fry the meat in a little oil till it loses its pinkness, then add the sliced vegetables and let them simmer thoughtfully for 10 minutes. Then add the tomato paste plus 2 or 3 cans of water (some like it wetter, some like it dryer) and the soy sauce. Simmer it covered for 45 minutes. Finally, cook the shell macaroni the way it says to on the package, drain it, add it, and serve.

KANSAS CITY BEEFBURGERS

(In Kansas City, when they grow weary of hamburgers plain, they sometimes spoon this sauce over the hot meat.)

Blend or otherwise mix thoroughly:

½ pound blue cheese
½ cup softened margarine or butter
¼ teaspoon garlic powder
2 tablespoons prepared mustard
salt and pepper as you like it

KIOWA INDIAN FRY BREAD

(The Kiowa Indians are an artistic tribe who painted their daring exploits and other things on buffaloskins. It may be that their Fry Bread was handed down on a buffaloskin, too.)

2½ cups flour
3 teaspoons baking powder

1 cup warm water
½ teaspoon salt

Knead the dough, roll it thinly, then cut it in squares, strips, circles, whatever you like. Then deep-fat-fry them like doughnuts—370°F— till they're brown on both sides. This makes the teepee smell good, as well as plenty of Fry Bread. I can't think precisely where it would fit into a menu, or, for that matter, where it wouldn't. It is good with soup, salad, chicken or ham. Or wherever you need ballast. Or just to eat.

LOUISVILLE LOBSTER (OR CRABMEAT)   *8 Servings*

*(This should be served with a Southern accent and a camellia.
It's rich and fairly expensive. But it is a good special supper with only a
salad and rolls, and it can be fixed completely ahead.)*

¼ cup butter
¼ teaspoon garlic powder
chopped parsley
1 large can tomatoes
½ cup flour
½ cup cream

2 tablespoons Worcestershire
    sauce
½ cup sherry
1½ lb cooked lobster or
    crabmeat
2 cans mushrooms, browned-
    in-butter, drained

Put the garlic powder in half the butter in a saucepan and simmer it
a minute. Then add the chopped parsley and two-thirds of the tomatoes.

While it cooks, mix the flour with the rest of the tomatoes till it's
a smooth paste, then add it to the first tomato mixture. Cook it just
a minute, then mix in the cream, Worcestershire sauce, and sherry.
Cook *that* 5 minutes, mix in the seafood and mushrooms, salt and
pepper it, and pour it into a casserole dish. Sprinkle it with any sort
of crumbs you have, dot it with the butter that's left, and STOP HERE.
Bake it, uncovered, for 20 minutes at 375°F.

MARY MARGARET'S SALLY LUNN

*(You can tell by the name of it that this is simply a good recipe,
not a difficult gourmet type, for the fancy recipes always put the
name of the inventor last—Chicken Gravy Mrs. Jones, instead
of Mrs. Jones' Chicken Gravy.)*

2 cups flour
2⅓ teaspoons baking powder
1 teaspoon salt
½ cup shortening

½ cup sugar
3 eggs, beaten
1 cup milk

Sift together the first 3 things so you won't have to do it when your
hands are sticky. Cream the shortening and sugar, and add the 3 eggs.
Add the flour mix to this, a third at a time, alternating with the milk,
a third at a time. Don't stir too much—it should be barely mixed and
a bit lumpy. Pour it into an average-size loaf pan—oiled—and bake
for half an hour at 425°F. Then test it with a broom-straw, and maybe
cook it another 5 minutes.

MAUI BANANA BREAD

(I think a Maui mama invented this when she let some bananas get a bit too ripe to eat. It's good toasted for Sunday breakfast, too. You can luau yourself a slice of ham to go with it.)

2 cups sugar
1 cup shortening
6 ripe bananas, mashed
4 eggs, well beaten

2½ cups flour
1 teaspoon salt
3 teaspoons baking powder

Cream the sugar and shortening, then add the mashed bananas and eggs. Sift the dry ingredients and add them, but don't overmix it. Bake it in a greased loaf pan at 350°F for about 35 minutes. (Test in the middle with a skewer.)

O'FLANAGAN'S SAUSAGE SUPPER   *4–5 Servings*

(Good and hearty for a cold night, and, with instant mashed potatoes, not much work.)

1 pound pork sausages, or sausage-meat
   shaped into cakes
2 apples, pared and sliced
2 onions, peeled and sliced
1 tablespoon flour
salt and pepper
1 cup bouillon (cube or powder kind)
1 to 1½ cups of hot instant mashed potatoes

Fry the sausages or sausage-meat till crisp. Drain, then put in a baking dish. In the fat that's left, cook the apples and onions until they're tender, then spoon them over the sausages.

Pour off all but a tablespoon of the fat now, and brown the flour in it. Add the salt, pepper, and bouillon, stir till it's a bit thicker, and pour it over the sausages and so forth. Top with the mashed potatoes. STOP HERE. Bake for 15 minutes uncovered, at 350°F.

PICAYUNE PECAN PIE
(or, Just a Dab for Me)

(This pie is astonishingly fast and easy. The hard part is finding the nuts and, once you have done so, parting with the price of them. However, owing to its richness, one pie serves 8 to 10 people, or the same 2 or 3 several times, for it keeps well.
A good way to serve it is to arrange small wedges on a plate and punctuate them with small clusters of cold white grapes.)

You need an unbaked pie shell. You also need:

3 eggs
½ cup whipping cream less
    1 tablespoon
1 cup sugar
1 teaspoon vanilla
2 tablespoons butter

1 tablespoon sherry
½ cup dark syrup
⅛ teaspoon salt
1½ cup pecans, plus enough
    to ornament the top

Put everything into the blender in that order, except for those decorative pecan halves. Turn the blender on for about 10 seconds.

Pour it in the pie shell and bake it at 400°F for 25 minutes, then decorate it with the pecan halves and bake for 10 minutes more. (If the middle seems shaky then, it might take another 5.) Cool it before serving.

QUICHE LORRAINE A LA SUISSE   *6 Servings*

(This isn't the classic quiche, because it contains Swiss cheese.)

Line a pie pan with pastry.
Fill it about half full with alternating layers of chopped boiled ham (or crisp bacon bits) and diced Swiss cheese, starting with the cheese. You'll need about half a pound of each.
STOP HERE.
Then beat together:

5 eggs
1 cup coffee cream
½ teaspoon salt

Pour it over the cheese and ham, then bake it at 350°F for 45 minutes. Serve it in wedges.

REALLY SOUTHERN CORN BREAD   *6 Servings*

*(This is from Texas via Oklahoma, and sugarless—which
classicists insist on—and fast.)*

Beat together with a fork an egg and a teaspoon of salt. Then add,
beating slightly with the same fork between additions

1 cup milk
2 heaped teaspoons baking powder
⅓ cup flour
1¼ cups corn meal

In a middle-sized frying pan melt 2 level tablespoons of shortening.
Pour most of it into the batter, leaving just a little. Pour the batter
into the frying pan, put the frying pan in the oven, and bake it for
25 minutes at 425°F. Cut it like a pie and serve it hot.

ROCKY RIVER APPETIZER PIE

8 oz package cream cheese
2 tablespoons milk
2½ oz jar dried beef, finely chopped
2 tablespoons instant minced onion
2 tablespoons green pepper, finely chopped
½ cup sour cream
¼ cup walnuts, chopped

Blend the cream cheese and milk. Add the onion, green pepper, dried
beef, and sour cream. Spread it in a presentable pie pan, sprinkle with
nuts, bake it for 15 minutes at 350°F and serve it hot with savory
biscuits.

SCOTCH SHORTBREAD

(For Scotsmen in a hurry. Good, too.)

½ lb butter
3 cups flour
¼ cup sugar

Cream the butter and sugar, then add the flour. It will be stiff and
rather crumbly but forge ahead, pressing it into a square 8-inch pan.
Bake it at 300°F for an hour. Cool it 10 minutes, then cut it in squares.

TOMATOES PROVENÇAL   *6 Servings*

(This seems to make a tomato go further than it normally would.)

First you scoop the seeds and some of the pulp out of 6 big tomatoes cut in half. Salt and pepper them, then turn them upside down somewhere so they'll drain.

Mix up:

a minced garlic clove	¾ teaspoon dried basil
2 tablespoons chopped green onions	¼ teaspoon thyme
	½ cup bread crumbs

with enough olive oil to hold it together and help stuff it in the tomatoes. STOP HERE. Then sprinkle a bit more oil on top and bake them, uncovered, for 15 minutes at 400°F.

VEAL SCALLOPINI   *3–4 Servings*

(This is a good non-sweet scallopini, which is rather hard to find.)

1 pound veal round steak, well trimmed
½ cup grated Parmesan cheese
salt and pepper

Pound the cheese into both sides of the meat with a blunt instrument. Keep pounding till the cheese is used up and the meat is a bare ¼-inch thick. Salt and pepper both sides, cut the meat in 2-inch strips, then sauté them in olive oil.

Now add:

a crushed garlic clove	½ teaspoon marjoram
½ cup beef broth	¼ teaspoon thyme
2 tablelspoons lemon juice	½ cup dry white wine

Cover it. STOP HERE. Then simmer for half an hour. If you like, you can add some sautéed mushrooms or sliced stuffed green olives, but you don't have to.

VIRGINIA PEANUT SOUP   *4–6 Servings*

2 cups chicken broth	4 tablespoons ground or chopped peanuts
2 tablespoons chopped onion	
2 tablespoons butter	¼ teaspoon celery salt
2 tablespoons chopped celery	½ teaspoon salt
2 tablespoons flour	1 teaspoon lemon juice
6 tablespoons peanut butter	

Sauté the chopped celery and onion in the butter till they're tender, add the flour and blend it, then add the chicken broth and simmer it for half an hour. Remove it from the fire, strain it, and add everything except the chopped peanuts. Heat it again to the boiling point, then serve it forth with the chopped peanuts on top.

WESTERN SANDWICH   *2 Large Servings*

(This is called Western in the East and Denver in the West. The other day I ran across a variation of it called an East-Western Sandwich, which was probably invented by a Chinese cowboy. It called for water chestnuts and soy sauce, but didn't taste as good as the classic version, which follows. It's too good a sandwich to forget, and the ingredients are usually around.)

4 eggs	2 teaspoons chopped onion
¼ green pepper, chopped	salt and pepper

Melt 2 tablespoons of butter in a frying pan. Sauté the green pepper and onion in it for a few minutes. Pour in the eggs, add the salt and pepper, and cook it till it's firm. Serve on buttered toast, open face.

YANKEE CASSOULET

(Beans with a French accent; good with caviar, fruit salad, Irish brown bread, and champagne.)

2 cups small dried navy beans	1 cup dry white wine
2 cups water	1 pound sausage meat
2 cups chicken stock	2 cups cubed meat (chicken,
1 teaspoon salt	beef, whatever you
1 onion, chopped	have)
1 teaspoon garlic powder	1 cup buttered crumbs
2 small cans tomato sauce	
1 tomato, skinned and chopped	

Bring the beans, water, and salt to a boil in an electric frying pan or a casserole and let them cook for 15 minutes, then stand for an hour. Add the onion, garlic, thyme, and the chicken stock. Cover, simmer for an hour, then add the tomato sauce and the wine. Re-cover it and simmer another hour.

Now brown the sausage meat and pour off the fat. Add it with the cubed meat and the beans. Pour it all into a bean pot or a casserole dish, sprinkle with crumbs and bake, uncovered, at 325°F for an hour.

If the top looks anemic, brown it under the broiler a minute or 3 before you bring it to the table.

ZABAGLIONE

(Or, Please, not while we're eating.)

I made zabaglione once for four people and it turned out nicely. Dizzy with success then, I decided to make it for ten people. But one absent-minded moment with zabaglione and you have Chinese Egg Soup, which is what I got.

Thus can Providence punish those who try to show off with za-baglione. It's best to try to show off with something else.

So, on second thoughts, I won't include the recipe, in case it gets someone else into trouble.

8. The Daily Anticlimax

ENTREES FOR THE SIMPLE-MINDED & THE PURE IN HEART

*"There is no lasting hope in violence,
only temporary relief from hopelessness."*
—KINGMAN BREWSTER, JR.

All days lead but to the kitchen, or so it often seems at 5 p.m. And there is an astonishing number of days in the average lifetime.

The uninspired but dependable recipes in Chapter 5 will see you through about three decades in the kitchen. But if you're going to be around out there for longer than that, you'll need another batch. This chapter, it is hoped, will provide them.

These recipes have all been reluctantly tested, and somewhat more cheerfully approved, by women who hate to cook. They call for no mysterious ingredients, and measurements are as clearly stated as possible. No "add a wineglass of Chablis" sort of thing.

Also, they try to explain what to expect—for instance, how long, if there's any doubt, a process takes. Recipes that don't are disconcerting. (Like "Beat egg yolk till thick and lemon-colored." I've never noticed that my egg yolks change color enough to get excited about, and as for thick they start out that way.)

Another thing: most of these recipes specify *covered* or *uncovered*. If they don't, it's because it doesn't matter. (By the way, it's good to remember the virtues of aluminum foil should you ever find yourself midstream in a recipe that demands covering and the pot you are using is lidless.)

Whether these recipes are completely free of land mines is of course another matter. The human element is involved here, and you know how that can complicate things.

I've tried to circumvent disasters like these, but I know they can happen.

HOW THEY TASTE

You will find an occasional clue, if it seems indicated, as to how something is going to taste. It is curious the way good ingredients can sometimes add up so bad (and vice versa), yet you can't make a hard-and-fast rule about it. That is, some recipes* run true to form and taste exactly as bad as you thought they would.

Then there's the fact that there's no accounting for taste buds. If you simply don't like saffron, no saffron recipe is going to taste really good. Along these paths we must walk with tolerance, as we pad out our little repertoires.

Only an occasional menu suggestion is given, by the way, because menus so often tend to peter out. What sounds good and even possible at nine in the morning often sounds like more trouble than it's worth at blast-off time, or 5:30 p.m.

So we'll wade into it now, with the following reasonably quick stand-by recipes, which taste good to us who make them. Some of them involve protein plus a vegetable or a starch, which eliminates cooking something else. They'll all do what they are expected to do, the Lord willing and the creek don't rise and they're grouped according to the main protein that's in them, starting with a small stampede of beef recipes right here.

Perhaps you remember Sweep Steak? This recipe appears in Chapter 5 (see page 43).

It is my pleasure, at this time, to present

---

* Only last week I carefully prepared a creamed-corn-and-water-chestnut recipe that gave every promise of being a mess and fulfilled it nicely.

SWIPE STEAK

which is the same thing except that you add a can of undiluted condensed mushroom soup *in addition to* the dry onion-soup mix. All this adds up to good gravy when you unwrap it.

Another interesting new development is:

SWOOP STEAK

This time, put the pot roast in a heavy iron pot with a lid. Put the dry onion-soup mix on the meat, then pour 2 cups of Burgundy wine on top of it all, replace the lid, and cook it in the same way.

With any of these 3 beef recipes, you can add potatoes, carrots, and celery—if you like, of course—for the last half hour, if you're cooking at 300°F; for the last hour if you're cooking at 200°F.

Now we'd better let that recipe rest. Either Sweep, Swipe, or Swoop will answer your modest pot-roast requirements, so let's not do anything else to it. There is an ever-present danger that enthusiastic cooks will take a recipe like this and fancy it up ("just throw in some fresh mushrooms, shallots, celery root, coriander, rosemary, oregano, basil, and seventeen artichoke hearts . . ."), and there goes your recipe.

HORSERADISH BRISKET

(This is good with or without the horseradish sauce, but the sauce is certainly easy.)

Settle a 3–4 pound fresh boneless beef brisket in a pot with a lid. Then add:

> enough water to cover the meat
> an onion cut in half
> a handful of celery tops or pieces
> salt and coarse-ground pepper

Put the lid on and simmer it 3 or 4 hours, or till it's tender. Then, for the horseradish sauce: Add a tablespoon of lemon juice and horseradish—to taste—to a can of cream sauce (or a cup of cream sauce you make yourself). A little more pepper is good in the sauce, too.

With any of these first 3 recipes, by the way, it's a good idea to buy a slightly larger piece of meat than you'll need. Then the next night's dinner can be:

POT-ROAST BUNS   *4 Servings*

(Which are good and not much trouble.)

Have about 2 cups of beef bits and 4 hamburger buns ready.
   For 20 minutes simmer together:

2 tablespoons vinegar	a lemon slice
¾ cup water	a medium onion, sliced
1 teaspoon sugar	2 tablespoons butter
2 teaspoons prepared mustard	

Then add ½ cup ketchup or chili sauce and 1½ tablespoons of Worcestershire sauce and the meat. Simmer it, covered, for 45 minutes. Then spoon it out onto the toasted buns.

Ground beef is the basis of the following 9 recipes, for the reason that when your intentions outshine your follow-through, you still have the hamburger there, ready to fry as usual, and no harm done.
   However, each of the following 9 has an additional point in its favor, and sometimes several. For instance, the next one is pretty, and uncomplicated, and tastes good with mashed potatoes.

ROSY MEATBALLS   *4 Servings*

To a pound of ground beef, add:

½ cup crumbs (packaged or homemade, see
   page 123)
an egg
1 teaspoon instant minced onion
¼ teaspoon dry mustard
salt and pepper

Shape them into Ping-Pong-size balls and brown them in butter, in something that has a lid.
   Now mix an 8 oz can of tomato sauce with a one pound can of whole cranberry sauce, to pour over the meatballs. Do so, and simmer them, covered, for half an hour. Reheat them just before serving.

Another cheerful variable ground meat recipe is called Cornish Pasties if you are English, and if you are a Scotsman,

FORFAR BRIDIES *4 Servings*

Makes 4 servings that would take care of 2 people as an entrée.

A package of pastry mix
½ pound ground steak (or chopped leftover
    cooked or uncooked beef, veal, or lamb)
a small carrot, grated or diced
a small potato, diced
a medium onion, ditto, or 1 tablespoon minced
    onion
salt and pepper—not too much
something to moisten it: 3 or 4 tablespoons of
    any soup or canned gravy or mushroom
    sauce; or ¼ cup bouillon, made with ½ cube

Roll out the pastry and cut 4 circles the size of side plates. Mix everything else, put a dollop of it on each circle, fold your Bridies into half-moons, and seal the edges with a fork. Prick them, and bake at 400°F for 25 minutes.

(If you brush them with egg white before you bake them, they'll have a shiny professional look.)

Those Bridies can be completely prepared ahead, right up to baking them.

And now we come to the matter of *when* to cook; for a valuable thing to know about cooking besides how to get out of it is when to get into it.

I wish I had learned earlier that for a girl who gets to the kitchen on reluctant feet, it is best to cook, whenever possible, at the more repellent times of the day. If those pastry circles in Recipe 6 had been cut out, say, at noon, the Forfar Bridies' chances of showing up for dinner would have improved immeasurably. Just which *are* the more repellent times of the day is, clearly, one's own decision.

I find that I am in general agreement with the old monastery maxim: "The morning is the Lord's and the evening is the angels' but the afternoon is the Devil's."

That is, I like to tend my own trade—writing—in the fresh morning hours 5 a.m. to noon, which is the time for a walk, lunch, and whatever else needs doing, till around 3 p.m. I wouldn't dream of spoiling an evening or a cocktail hour with cooking. So, midafternoon is my time to cook when I do, for I seldom can think of anything bright to do with midafternoons anyway.

If my office were elsewhere, or if I had very small children now, this wouldn't work. I'd have to think of something else. But I would still choose, to the extent that I could, whatever hour seemed most generally pointless. Hour is about it, too. It is astounding what you can do in an hour if you have to.

The next recipe—a domesticated version of a well-known San Francisco specialty—is good, fast, and highly expandable or retractable. Just add more eggs, or less spinach, or more meat.

CASUAL JOE'S SPECIAL   *4 Servings*

some ground beef—½ to 1 pound
some chopped spinach—a package of frozen,
      cooked and drained; or a can of spinach,
      drained; or cooked drained chopped
      spinach, though that is a lot more trouble
some olive oil—say, 3 tablespoons
some onion or garlic—a cut garlic clove sizzled
      in the oil and then removed, or a teaspoon
      of minced onion, or half a chopped onion—
      whatever you feel up to
some eggs—say, one per customer, beaten
      slightly
salt and pepper

Heat the olive oil in a pan with the onions or the garlic. Add the ground beef in small bits. Pan fry* it till it's as done as you like it. Then add the spinach, STOP HERE, and stir it around till it's hot. Then add the eggs and stir till they're cooked. Salt and coarse-grind pepper it, and serve it.

The last ground beef affairs here are Combinations or Casseroles, and it might be well to look hard at the casserole before we get into it.

Most men don't regard the casserole too highly. You seldom hear a man reply, if you're so foolish as to ask him what he'd like for dinner, "Why don't you make that good prune-chicken-broccoli whatcha-macallit?"

If you retitle it a Stew or a Goulash, it stands a slightly better

---

* I'd rather say "fry" because I get tired of "sauté," and I think I was happier before I knew "fry" means "deep-fat fry" as in doughnuts. Now I feel duty-bound to say "pan-fry" when I mean "use a greased pan," for fear someone will think I don't know any better. Thus education doth make cowards of us all.

chance with him. Even so, he'd rather have a piece of meat, in recognizable form.

Remember, too, that a casserole is economical only when it's to serve a lot of people, or when it is creatively concocted out of odds and ends by a good cook who loves to. She also knows how to serve it with aplomb, but unfortunately this doesn't come in cans.

The rest of us wouldn't dare clean out the refrigerator for a casserole, or want to. We simply buy the pimentos and all the other things the recipe demands. Which doubles or triples the cost of the ground beef we could have served plain.

Fatalistically, we realize when buying these things that it will probably be a long old time before we need pimentos (and the other things) again. So far as those pimentos are concerned, you can keep them healthy for a considerably longer time if you transfer them into a small glass jar and add a teaspoon of vinegar and cover them with water. But this probably won't get done; and so the rest of the pimentos will idle themselves into a hairy old age if you don't promptly throw them out.

Yet there are times, even in the life of the reluctant cook, when she feels an inner need to make a casserole. After she's tasted a good one somewhere else, perhaps. Or when she is in a rare nesting mood and the wind is right. A man is wise to let his wife have these occasional marabou moments, too. He probably isn't 100% perfect himself.

BOEUF AND OEUFPLANT   *4 Servings*

(What this is, actually, is good eggplant and ground beef sandwiches baked in sauce. Presently, if you stay with it, you'll come to eggplant sandwiches without the boeuf, which will prove equally exciting in a different way.)

An eggplant, or aubergine if that's what you
        prefer to call it, sliced in half-inch slices,
        salted and peppered
olive oil
1 pound ground beef shaped into flat patties
a can of spaghetti sauce (1 pound size)
        preferably with mushrooms in it. If it
        has no mushrooms, add a can
¼ cup grated Parmesan cheese

In a little oil, pan fry the eggplant slices on both sides till they're light brown. Drain them on paper towels while you pan fry half as many patties as you have eggplant slices. (You'll have to add more oil, because the eggplant really soaks it up.)

In a shallow casserole dish, layer the eggplant slices, with beef patties between them. Cover it all with the sauce; top with the cheese. STOP HERE. Bake it, uncovered, for 20 minutes at 350°F.

7-HAPPINESS BEEF AND RICE   *6–8 Servings*

1. It is meat and starch combined.
2. Neither has to be cooked first.
3. Everything goes together at once.
4. Very young people and very old people like it and the others don't mind it much.
5. The amount of meat depends on what's there.
6. Odds-and-ends of vegetables can go into it.
7. Though it looks like dogfood when it goes into the oven it doesn't when it comes out.

¼ cup vegetable oil
6 oz / 1 cup uncooked rice
½ to 1½ pounds lean ground beef
small bottle stuffed olives, sliced
1 teaspoon each salt, pepper, paprika
1 medium onion, chopped
1½ cups V-8 or tomato juice
1½ cups boiling water
Grated cheese to spread on top

Crumble the raw beef in a big bowl. Add everything but the cheese and mix it up. Pour it into a 9 × 13 inch baking pan and bake for an hour at 350°F. Then reduce the heat and bake for an hour longer. Half an hour before serving time, sprinkle the grated cheese on, and finish baking.

4-HAPPINESS SPAGHETTI   *6–8 Servings*

1. People with hearty, uncritical appetites like it and eat it—little kids, football players, and guests who had a third drink.
2. It is quickly put together ahead of time.
3. It doesn't cost much.
4. It will sit in a 200°F oven for an hour or longer without being noticeably affected.

2 pounds lean hamburger crumbled and browned in a little oil
2 large onions, chopped and sautéed till transparent

2 cans Heinz or similar spaghetti
8 oz can of petite peas, the petiter the better
1 or 2 cans drained mushrooms, the more
    the merrier
1 cup tomato juice (or enough that it comes
    about half-way up through the food)
½ pound sharp cheese

Layer these things in this order: beef, onion, spaghetti, mushrooms, peas. Sprinkle it well with garlic salt and pepper, plus several squirts of Worcestershire sauce. Put the cheese on top and pour on the tomato juice. Freeze it if you like, or keep it in the refrigerator as long as 36 hours. (Either way, warm it to room temperature before you cook it.) Or bake it immediately, covered, in a 325°F oven, for at least an hour.

If you like curry, this next one is handy to know. Most curries seem to involve lamb, chicken, or fish, but this is how you can

CURRY HAMBURGER   *4 Servings*

In a pan that has a lid, sauté a chopped onion in oil or butter, then add:

1 pound ground beef   1 teaspoon curry powder
salt and pepper   ¼ teaspoon garlic salt

Stir it around till the meat is brown. Then add

Two 8 oz. cans of tomato purée
1 cup water

Simmer it covered for 10 minutes. STOP HERE. Then, 5 minutes before dinnertime, add a squirt of lemon juice. Serve it on rice with whatever trimmings are available: chutney, sliced green onion, crumbled bacon . . .

Finally, in the beef department, a Mexican-orientated dish which children like. (Adults like it all right; they're just not writing home about it.)

TAMALE BEAN POT

*6–8 Servings as is,
and easy to double
or triple*

*(You can bake this 4 hours at 200°F, which would be handy on a
football afternoon; or 2 hours at 350°F, as you like it.)*

Brown 1 pound of ground beef with a minced garlic clove and 1½
teaspoons of chili powder. (If you like a more distinctly south-of-the-
border taste, add another teaspoon.)
Then mix it with:

1 can chick peas (garbanzo beans)
2 cans red kidney beans, drained
1 can Mexicorn, drained
1 can tomato sauce
a spatter of Tabasco sauce
2 cans of tamales, papers peeled off, and cut
    in 1-inch chunks

Bake it, covered, for an hour at 325°F.

So endeth the beef section. And perhaps right here would be a good
place for an eggplant affair which is not only beefless but wholly
meatless, though it's a good hearty main dish.

ARMENIAN SANDWICHES

*3 Servings as an entrée,
6 as a vegetable
accompaniment*

Slice an eggplant* in half-inch slices. Pan fry them a little in olive oil,
and lay them out neatly on a paper towel.
Now pour half the beaten egg into a small bowl and add enough
grated Parmesan cheese for a thick paste. Spread it on half the eggplant
slices, and top them with the others.
Dip these sandwiches in the rest of the egg, then in some crumbs.
STOP HERE. Pan fry them, both sides, in olive oil till they're a pretty
light brown.

Now for a few PORK things.

---

* You needn't peel it unless it's an elderly eggplant with horrid age spots and wrinkles. This
would be one you bought some time ago and forgot about, because it would be foolish to start
with an antique.

THE PARSON'S HAM   *2–3 Servings*

*(A good fast dinner when you've an eye on the clock
and a foot in the flypaper.)*

Cook ⅔ cup of rice.
Lightly pan fry a 1 pound ham slice.

Put it on an oven-proof platter if you have one, and on a pan if you
haven't. Pile the rice on it, grate yellow cheese generously on top of
the rice, and place it under a hot broiler for a few minutes till the
cheese melts.

To round things out, you could arrange canned peach halves around
it before you broil it, first putting a little brown sugar and butter into
their hollows. But there isn't always time to round things out.

THE EASIEST RIBS*   *4–6 Servings*

Allow a pound of spareribs per person, or ¾ pound of the small
meatier back ribs.

Mince or crush a garlic clove in a bowl then add ¼ cupful each of:

prepared mustard	bourbon whisky or dark rum
soy sauce	brown sugar

Add 1 tablespoonful of grated orange rind, though this is not essential.

This will take care of 4 to 6 pounds of ribs. Spread it on both
sides of the ribs and roast at 325°F for 2 hours. Turn them once and
baste them if you think of it.

Next comes a slightly different approach to pork chops.

Certainly, different doesn't always mean better. Recipes that boast
like that always remind me—well, not always, but they did right
then—of the inscription on the Scottish tombstone: "Lay down your
burden and follow me." To which a shrewd passer-by had appended
a neat sign:

"To follow you I won't consent
Until I know which way you went."

What is different about the next recipe is the soy sauce, which gives
a slight Oriental aura to the chops, and some think it improves them.

---

* A virtually non-cooking friend of mine, reading proofs here, said, "But they're not as easy as
roasting them plain at 500°F for 10 minutes and then 350°F for an hour without any sauce at
all, and mine are easier to eat." I couldn't think of a thing to say.

APRICOT PORK CHOPS

6 Servings

6 reasonably thick pork chops
1 medium onion, finely
    chopped
medium can apricot halves

2 tablespoons soy sauce
a green pepper, thinly sliced,
    if you like it

Into a plastic bag put a little flour, salt, pepper, and then the chops. Shake them firmly. Brown them in the fat you trimmed off, then add the apricots, onions, and soy sauce. Simmer it half an hour covered, STOP HERE, and half an hour uncovered. If you want to add the green pepper, do it 15 minutes before the chops are done.

If you occasionally cook a pork roast, the following dish will help use it up. (It's a good easy goulash anyway, made with 2 or 3 good-sized pork chops, boned, cubed, and browned.)

TOMORROW'S GOULASH

4 Servings

Brown a small chopped onion in 2 tablespoons of bacon fat.
    Add 1 tablespoon of paprika, and simmer it while you cube 2 to 3 cupfuls of the cooked pork.
    Now add the pork, plus:

2 cups sauerkraut
1 tablespoon caraway seeds

Cover and simmer it for an hour. STOP HERE and reheat it when you're ready to serve. If it seems dry, add a little water. And just before dinnertime, stir in ½ cupful of yogurt.

OH DAD, POOR DAD
Or, Spam and Cheese

4–6 Servings

(But if you don't tell him, he'll probably think this is ham.)

Chop up a can of Spam. Then mix it with:

2 beaten eggs
20 small soda crackers crushed
2 cups milk
¾ cup grated sharp Cheddar, plus a little
    more for the top

Bake this, uncovered, in a casserole dish for an hour at 350°F.

SEAFOOD will be the next consideration, with 2 recipes, the first being a well-bred little sole recipe.

Sole is an In fish, as you may have noticed. Many a cook depends on her little sole recipe as many another girl counts on her basic black. You might try counting on this one if you're not already committed. It's only a 10-minute operation—mixing the sauce, spreading it on the fish fillets, and rolling them up. But the results are rather impressive. And taste good.

RIVIERA SOLE
6 Servings

Mix together:

1 cup yogurt
½ cup mayonnaise

1 tablespoon lemon juice
½ teaspoon curry powder

After you rinse 2 pounds of sole fillets, and pat them dry with paper towels, spread half the mixture on them, salt and pepper them, and roll them up. Put them in a shallow buttered casserole and pour the rest of the sauce on.

Over it all, sprinkle a can of drained browned-in-butter mushrooms and a can of drained white grapes. (Or you could use raw mushrooms and fresh grapes. If you do, sauté the mushrooms first in a little butter, then add the grapes and cook 2 or 3 minutes more.)

All this can be done at any time. Then bake at 350°F for half an hour.

BODDIAN SOLE
3–4 Servings

(Not quite so well bred, but just as easy.)

You start with a pound of sole, or 4 large fillets. Lay them out nicely in a baking dish.

Mix:

1 can undiluted mushroom soup
½ cup cooked shrimps or prawns
½ cup white wine

and pour it over the fish. STOP HERE. Let it stand 3 hours, and more wouldn't matter.

Finally, sprinkle it with ½ oz Parmesan cheese and bake it, uncovered, for 20 minutes at 400°F.

A word about WINE, by the way, inasmuch as we just passed some.

There is a great deal of it around, and those little old wine makers are understandably anxious that we use it up.

Sometimes their efforts remind you of the soap-selling genius a while back who persuaded people to carve statues out of soap as well as wash with it. This got rid of a lot of soap. And after the recent spate of wine makers' recipe books and kitchen manuals, we mustn't be alarmed if they now tell us to use a robust Burgundy to dampen the silage as well as the swordfish.

As it is, one finds some fairly improbable wine recipes. The wine makers like wine on cinnamon toast (you mix sugar, cinnamon, and butter into a paste with Marsala or sherry).

Or wine on pork chops (roll them in dry biscuit mix, sauté them in butter, then simmer them in sherry). And they like wine in baked beans, in tuna salad. . . .

But not everyone does. Here you must keep a cool head, and taste it on your mind's tongue first. If it tastes good there, then try it. But be cautious about quantity. Here again, they like you to pour it on. There is a Let's-throw-away-the-chicken-and-drink-the-gravy School that it's best to steer clear of.

As to the grade of wine to use in cooking, there is a disagreement. Some good cooks say, *Any* kind. Other cooks say, Use the same wine in cooking that you'll serve later at the table. (I'll bet they don't always do it themselves, though, when it's a matter of a fine old vintage Bordeaux.)

The main consideration, it seems to me, should be the basic flavor—strong or slight—of the dish itself. Nuances are lost in a hearty beef stew that's redolent of onions and garlic. But a custard or a delicate fish or chicken is only as good as the wine is.

Several nice things have been happening to CHICKENS around the country while my back was turned. I'm glad to have this chance to pass them along. Neither one messes up a broiler the way broiled chicken does, or the ceiling, as fried chicken does.

The first is:

INNOCENT CHICKEN

6 Servings

(If you follow the crumb suggestion on page 121 this will taste a bit different every time, but still innocent. There's no point trying to complicate it, either, with herbs or sauces, because many recipes, like this one, are born uncomplicated and should remain so.)

You'll need:

about 2 pounds chicken
  pieces, fresh or thawed
¾ cup melted butter

3 cups crushed cornflakes
  (or crumbs)
½ teaspoon seasoning salt
salt and pepper

Sprinkle the salt, pepper, and seasoning salt all over the pieces, dip them in the butter, then the crumbs, and lay them skin side up in a baking dish. STOP HERE. Bake, covered, for half an hour at 350°F. Then baste it with the rest of the butter and bake uncovered an hour longer at 250°F.

The second, not quite so innocent but nearly, is:

5-MINUTE CHILI CHICKEN

4–5 Servings

(The 5-minute preparation-time depends on how fast you can cut up aluminum foil; and if someone stole the kitchen scissors again, it's more like 7.)

Line up:

8 to 10 chicken thighs or drumsticks
¼ jar of Chili Seasoning
¼ cup cider vinegar
some aluminum foil

Then salt and pepper the chicken. Next, mix the seasoning with the vinegar, paint each piece neatly with it, and wrap each one snugly in a square of aluminum foil, so you won't have to wash the baking dish later. Then bake them at 400°F for 40 minutes.

Four real quickies involving chicken:

SOUPER CHICKEN

4–5 Servings

Mix

    1 can condensed mushroom soup
    1 can condensed onion soup
    ⅔ cup dry white wine

Pour it over 2 to 3 pounds of chicken pieces, cover, and bake at 300°F for 2½ hours. Serve it. It you want gravy instead of sauce, thicken the juice with 2 tablespoons cornflour mixed in a little cold water. And if you want stew, add some little onions and carrot chunks about 30 minutes before it's done.

COCA-CHICKEN

4–5 Servings

Salt and pepper a flock of chicken pieces—2 or 3 pounds—or a whole chicken, cut up. In a casserole, warm ¾ cup ketchup, add the chicken, and pour one cup of Coca Cola over the whole thing. Cover it, cook for half an hour. Then uncover it, cook for another half-hour, and it's done. And don't knock it till you've tried it. Then you can, but fair's fair.

Don't knock bottled barbecue sauce either. There are some good brands around—some smokier, some spicier. Get one you like, to keep handy for:

BARBACHICKEN*

Simmer the chicken pieces in a little water for 10 minutes, then drain them. Lay them out in a shallow pan, pour some sauce on top, and bake at 350°F for about 40 minutes.

BASTARD BARBECUE

3–4 Servings

*(You will probably be suspicious, as I was at first, of the
brown sugar. But go ahead.)*

Salt and pepper and lavishly garlic-salt a cut-up frying chicken.
    Put it in a shallow pan and sprinkle it generously with soft brown sugar. Dot it with lots of butter and bake it, uncovered, about an hour, at 350°F.

---

* That same barbecue sauce is good on any leftover roast meat if you've eaten it plain too long. Cut the meat in small chunks and heat them in it.

Two Dependable Chicken Things to Freeze:

MC CORMACK'S CHOICE   *8–10 Servings*

*(The idea here is four items, layered and baked: broccoli,.
chicken-in-gravy, cottage cheese, and noodles.)*

a 4-lb chicken, cut up
a celery stalk
an onion slice
1 stick butter
½ cup flour
½ teaspoon salt

½ teaspoon dried basil
1 package frozen chopped
  broccoli
8 oz egg noodles
16 oz cottage cheese
1 egg

Take the broccoli out of the freezer to thaw while you simmer the chicken in water to cover, with the celery and onion. Then get the meat off the bones and dice it. Next, make some gravy: melt the butter, stir in the flour gradually, and add salt, basil, and 2½ cups of the water you cooked the chicken in.

Cook the egg noodles for 8 minutes and drain them. Then beat the egg a little and mix it with the cottage cheese. Finally: layer these things like this, in a big casserole dish: *chicken mix, noodles, cottage cheese, broccoli.* Do it again, ending with chicken mix. Bake for 45 minutes at 350°F, wrap it, and freeze. When you eventually reheat it, sprinkle Parmesan cheese on top and reheat it, frozen, for 2 hours at 350°F.

PHOEBE'S CHICKEN TARRAGON

(quicker and very good too)

4 pounds chicken pieces
salt, pepper, garlic salt
½ cup mushrooms, fresh or
  canned

¼ cup butter
3 tablespoons tarragon, dried
¾ cup dry white wine

Sauté the seasoned chicken pieces in the butter. Take them out, sauté the mushrooms in the same butter for 4 minutes, and replace the chicken. Sprinkle it with the tarragon, both sides, so it is elegantly speckled. Then add dry white wine, replace the mushrooms, cover, simmer half an hour. Freezes well.

The next recipe is a bird of a different feather. It is here because it uses up leftovers the week following Christmas. (Should you ever feel like making it from scratch, the easiest way to cook the chicken is on page 258.)

LEFTOVER FOWL SOUFFLÉ

6 Servings

You need about 4 cups of diced cooked turkey or chicken.

Sauté 4 spring onions, chopped, in 2 tablespoons of butter. With the other hand, cook ½ cup of raw rice, which makes a cup of cooked. Or use enough pre-cooked rice to make one cup.

Now combine:

4 beaten eggs
1 can chicken broth
1 small can condensed milk

4 slices bread, torn in small
    pieces
2 tablespoons chopped parsley
½ teaspoon herb seasoning

To this reasonably damp mixture add the diced chicken, onions, rice, and a teaspoon of salt. Put it in a baking dish, cover it generously with grated sharp cheese, and bake it at 350°F for 45 minutes.

Next, a little lamb, which somehow straggled behind.

A GOOD THING TO DO WITH LAMB CHOPS

For 4 chops, mix about ¼ cup blue cheese with a few drops of Tabasco and a teaspoon of Worcestershire sauce. Have this at the ready.

Rub the chops with a cut garlic clove and broil them, about 4 inches from the heat. If they are an inch and a half thick, broil 10 minutes, a little less if they're thinner. Turn them over then, spread the cheese mixture on the up side, and broil them another 5.

LAMALOHA LOAF

6–8 Servings

*(A good different meat loaf. When you slice it, don't be upset if
it falls apart a bit, for that can happen to anyone. It does so because
it's tender and 2-layered.)*

Mix all together:

2 pounds ground lamb, lean
    as possible

¼ cup chopped parsley
2 eggs, unbeaten

1 cup cracker crumbs (that's
    28 soda crackers)
¼ teaspoon garlic powder (or
    1 crushed garlic clove)
½ teaspoon cumin

2 or 3 tablespoons soy sauce
½ teaspoon salt, or seasoned
    salt
½ teaspoon sugar
½ cup ketchup

Divide this into 2 longish patties (so it will eventually add up to a loaf) and put one of them in a loaf pan. Down the middle, line up

an 8 oz can of drained mushrooms, browned-in-butter.

Along the sides, arrange

½ small can of pineapple tidbits.

Cover it with the second long patty. Seal the edges now and spread some ketchup over the top. STOP HERE. Then bake for 1¾ hours at 350°F. (This is longer than a beef loaf would take because most people like the lamb more well done.)

SHOULDER BAGS

Cut aluminum foil in 10-inch-square pieces.
    On each, place:

a salted-and-peppered lamb
    chop
an eggplant slice

a slice each of onion, green
    pepper, tomato

Pour a tablespoon of sherry on top, wrap them up swiftly (so the sherry doesn't run out) and snugly, then put them in a baking pan. Bake them an hour at 350°F.
    These are good with any sort of rice or pilaff.

LAMB AND LEMON   *4 Servings*

*(An unexpectedly good flavor combination, and a
nice change from garlic.)*

Mix together:

¼ cup olive oil
¼ cup lemon juice
1 teaspoon grated lemon rind

Brush 8 1-inch-thick loin or rib chops with this, and broil them about 4 inches from the heat, 7 to 10 minutes on the first side, depending on how pink you like your lamb. Brush them occasionally as they broil and after you turn them over. Give them about 6 minutes on the second side. You may garnish each chop with a lemon slice if you have another lemon.

These should do it, then, for the next three decades. But just a word on the important matter of:

KEEPING A STIFF UPPER LIP

When you hate to cook, another ailment you probably suffer from, besides apathy, is the inability to judge correctly your own work.

In these low moments, should the whole dinner taste a little seedy, you must remember that it probably doesn't to other people. You had a better chance than they did to get tired of the ingredients.

Neither is the meal quite so glorious as you may think in those rare euphoric moments when the soufflé soars and the salad dressing sings. (Remember, you're exceptionally fond of anchovies.) The truth usually lurks somewhere in the middle.

It can also help if you will scrutinize critically an occasional restaurant meal. Then, after you've eaten a slice of tired salami with a pickled mushroom—which passed for antipasto—plus a cardboard cutlet, a too-vinegary salad, and grocery-store ice cream that's been given a fancy name, ask yourself if you could unblushingly have charged $25 for that.

As a last resort, should these things fail you, you may turn to Dr. Bryan's truly astonishing words of aid and comfort on page 241.

9. Vegetables, Salads, Salad Dressings

OR THIS SIDE OF BERIBERI

Once I knew a girl who just loved vegetables. You didn't dare leave this little bunny alone with a relish tray or it would be instantly deflowered of its cauliflowerlets and stripped clean of its carrot strips.

But this girl is in the minority. For cold scientific proof, do this: On one side of a plate, put a stack of marinated string beans; on the other side, put a heap of smoked oysters. Then observe carefully which gets left. You needn't even be that fancy. A can of salted peanuts will win over the string beans, hands down, every time.

Facts must be faced. Vegetables simply don't taste as good as most other things do. And there isn't a single vegetable, hot or cold, that stands on its own feet the way a ripe peach does, or a strawberry. Even sweetcorn needs butter and salt. (It is interesting to note that vegetables beginning with A are the most self-sufficient: artichokes, asparagus, avocados, which have really slithered out of the fruit kingdom by this time into the vegetable kingdom no matter what the botanists say. But the farther down the alphabet you go, through spinach and turnips, the more hopeless they become, given all the butter and salt you've got.)

Actually, the food experts know this, deep down. You can tell they do, from the reliance they put on adjectives whenever they bump into a vegetable. "And with it serve a big bowl of tiny, buttery, fresh-from-the-garden beets!" they'll cry. But they're still only beets, and there's no need to get so excited about it.

Never make the mistake of combining two rather repulsive vegetables in the hope that any good will come of it. *Two wrongs never make a right.* Once I knew a lady who cooked big carrots and hollowed out their middles and filled the resultant canoes with canned peas.

In order to make most vegetables fit to eat, you must cover up the basic taste of the vitamins with calories. You use butter, oil, sour cream, nuts, chopped bacon, mushrooms, and cheese, as well as lemon juice, vinegar, herbs, and a lot of other things which we shall come to presently.

This is not only fattening, for the most part, but it is also a lot of trouble. You're certainly not going to do it very often. There is no reason you should, either. The children must learn sooner or later that life isn't all beer and skittles, and your husband knows it anyhow. It won't hurt them a bit to eat their plain buttered vegetables at gun point, with a running commentary by you on what will happen to their teeth and complexions and bottoms if they don't.

Moreover, there is a certain social cachet to serving your vegetables plain. Indeed, if your entrée is in any way fancy, the *haute cuisine* crowd frowns on anything but the simplest vegetable as an accompaniment, which should be a load off your mind and off your back.

So just gird your loins and serve that big bowl of tiny, buttery, fresh-from-the-garden beets, murmuring—if you care to—"After all, there's nothing like good butter, salt, and coarse-ground pepper." (Always be sure it's coarse-ground, because a lot of people feel that anything peppered should look as though it had been fished out of a gravel pit.)

However, just once in a while, when you are serving a very easy main dish, like something thawed, or when you yourself get so tired of plain vegetables that you cannot stand them any more, it is nice to know a few things to do.

First of all, find a seasoning you like, and add it to the melted butter. This is an easy way to improve vast hordes of vegetables.

Second, you can also add a bouillon cube to the water you cook them in. This helps a bit, too.

Third, the authorities maintain that a wee pinch of sugar, in addition to your other seasonings, brings out the flavor of *any* vegetable. The debatable point here is whether you want to bring it out or cover it up; but this is every girl's own personal decision.

Fourth, there is an easy cheese sauce you can make and keep on hand to give gentle assistance to cauliflower, cabbage, asparagus, French beans, et cetera.

EASY CHEESE SAUCE

1 pound sharp processed cheese, diced
1½ cups evaporated milk
1 teaspoon salt
2 teaspoons dry mustard

Melt the cheese in the top of your double boiler over hot water, add everything else, and stir it till it's smooth and hot. Then pour it into a jar, cover it, and keep it in the refrigerator. When you want to use some of it, put the amount you want in the top of your double boiler again, thin it with a little milk, and heat it.

Fifth, there is an easy fake hollandaise which is good with artichokes, asparagus, and whatever else you think you'd like hollandaise on.

FAKE HOLLANDAISE

¾ cup mayonnaise   salt, pepper·
½ cup milk   1 teaspoon lemon juice

Cook the milk and mayonnaise together in the top of your double boiler for 5 minutes, stirring constantly. Then add the other things and stir just long enough for one good chorus of "Clementine," and it's done.

Or sixth, you might feel daring and try:

BLENDER HOLLANDAISE

*(Which isn't the ugly word it used to be if you have a blender,
though if you don't, make the preceding recipe.)*

Heat slowly ¼ pound of butter in a saucepan till it bubbles. But don't
let it brown.

At the same time, in your blender put:

3 egg yolks	¼ teaspoon salt
2 tablespoons lemon juice	pinch of cayenne pepper

Cover the container and turn motor on at low speed. Immediately
remove the cover and pour in the hot butter in a steady stream. When
all the butter is added, turn off the motor. This makes enough for 4
or 5 people.

And so to the recipes.

COMPANY CARROTS   *3–4 Servings*

*(Through the ages, people have gone to enormous trouble to
camouflage carrots. Once I saw a recipe that called for carrots, strained
honey, marjoram, grated cheese, and chestnuts, which is like sewing
diamond buttons on denim jeans.)*

Cut a reasonable number of carrots into strips—so you have 2 cupfuls,
say. Cook them till they're tender and drain them. Then mix these
things together in a heavy pan:

3 tablespoons butter	½ teaspoon paprika
2 tablespoons sugar	juice of half a lemon

Add the carrots and sauté them about 10 minutes, stirring so that all
the strips get well acquainted with the sauce.

OVEN CARROTS   *4–5 Servings*

*(If you're out of lemon juice and feel that you must do something
about carrots anyway, you can do this. It is more trouble, but it
demands no last-minute attention, the carrots stay crisp, and the
dish looks quite polite.)*

4 green onions chopped, tops and all	3 tablespoons minced parsley
3 tablespoons butter	½ teaspoon salt
	dash of pepper

10 to 12 small carrots, or 5   ¼ cup light cream
    big ones, cut in strips

Fry the onions in the butter till they're tender. Add the carrots, parsley, salt, and pepper, and put it all into a buttered casserole dish. Pour the cream on top, cover, and bake at 350°F for 45 minutes.

KIDS VS. CARROTS

Children who raise Cain about carrots will sometimes eat them if you boil them along with potatoes and mash the two together. Not always, but sometimes.

And now for the swift little hot green vegetable, which has a tendency to finish cooking faster than the rest of the meal does.

There is a mystique, by the way, about serving hot things smoking hot and cold things icy cold which is hard on the tooth enamel, as well as on the people who are doing the cooking.

It's a neat trick when you can do it because it makes things taste a notch better. Plates you've chilled make a salad more effective, somehow. And the reputation of many a steak house has been built on the sizzle.

But sometimes—especially in the matter of hot food—the food and the people don't synchronize. That's because real life is different from gourmet-cookbook life.

In real life, the clarion call to dinner is often the signal for the man of the house to start taking apart his outboard motor in the basement while the daughter of the house disappears in a panic search for hair curlers.

However, next to the family, vegetables are the stickiest wickets, because so many of them take so little cooking. Here we must go back to the prime fact in Chapter 5. *Few things cannot be interrupted while cooking.* It's simply a matter of deciding who's in charge—the cook or the dinner.

Therefore, the thing to do, when you think of it, is to cook a green vegetable a few minutes less than it's supposed to be. Then pull it off the burner, remove the lid, so it won't steam, pour off the water, if any, and add the butter, and seasonings. You can reheat it at any time in the butter, for another couple of minutes, and it won't be overcooked.

VERY EDIBLE STRING BEANS   *6 Servings*

(Many string bean recipes, too, call for expensive ingredients like fresh mushrooms and toasted almonds, and even so, you can still taste the string beans. Simmering them with a ham bone works as well as anything, but remember, they didn't give that ham bone away. This recipe calls for no exotic extras, and it tastes good.)

2 packages frozen string beans, cooked and drained (or 2 pounds fresh ditto)
5 tablespoons butter
salt and pepper

1 tablespoon finely chopped parsley
1 clove garlic, minced
juice of half a lemon

Sauté the cooked beans in the butter, along with the salt, pepper, parsley, and garlic, for 7 to 10 minutes. Just before you serve them, sprinkle the lemon juice on. (Note: These beans are the exception that proves the Leftover Rule, p. 65. If there are any beans left over, known as has-beans, you had better keep them, because they are good in a green salad.)

BEN'S BEANS

All he does is this: He sautés a little can or two of mushroom pieces in a little butter, adds cooked French beans, salt, pepper. Then, over low heat, he stirs in enough sour cream or yogurt to make a sauce, heats it through, and serves it up.

If you are roasting meat in a 300°F oven and want a vegetable to bake along with it, you can make:

SIMPLE BEANS   *3–4 Servings*

Cook and drain a package of frozen string beans and add:

1 tablespoon minced onion
½ teaspoon salt
1 can condensed mushroom soup thinned a bit with milk
2 tablespoons chopped pimentos if you have them

Put this in a casserole dish and bake it, uncovered, for an hour in that 300°F oven. Longer won't hurt.

If you want to take care of two nights' greenery in one go, make:

BAIL BOND BEANS

Cook more French-cut green beans than you can eat tonight till they are just tender. In a little saucepan, heat together:

2 tablespoons lemon juice
2 tablespoons olive oil
¼ cup sliced black olives
some garlic salt and oregano

Pour it over the hot green beans and serve them.

Add first night's leftover Bail Bond Beans to a green salad for the next night. Very good.

BEETNIKS

Should you happen to fish the final sweet pickle out of the juice in a pickle jar and, at the same instant, notice a can of baby beets on the pantry shelf (admittedly an unlikely chain of events), you can put the beets into the pickle juice, put the lid back on, and the next morning they will be pickled.

SOUR CREAM CABBAGE   *5–6 Servings*

(You wouldn't cook this for company unless your kitchen is 200 yards from the living room, but it's easy and it tastes good.)

1 firm green cabbage	½ teaspoon nutmeg
1 egg, well beaten	salt and pepper
2 tablespoons sugar	1 cup sour cream or yogurt

Shred the cabbage finely, and throw the stump away. Cook it in as little water as possible till it's tender—5 to 10 minutes. Drain it, then add the other ingredients, mixed together, and put it on a low burner to heat through.

THE SOLUTION TO CANNED OR FROZEN PEAS

4 Servings

First, buy a pound of little tiny peas. (Petits pois.) If canned, drain them. Then slice 3 green onions and sizzle them a minute in 1 tablespoon of olive oil. Add the peas, and

¼ teaspoon thyme
dash of salt, pepper

¼ head lettuce, chopped

and stir it once in a while as it sits on a low burner and heats through.

BROILED ONIONS

4 Servings

1 pound small cooked onions
2 tablespoons butter

¼ cup bread crumbs
¼ cup grated Parmesan
salt, pepper

You drain the onions first, then melt the butter in a pie dish and roll the onions in it. Now mix the bread crumbs and Parmesan together and sprinkle the mixture all over the little fellows, before setting them 4 inches beneath a hot broiler for 7 minutes.

CRISP TOMATOES

Cut some firm peeled tomatoes into thick slices, salt and pepper them, dip them in cornmeal, and fry them in bacon fat or butter until they're light brown.

PAINLESS SPINACH

4 Servings

1 package frozen spinach
1 cut garlic clove
1 tablespoon butter

salt
pepper
half a lemon

First, cook the spinach and drain it. Then sizzle the garlic clove in the butter, remove the clove, and put the spinach in. Let it simmer for 5 minutes. Just before you serve it, salt and pepper it lightly and add a good squeeze of lemon juice.

SPINACH SURPRISE
4 Servings

(The surprise is that there's usually none left, even with dedicated anti-spinach people.)

1 package frozen chopped
  spinach
¼ cup chopped onion
½ cup sour cream or yogurt

4 tablespoons butter
pinch of salt
1 teaspoon vinegar

Cook the spinach with the onion. Melt the butter, add the spinach, well drained, and stir it. Then add the salt and sour cream or yogurt, and blend it together. Finally, stir in the vinegar and serve.

Forward now to some swift vegetables with rather a company taste.

SWIFT MUSHROOM SPINACH
4 Servings

Mix a can of undiluted condensed mushroom soup with a package of frozen cooked drained spinach. Add a teaspoon of vinegar. Heat it till it's hot.

Sliced water chestnuts or chopped walnuts would be good in this. Still, that's one more step, and it's good without it.

GUEST CHOKES
6 Servings

(You could serve these cold, too, as an upgraded pickle on a picnic.)

First, simmer a small minced onion and a garlic clove in a little butter for 5 minutes. Take the garlic out and add:

½ cup chicken stock (the bouillon-cube kind)
Two 15 oz cans artichoke hearts, drained
3 tablespoons lemon juice
1½ teaspoons salt
1 teaspoon oregano

Simmer with the lid on for another 10 minutes. Reheat and serve. Grated lemon rind would be a thoughtful note on top.

ZUCCHINI BOATS

6–8 Servings

(The general principle here is the simple one of scooping out the innards to improve them, then piling it all back in to bake)

6 medium zucchini
1 chopped onion, sautéed in butter till tender
1 tablespoon additional butter
1 tablespoon flour
⅛ teaspoon pepper

½ chicken bouillon cube dissolved in ¼ cup hot water
¼ cup single cream
¼ cup breadcrumbs
2 tablespoons Parmesan cheese

While the chopped onion bubbles gently in the frying pan, make boats out of the zucchini: slice off the ends and cut a long vertical slice off each, a third of the way down. Simmer both tops and bottoms in salted water for no more than 10 minutes, then scoop out all the meat but throw away the tops. Chop it, dry it a bit with a towel, and add it to the pan.

Now make a cream sauce: melt the additional butter in a small saucepan, stir in the flour, cook till bubbly, then add the chicken stock and cream. Stir till medium thick, then put in the frying pan along with the breadcrumbs, cheese, and pepper. Simmer for 5 minutes, then pile it into the zucchini shells, put them in a greased pan, top with more Parmesan, and bake at 400°F for 15 minutes. Serve with a lemon wedge.

GREEN PANCAKES

6 Servings

(pronounced *Frittaten*)

2 lb grated raw zucchini
1 cup flour
2 teaspoons baking powder
2 eggs, well beaten

salt, pepper
½ teaspoon thyme
butter for frying

Put the grated zucchini in a bowl. Sift the flour and baking powder together and beat the mixture into the vegetable. Then beat in the eggs, salt, pepper, and thyme. Blend it till it's a thick pancake batter, then drop by the spoonful into a frying pan containing some good hot butter. What you're aiming for is pancakes about 3 inches wide. These are a good accompaniment for the Sunday roast.

SPINACH-AND-LOVE APPLES   *6 Servings*

Get 3 or 4 big *tomatoes*, peel them and slice them into 8 thick chunks. Lay them out in a flat buttered baking dish. Sprinkle with *garlic salt*. Now cook 2 packages of *frozen spinach* and drain it. With it, mix:

¼ cup breadcrumbs	⅓ cup grated Parmesan cheese
1 small chopped green onion	½ teaspoon garlic powder
4 tablespoons melted butter	½ teaspoon thyme
¼ teaspoon salt	2 beaten eggs

Spoon this on top of the tomato slices, shape into neat little humps, sprinkle more crumbs and Parmesan on top, and bake at 350°F for 15 minutes.

GUEST SPROUTS   *5–6 Servings*

Cook 2 packages of frozen (or 2 pounds fresh) Brussels sprouts according to directions, and drain them.

In a little saucepan, heat:

¼ cup butter
1 tablespoon prepared mustard
2 tablespoons lemon juice

Pour the sauce over the Brussels sprouts. STOP HERE. Heat it all together, then serve.

So here we are, as ready as we'll ever be to deal with the hot vegetable casserole.

The reason we must do so is this: The truculent cook operating on a short culinary tether never gets too far away from the chop, the steak, and the hamburger. And not only does a hot vegetable casserole round out that sort of meal in an authoritative way, but it also often enables her to dispense with something—a starch, a salad, or rolls.

That is what these 7 casseroles do. And another big point: They all bake in a 325°F oven. That means that if you roast beef at 325°F for 20 minutes to the pound you can bake the vegetables right along with it.

EXTRAORDINARILY GOOD EGGPLANT   *6 Servings*

1 eggplant, unpeeled
2 chopped onions
¼ cup butter
1 tin smoked oysters, coarsely chopped
⅔ cup crushed Ritz crackers (plain or cheese)

Cut the eggplant into small pieces and simmer them, covered, in salted water till they're tender—about 10 minutes. With your other hand sauté the chopped onions in the butter till they're tender, too.

Drain the eggplant thoroughly in a colander, pressing it with paper towels to dry it thoroughly. Then mix together everything except half the cracker crumbs, and put it in a casserole dish. Put the rest of the crumbs on top. STOP HERE. Bake for 35 minutes at 325°F.

CORN CHIP CASSEROLE   *6 Servings*

(A nice idea with chicken, ham, hamburgers.)

Sauté:

2 sliced green onions
3 stalks sliced celery

in:

1 tablespoon butter

till they're tender.
Then mix:

2 slightly beaten eggs   ¼ teaspoon salt
⅓ cup milk   a 17-oz can of cream-style corn
½ teaspoon crumbled oregano

Add the cooked onions and celery to the second mixture, and have 6 oz of corn chips ready as well as ¼ pound of grated cheese.

In a casserole dish, layer the corn mixture, the chips, and the cheese till you run out of material, ending—if you can—with the chips. STOP HERE. Bake at 325°F for 40 minutes, uncovered.

JOAN'S CONTRIBUTION   *6–8 Servings*

(This includes—as you will see—5 vegetables, and it's good anyway.)

1 package frozen chopped
  spinach
1 package frozen broccoli,
  chopped (or 2 packages
  of either)
1 can condensed mushroom
  or celery soup

½ teaspoon salt
¼ teaspoon tarragon
¼ teaspoon pepper
some French-fried onion rings
¼ cup grated cheese
2 middle-sized tomatoes,
  peeled and quartered

Cook the spinach and the broccoli a little less than the box says you're supposed to, adding a tablespoon of vinegar to each.

Add the seasonings to the soup, then fold in the drained spinach and broccoli. Pour it into a flattish buttered baking pan, and arrange the onions and tomatoes on top. Sprinkle on the cheese. STOP HERE. Bake it at 325°F for 35 minutes, or 250°F for 45 minutes, whichever is handier.

N.B. You can double this easily should you need to. If you do, make it one can of mushroom soup *and* a can of celery soup.

CHEESE CELERY SPECIAL   *4–5 Servings*

(A good way to use up the large ungainly stalks.)

Cook 1 lb of coarsely chopped celery in water till it's tender but crisp. Drain it.

Then sauté:

½ chopped onion
1 chopped green pepper

in 2 tablespoons of butter. Into this, stir:

about ¼ cup blue cheese
½ cup heavy cream

Now add the drained celery, put it all in a baking dish, and cover with:

¾ cup of crumbs

The crumb topping is better if you use coarse crumbs fried in a little butter. But those out of a box are all right dotted with butter. STOP HERE. Heat it through, about 15 minutes, in a 325°F oven.

GREEN-BEAN CASSEROLE   *6–8 Servings*

(I think a polite-tasting canned-bean recipe is handy to have.)

2 cans green beans, drained
   (or an equal amount of
   any other kind, but
   canned is easiest)
2 tablespoons vegetable oil
2 medium chopped onions
a few parsley sprigs (or a
   teaspoon of dried)

1 teaspoon garlic powder
½ small container cottage
   cheese
¼ cup grated Cheddar cheese
4 eggs, slightly beaten
1 teaspoon salt
dash of pepper
¾ cup of soft breadcrumbs

Sauté the chopped onions in the oil till they're tender. Then add everything but the beans and stir it.

In a greased casserole dish, layer this mixture with the beans, trying to end up with the cheese mixture, though the sky won't fall if you don't. STOP HERE. Bake it, uncovered, for 30 minutes at 325°F.

MACADANGDANG SPINACH MEDLEY

(Which provides a starch, too.)

1 pound (fresh or frozen
   and thawed) spinach
2 tablespoons butter
1 chopped onion
1 teaspoon garlic powder
3 cups cooked rice
4 eggs, slightly beaten

½ cup milk
2 teaspoons salt
¼ teaspoon pepper
1 cup shredded Mozzarella
   cheese (about 4 oz)
½ cup grated Parmesan
   cheese

Melt the butter, add the chopped onion, and cook till it's tender. Add the spinach, garlic, rice and Parmesan, and mix it well. Now combine the eggs, milk and seasonings and stir this into the rice mixture. Turn it into a shallow rectangular baking dish, top it with the Mozzarella, and bake at 325°F for half an hour.

SPICY BAKED EGGPLANT

Get a good-sized eggplant and don't peel it, just cube it. Sauté it in ¾ cup olive oil for about 5 minutes. Then add:

a 15 oz can of tomatoes
small jar of pimentos drained
    and coarsely chopped
2 medium sliced onions

1 teaspoon garlic powder
2 tablespoons chopped parsley
1 teaspoon capers

Cook all this about 15 minutes more, then pile it into a casserole dish, put crumbs on top, heat it half an hour at 325°F and double-check to be sure it's hot right through. This freezes well.

Finally, to taper off, here are two generalized approaches to the vegetable that seem to improve most of them.

ALL-AROUND CRUMB TOPPING

Fry a cup of rather coarse breadcrumbs in one stick of butter till they're brown. Sprinkle them on hot precooked salted-and-peppered asparagus, string beans, broccoli, cauliflower. . . .

If you wanted to sprinkle Parmesan cheese on top of that, and put the dish under the broiler for a minute, you could. But you're not supposed to if there's cheese elsewhere in the dinner, for that would be a sort of culinary stutter. Anyway, we must cut corners where we can.

The second useful generalized approach is Blender Hollandaise which you will find on page 112.

And so to the SALAD department.

Many dishes have been called salad, including canned peach slices in lime jelly, bananas, walnuts and whipped cream, and cottage cheese. Once, I knew a lady who pitted cooked prunes and stuffed them with peanut butter.

But when you hate to cook, you need concern yourself mainly with only two kinds: vegetable salads and fruit salads. Of the two, the vegetable salad is the more important because you don't have to cut up all that fruit; and first and foremost among the vegetable salads is the GREEN SALAD.

It is important to fix firmly in your mind the proper proportions of the classic vinegar-and-oil dressing for the green salad. These are, roughly speaking,

1 part wine vinegar
and
2 parts olive oil

or, to put it another way.

2 parts olive oil
and
1 part wine vinegar

(These proportions are stressed here because, when you hate to cook, it is easy to reverse them, and the result would pickle herring.)

Also, if you are serving wine with dinner, you should use lemon juice instead of the wine vinegar, although, if your friends are like my friends, they wouldn't be able to tell the difference, and they wouldn't tell on you if they could.

Of course, you need a little salt and coarse-ground pepper, and you can rub the bowl with garlic if you like it, or crush half a garlic clove with the salt if you like it a lot. And that's *it*: a nice, easy, understated dressing to use on endive, lettuce, fresh raw spinach leaves, or whatever you have around.

You may also add, if you like, anchovies and thin-sliced unpeeled cucumbers or artichoke hearts, sliced or unsliced, or chopped tomatoes, cucumber, and green onions or, improbably enough, canned mandarin orange segments, which are quite good with the vinegar-oil dressing, and pretty against the greenery.

And of course you may add croutons. You make them like this:

CROUTONS

¼ cup olive oil   1 garlic clove, cut in half
4 slices bread, diced

You put the olive oil in a pan over low heat, add the garlic, and when the oil is hot, add the bread squares. Stir it so that each square is coated. As a matter of fact, you might as well stand there and shake that pan, because those bread squares would just as soon burn as look at you. Remove the garlic halves after a bit, and when the bread squares are nicely browned, drain them on absorbent paper. They'll keep in a covered jar in the refrigerator. Just freshen them about 10 minutes in a 300°F oven before you use them.

But of course you will probably prefer to buy the ones which come in packages in a variety of flavors.

Then there are these 3 sour-cream dressings, which are good to know about because they're so easy.

SOUR CREAM CINCH NO. 1

Add the juice of half a lemon to 1 cup of sour cream or yogurt (the yogurt is cheaper and less fattening and works quite as well here) and salt and pepper it to taste.
    If you add ketchup to this, it's also good with seafood.

SOUR CREAM CINCH NO. 2

Just combine:

½ cup mayonnaise	sprinkle of paprika
½ cup sour cream or yogurt	1 teaspoon fine minced onion
½ teaspoon salt	2 teaspoons caraway seeds

Or try:

CHUTNEY SOUR CREAM DRESSING

1 cup sour cream
¼ cup chopped chutney
juice of ½ lemon or lime

On the subject of dressings here are 5 more dependables:

JUNE SALAD DRESSINGS

(History doesn't relate why this should be made in June but it makes plenty and lasts for weeks, whenever you make it.)

Blend together:

1 cup sour cream	2 teaspoons celery seed
½ teaspoon garlic powder	½ teaspoon salt
2 tablespoons lemon juice	a dash of pepper
1 teaspoon dry mustard	

See that it's smooth, then chill it to serve later with fresh lettuce.

JOHANNA'S DRESSING

In a blender, blend:

1 cup olive oil
3 tablespoons minced onion
1½ tablespoons Parmesan
    cheese
3 teaspoons salt

1 teaspoon each
    Worcestershire sauce,
    dry mustard, basil,
    oregano, sugar, pepper

Then add and blend for another 30 seconds:

½ cup red wine vinegar
2 tablespoons lemon juice

Keep it cold and count on it.

FREEZABLE DRESSING

Over simmering water, mix well:

2 tablespoons sugar
1 teaspoon salt
1 teaspoon French mustard
1½ tablespoons flour

Then beat an egg in ½ cup milk and blend it in. Now stir in ¼ cup
vinegar and keep right on stirring, over the hot water, till it's thick—
about 12 minutes. Blend in 1 tablespoon butter, then cool it and
refrigerate in a covered jar.

This next one is the well-known San Francisco salad dressing named
after the old George Arliss play. There are dozens of variations of it.
I like this one the best of those I've tasted. In these proportions it
dresses 10 servings, and if you're not serving 10, so much the better.
It keeps well, and you use the rest as a dressing for broccoli or asparagus. It's also a good dip for artichoke leaves.

GREEN GODDESS SALAD DRESSING

Mix 1 tablespoon lemon juice with ½ cup heavy cream. Then add and
mix:

1 cup mayonnaise*
3 tablespoons cider vinegar

---

* The recipe actually calls for "good mayonnaise," a term that always makes me feel truculent
as well as defensive. What kind do they think you buy? I'm sure whatever you have is all right,
so long as it's mayonnaise.

1 crushed garlic clove
1 rounded tablespoon anchovy paste
¼ cup fresh parsley
2 tablespoons onion powder (or
    1 tablespoon dried minced onion)

(As to what you put the dressing on—classically speaking—it's greenery: any lettuce or watercress or whatever you have, with tomato wedges on top. If it's to be the main course, add crabmeat, shrimps, or chunks of cold chicken along with the tomatoes.)

Easiest of all, perhaps, is:

ROQUEFORT DRESSING

Simply add crumbled Roquefort or Danish Blue to your classic vinegar-and-oil dressing.

One more good thing to know is how to make a Caesar salad without the last-minute raw-egg business.

READY CAESAR SALAD

(It's good without the anchovies, too; it's just a different salad then.)

Into a pint jar put:

the juice of 1½ lemons
    (4 tablespoons)
¼ cup olive oil
½ teaspoon ground pepper
1 teaspoon Worcestershire
    sauce
½ teaspoon garlic powder

½ teaspoon salt
1 beaten egg
¼ cup Parmesan cheese
4– 6 anchovies, chopped, or
    more if you like them
    very much

Shake the jar with vigor, once you've put the things in and the lid on. Then keep it in the refrigerator till dinnertime. At serving time, pour it over crisp lettuce (ideally, romaine) and add croutons, say half a cupful to a cup.*

The next six salad recipes can be done ahead, too. Indeed, the first 3 should be, keeping in mind how comforting it will be later, as you

* See pages 124–125 for recipe.

drag your wagon into the kitchen, to know your salad is all ready. Should you lose your impetus and not make it, you can still—at the last moment—simply slice the cucumbers and peppers as always and serve them with whatever dressing is around.

SIDE-DISH SALAD   *4 Servings*

1 green pepper
2 cucumbers, unpeeled
some onion rings, if you like
1½ teaspoons salt

2 tablespoons vinegar
1 cup sour cream or yogurt
paprika or coarse-ground pepper

Two or three hours or longer before serving, slice the pepper, onion, and cucumbers very thin. Put them in a bowl, sprinkle with salt, and refrigerate them. Mix the vinegar with the sour cream, too, so it will be ready.

Before dinner, drain the vegetables, stir them about in the dressing, and decorate with paprika or coarse-ground pepper.

GOOD SPINACH SALAD   *6 Servings*

(Spinach is sometimes a nice change from lettuce, and it is especially becoming to a pale dinner.)

First, mix:

2 tablespoons wine vinegar
6 tablespoons olive oil

1 teaspoon garlic powder
salt to taste

Or, if you keep a bottle of vinegar-and-oil dressing around, use ½ cup. Just be sure it's well garlicked.

Now hardboil 3 eggs and fry 8 strips of lean bacon. Drain the bacon on paper towels. Wash a pound of spinach thoroughly, dry it, tear it in pieces, put it in a bowl, and refrigerate it.

When you're ready to serve dinner, chop the eggs and crumble the bacon into the bowl, then toss it all with the dressing. Parmesan cheese is good on this, and so are croutons, but neither is vital.

This next one uses up radishes and some of your canned beans.

ROSY RADISH SALAD

4–6 Servings

Fry, drain, and crumble 4 strips of bacon.
  Mix them with:

a middle-sized chopped onion
2 tablespoons vinegar
1 tablespoon sugar
½ teaspoon salt

⅛ teaspoon pepper
1 pound can of french
  beans, drained
1 cup of sliced radishes

Leave it in the refrigerator several hours so the flavors get friendly, then serve it on lettuce.

Here's one that's handy because it's also a dip if you want it to be. Increase the sour cream to make it dippable and skip the tomato shells—just use a finely chopped tomato.

GUACAMOLE TOMATOES

4 tomatoes hollowed out
  (save the pulp)
1 large ripe avocado

a small chopped onion
1 tablespoon lemon juice
½ cup sour cream

Mash the avocado, then mix it with the tomato pulp and the rest. Spike it if you like with Tabasco, salt and pepper. Stuff it into the tomatoes and serve it on lettuce.

PETER ABBOTT SALAD

(To serve on a lettuce leaf or in sandwiches.)

Slice about 10 hardboiled eggs. Then slice thinly, on the diagonal, about 6 celery stalks. Drop it in boiling water for about a minute and drain it. Cut half a green pepper in thin strips. Then mix together

a green onion, chopped
½ cup mayonnaise
1 tablespoon Dijon mustard
1 tablespoon vinegar

and combine everything. STOP HERE. Decorate it if you like with more green pepper strips or pimento, chopped stuffed olives, sliced black olives . . . whatever is handiest.

CHILLED DILLED CUCUMBERS

Slice a large cucumber thin enough to read through, but instead of doing that, beat together:

5 tablespoons vegetable oil	½ teaspoon dill weed
3 tablespoons vinegar	¼ teaspoon each sugar and salt

and pour it over the cucumbers. Chill it till dinnertime.

FANCY SLICED TOMATOES

*(Make this a few hours ahead if you can, so the
flavor has a chance to mature.)*

tomatoes	dried basil
green onions	sugar
salt	vinegar
pepper	olive oil

Put a layer of sliced unpeeled tomatoes in a shallow pretty bowl about 8 or 10 inches in diameter, and put a layer of sliced green onions on top of it. Sprinkle a bit of salt and pepper around, a pinch of basil, ½ teaspoon of sugar, and 1 teaspoon each of vinegar and olive oil. Add another layer of tomatoes and onion slices and repeat the seasonings. Keep going in this fashion, depending on how many people you're serving and how tired you get.

POSH SALAD   *6 Servings*

½ head cauliflower	⅓ cup crumbled Blue cheese
½ large mild onion	black pepper
¼ cup sliced stuffed olives	small head of lettuce
½ cup oil-vinegar dressing	

Separate those little cauliflowerlets and slice them thin. Slice the onion now, separate the slices into rings, and add them to the cauliflower slices together with the sliced olives. Now marinate it all in the dressing, with a good sprinkling of pepper, for anywhere from half an hour to overnight.

When you serve the salad, cut or tear the lettuce into small pieces, put it in a bowl, pour the marinated mix over it, and crumble the cheese on top.

TOMARTICHOKES

6 Servings

6 big red tomatoes
6 artichoke hearts
salt, pepper
powdered dill

mayonnaise
sour cream or yogurt
lemon juice
curry powder

Drop the tomatoes into boiling water for a minute, so the skins will slip off easily. Then cut off the tops, scoop out the seeds and juice, and season them inside and out with salt, pepper, and the powdered dill if you have it. Don't fret about it if you haven't. Into each and every tomato put a canned artichoke heart. (You could use frozen ones, too, but then you'd have to cook them first.) Then put them in the refrigerator and make a dressing from equal parts of mayonnaise and sour cream, with a bit of lemon juice and ½ teaspoon of curry powder. Put this in the refrigerator, too. Just before you serve the tomatoes, spoon some of the dressing over each.

TOTALLY ADMIRABLE ASPARAGUS

For the loveliest, greenest, tender-crisp asparagus you ever tasted, do this:

If you want to be extra polite, take the claws off the stalks, using a vegetable parer. Otherwise don't bother.

Break off the tough end of each spear at the joint where it wants to break, and either throw these away or save them for soup.

Now wash them and cover them with ice cubes till they are VERY cold. Say 15 minutes.

Heat water in a kettle to a rolling boil, and into it drop the shivering asparagus, which will immediately cool the water. When it once again comes to a rolling boil, wait 30 seconds, then remove the spears immediately to another panful of icecubes to stop the cooking process. In 10 minutes or so, dry your asparagus tenderly in paper towels and keep it chilled till serving time.

A good easy dressing to serve with it is mayonnaise to which you've added a lot of lemon juice.

10. Spuds and Other Starches

OR BALLAST IS A GIRL'S BEST FRIEND

Just say POTATO to the lady who hates to cook, and ten to one she'll think BAKED.

No wonder. The honest baked potato is a noble thing. And like your Little Basic Black Dress, nobody notices it especially but nobody objects to it either, and you can dress it up or down.

Also, it is easy to bake a potato this way, because you just scrub it and butter it and put it in the oven, where it will bake from 350°F to 475°F, depending on what else is in there. And it doesn't dirty a single pan!

Now, it often happens, while you're preparing dinner, that your mind is on higher things, or lower, as the case may be, and presently you notice that you *forgot to put the potatoes in*. When this happens, you can parboil them for 5 minutes before putting them in to bake, or you can stick an aluminum skewer or an aluminum nail into each potato. Either of these maneuvers speeds up the baking process a good 15 to 20 minutes.

Or, in the case of potatoes that you forgot to put round a roast in a 300°F oven, you can parboil them 15 minutes and then put them round the roast, and they'll be done in about 45 minutes.

Never believe the people who tell you that pricking potatoes with a fork keeps them fresh and flaky if you're going to let the potatoes sit around for a while after they've baked. These people are dreamers, for the potatoes will be only *slightly* less soggy if pricked than if unpricked. Actually, the only thing to do is to eat the potatoes as soon as they come out of the oven, or else let them go on merrily baking —in which case the skins will be crisper and harder, but many people prefer them that way. However, all this is a minor matter; and if a somewhat soggy potato is the worst thing that ever happens to you, you are Lady Luck's own tot. The butter and salt and pepper will make them taste good anyway.

" . . . As for the foil-wrapped baked potato, sloshed with sour cream and laced with onions so that no trace of potato flavor remains, I give up. You find this culinary dead end everywhere, served with a proud flourish (and bits of bacon, if you don't watch out). They put foil around it to render the jacket damp and soggy, which I guess is the way people like it. I didn't come here to argue."
—HERB CAEN

How to Dress Them Up if You Care To. Slash and squeeze each baked spud and put in it a chunk of anchovy butter (butter creamed with anchovy paste) or Roquefort butter (butter creamed with Roquefort cheese), or else pass a bowl of sour cream or yogurt (beaten a bit to mayonnaise consistency) or sour cream or yogurt combined with onion soup mix, or chopped parsley, chopped chives, chopped green onion tops, or crisp crumbled bacon.

How to Dress Them Up Even More

CRISSCROSS POTATOES

Cut middle-sized baking potatoes in half, the long way. With a knife, score the cut sides crisscross fashion, about a quarter of an inch deep. Mix a little salt and dry mustard with butter—allowing a scant tablespoon of butter for each potato half—and spread this on the potatoes. Bake them as usual, anywhere from 350°F to 475°F for an hour.

Now, it's true that sometimes—say, once a decade—it seems imperative to serve a starch that isn't a baked potato. When you are faced with this, you may find the next few items handy.

SPUDS O'GROTTEN

*(A fine old Irish recipe originated by Mother O'Grotten,
who recently emigrated from County Cork.)*

Cook and mash your potatoes as usual (they're best if you mash them
with hot milk). Then pile them into a greased casserole dish and
sprinkle grated sharp Cheddar cheese on top. Don't be mingy with
the cheese. Put on plenty. Bake them, uncovered, at 350°F for 15
minutes.

FLUFFY ONION SPUDS   *6–8 Servings*

*(Handy if you are roasting meat in a 300°F oven and for some odd
reason are not roasting your potatoes around it.)*

Cook and mash 5 good-sized potatoes, using cream, salt, and pepper.
Now chop and sauté a middle-sized onion until it's tender, in 5T of
butter. Add it to the potatoes. Put all this in a pretty, greased, oven-
proof dish and set it, uncovered, in that 300°F oven where the roast
is, for 45 minutes.

MUSHROOM SPUDS   *5–6 Servings*

You find your grater with the big holes in it and you grate 4 middle-
sized potatoes. Then you mix a can of condensed cream of mushroom
soup (or celery soup, in which case you call the whole thing Celery
Spuds) with half a can of milk, heat it, pour it over the potatoes, and
bake, uncovered, at 350°F for 1¼ hours.

FAST FRIES   *3–4 Servings*

Take a can of small white potatoes and drain, rinse, and slice them.
Melt a little butter in a heavy pan, then add the potato slices, onion
salt (or half a teaspoon of onion juice), and pepper. Cook them over
medium heat till they're brown, then pretty them up with chopped
parsley.

The next two use baking potatoes but the end results bear no resem-
blance to baked potatoes.

FANCY BAKED FRIES   *4 Servings*

Scrub 3 baking potatoes but don't peel them. Cut them so they vaguely resemble french fries, and spread them out on a baking sheet. Now heat ¼ cup butter with 2 teaspoons of anchovy paste and a dash of salt and pepper until the butter melts. Brush the potato strips with this and bake them in a 340°F oven for 35 minutes.

SWISS POTATOES   *4–6 Servings*

(It's best to make more than you need because they're good fried the next day.)

1½ big baking potatoes, sliced thin as possible
1 teaspoon salt
1 teaspoon minced, dried onion

2 beaten eggs (plus a little more)
¼ pound Swiss cheese, grated

Mix it all together in a medium-sized baking dish, sprinkle more cheese on top and bake uncovered at 350°F for an hour, or 300°F for an hour and a quarter.

Or you could make:

FAST CHEESE SCALLOP   *3–4 Servings*

You make about 1½ cups of cream sauce with dry mustard and a bit of Worcestershire (or use somewhat thinned condensed celery soup) and pour it over a pound of cooked potatoes in a casserole dish. Put plenty of grated cheese on top, and bake, uncovered, at 350°F for 25 minutes.

PARMESAN POTATOES
6–8 Servings

(Lovely and creamy and fattening, and good in the summertime with a barbecued steak.)

4 large peeled potatoes, sliced thinly
1½ cups milk
½ cup heavy cream

¼ cup Parmesan
½ teaspoon salt
dash of pepper

Put the potatoes, milk, salt, and pepper in the top of your double boiler over boiling water, and cook for 30 minutes. Now pour this into a baking dish, pour on the cream, and top it with the Parmesan. Bake at 350°F for 20 minutes.

Something else to do with new potatoes besides boiling them and rolling them in melted butter and parsley is to boil them, unscraped. After they're tender, slice them, still unscraped, into a pan that contains a lump of butter, melted, and some chopped green onions. Fry them gently, stirring once in a while, and chop some parsley into them, just before serving.

Don't fret too much about NOODLES. Whatever you do to them, they remain noodle-like, which Providence probably intended. For a slight change of pace, you can put a good teaspoonful of instant bouillon into the noodle water, and serve them with lots of butter and lots of paprika. Or you can skip the paprika in favor of poppy seeds, enough to speckle them thoroughly. But don't expect too much.

As for MACARONI, the following recipe is handy, because it will stretch a meal when the pork chops turn out to be smaller than you thought they were. It's a good main dish, too.

MAMA'S MACARONI
4 Servings

4 strips bacon, chopped
½ green pepper, chopped
1 large onion, chopped

1 small jar pimento-stuffed olives, sliced
8 oz macaroni, cooked

Fry the bacon bits till they're crisp, then add the onion and green pepper, and cook over low heat until they're tender. Add the olive slices, and mix the whole works with the hot cooked macaroni. Taste it, then salt it. You may serve it with parsley, and tomato salad on the side.

RICE presents no real problems, but when you get tired of looking at it plain, you can make:

ROSY RICE

Substitute tomato juice or V-8 juice for half the water you would ordinarily use in the cooking. Before serving, add a little butter and a dash of garlic salt.

Incidentally, if your rice usually turns out soggy, and if this bothers you, it is handy to know the following system for cooking rice so it's dry, with each grain separate. This system has two disadvantages. You can't use any saucepan; it must be a thick-bottomed one, heavy iron or enamelled iron. You will have to soak the pan, too, before you wash it afterwards. But in this world we can't have everything.

DRY RICE

Use 1½ cups of cold water to 1 cup of rice, and bring it to a fast boil in that thick-bottomed pan. Boil it with the lid off for 5 minutes. Then turn the heat to medium and cook until the water has apparently boiled away. Now turn the burner to its lowest possible heat, or flame, cover the pan, and cook it for 20 minutes *without stirring*.

That's the big thing. Don't stir. You can muss it around a bit on the surface with a spoon, if you care to, but you must not disturb the crust that's on the bottom. This apparently does something magical, to make the rice dry and the pan hard to wash.

Should you ever use this method, allow a little more rice than you normally would, because it doesn't expand quite so much.

CHEESE RICE   *6 Servings*

3 cups hot cooked rice   3 tablespoons melted butter
¼ cup grated Parmesan   dash of pepper

Just toss these things together.

RAISIN RICE

6–8 Servings

(Easy, and good with anything curried.)

8 oz rice
1 teaspoon salt
¼ large onion, thinly sliced

2 tablespoons sliced almonds
2 tablespoons butter
½ cup seedless raisins

Cook the rice. While it cooks, sauté the onions and almonds in the butter till they're a gentle brown. Then add the raisins, heat thoroughly, and when the rice is done cooking, mix everything together. Now taste it—it may need a little more salt.

ONION RICE

In a saucepan put 1½ cups of *water*, a tablespoon *oil*, a package of *Onion Soup Mix*. Bring to a boil, add ¾ cupful long grain *rice*. Turn to low, simmer for 20 minutes, and don't peek while it cooks.

A Nice Change From Spuds And Rice Is:

BARLEY SHIMMELFENNER

6 Servings

(To bake along with a roast or serve with any cold meat.)

¾ cup barley, rinsed and
  drained
3 tablespoons butter
1 celery stalk, chopped

1½ teaspoons salt
¼ teaspoon pepper
1½ cups chicken stock
1½ teaspoons parsley, chopped

First melt the butter in a frying pan and sauté the barley briefly, not enough to brown it, then add everything else and heat it to boiling. At that point pour it into a casserole dish, start to cover it. When you notice the dish doesn't have a lid, mutter some basic English to yourself while hunting up the aluminum foil. When it eventually appears, cover it with that and bake it for an hour at 350°F.

11. Luncheon for the Girls

OR WAIT TILL YOU TASTE MAYBELLE'S
PEANUT BUTTER ASPIC

Few things are so pleasant as a Ladies' Luncheon, when the ladies meet in some neutral corner like the Carioca Room at the Sherry-Hinterland, or at Harry's Bar and Grill.

There they may relax and swap tatting patterns, serene in the knowledge that they needn't eat anything molded unless they order it. There, too, a lady can have an honest Scotch-and-soda instead of something pink and sweet without losing her Brownie badge; and not one lady needs to jump up to change plates and miss hearing what Harriet said when Charlotte told her what Thelma said when she saw that awful Henderson woman at the movies with that boy who used to go around with Eloise's neighbor's niece.

Furthermore, someone else is left to get the lipstick off the napkins, which, incidentally, is something *not* to worry about. It is appalling, though not serious, how much glamor comes off on the napkins. But you merely pick up the napkins gingerly by one corner and put them aside till washday. Then, about 15 minutes before washing a load, rub salad oil on each red stain till it soaks through the material, and put them in the wash. The oil melts the lipstick, you see, and the laundering removes the oil.

However, as to the Ladies' Luncheon at home, about the best thing that can be said for it is that—like the whooping crane—it is definitely on the downward path to extinction. More and more ladies are discovering that with only a little fast footwork they can turn a luncheon into a Morning Coffee (with a lot of good little pastries) or Afternoon Tea (sandwiches and rich cookies) or a Cocktail Affair (see Chapter 4)—any one of which is a lot easier. And when you hate to cook, your agility in this respect is truly remarkable. It is only once in a long long month of Sundays that the woman who hates to cook finds herself stuck with a Luncheon for the Girls.

This, accordingly, is a brief chapter. It consists of six luncheon menus: 1. The Soup-Sandwich; 2. The Soup-Salad. 3. The Salad-Sandwich; and if you are so unlucky as to find yourself on the Patty-Shell Circuit, 4, 5, 6. The Hot Main Dish.

In each menu (with one exception), only one thing takes any doing. Also, each menu, in its entirety, can be made in advance, which enables you to be with your friends in the living room until a minute or so before you eat. After all, if they're your best friends, you want to be with them; and if they're your second-best friends, you don't dare not.

First, a general word about DESSERT.

It is wise to keep in mind that in any group of two or more women, at least one is on a diet, and several others think they ought to be. If you serve them a rich dessert which you spent considerable time making, they will probably eat it, but they will be annoyed with you. If they do *not* eat it, you will be annoyed with them. And, on the other hand, the nondiet-minded ladies will look at you squint-eyed if they have dutifully ploughed through the main part of the luncheon only to find that there's no dessert at all.

This poses a pretty little problem, which is best solved by a fruit dessert (see Menu No. 1, below) *plus* a plateful of shop-bought petit-fours (or cakes), or a dish of good chocolates, or a bowl of nuts and raisins, or all three, hereinafter known as Oddments.

Everyone can eat the fruit dessert, you see, and you, as hostess, will not be offended if they pass up the rich goodies. After all, you spent no time making them, and, also, there will be more left for you and the family to enjoy when the ladies finally go home.

Remember, too: if your luncheon is reasonably substantial or contains a good deal of fruit anyway, you can even skip the fruit dessert and just bring out the Oddments.

And so to Menu No. 1.

Luncheon Menu No. 1. Soup-Sandwich

Cheese-Chicken Soup
Chicken, Ham or Beef Sandwiches
(or all three)
Honeydew Melon
Oddments
Coffee

CHEESE-CHICKEN SOUP · 6 *Servings*

2 cans condensed cream of chicken soup
1½ small jars tasty processed cheese spread
parsley

Blend a can of water with the soup, in the top of the double boiler. Then stir in the cheese spread, and keep stirring until it's all smooth and hot. You can keep this waiting as long as you like, over hot water. Parsley it with a lavish hand before you serve it.

Luncheon Menu No. 2. Soup-Salad

India Chicken Soup
with slivered almonds
South-of-the-Border Salad
Hot Rolls
Oddments
Coffee

INDIA CHICKEN SOUP · 4 *Servings*

1 teaspoon curry powder
1 can condensed cream of chicken soup
1 chicken-bouillon cube dissolved in ⅔ can
    hot water
⅓ cup cream
slivered toasted almonds

First mix the curry powder with the soup, using the top of the double boiler. Then add and blend everything else, heat it through, and when you serve it, sprinkle the almonds on top.

SOUTH-OF-THE-BORDER SALAD   *6 Servings*

After breakfast, mix and chill:

½ cup mayonnaise   1 teaspoon seasoning salt
½ cup chili sauce   several drops Tabasco
1 teaspoon chili powder   1 teaspoon vinegar

Just before lunch put these things in a bowl:

a medium head of iceberg lettuce, in bite-size
    pieces
¼ cup sliced pitted black olives
½ cup grated Cheddar cheese
1 small purple onion, sliced thinly
seasoned salt, and pepper
a large avocado, cut in chunks
2 cups crumbled corn chips

Add the dressing, toss, and serve.

Luncheon Menu No. 3. Salad-Sandwich

Friday Night Sandwich
Small Green Salad
with Vinegar-Oil Dressing
Oddments
Coffee

Friday-Night Sandwich is the rich crabmeat-cheese-bacon affair on
p. 39. You can make them well in advance, then shove them under
the broiler just before you call the ladies to lunch.

Luncheon Menu No. 4. Hot Main Dish (A)

Beef à la King
Fresh Fruit Salad
with Orange-Mayonnaise Dressing
Oddments
Coffee

Beef à la King is that fantastically easy dish on p. 47. It will stay hot
and good in your double boiler for a long, long time.

ORANGE-MAYONNAISE DRESSING

Thin mayonnaise, to taste, with fresh orange juice.

Luncheon Menu No. 5. Hot Main Dish (B)

Hurry Curry
with Rice and Chutney
Green Salad
with Mandarin Orange Segments
Oddments
Coffee

Hurry Curry is the ultraswift curry on p. 54. It, too, keeps nicely in the double boiler if the ladies happen to want another drink before they eat.

Luncheon Menu No. 6. Hot Main Dish (C)

Chicken-Rice Roger
Fancy Sliced Tomatoes
Hot Rolls
Oddments
Coffee

Chicken-Rice Roger is the simple chicken dish on p. 53, which you can prepare any time, then put in the oven before you eat. The tomatoes (p. 130) can be prepared, if you like, even the night before.

12. Company's Coming

OR YOUR BACK'S TO THE WALL

When you hate to cook, you should never accept an invitation to dinner. The reason is plain: Sooner or later, unless you have luckily disgraced yourself at their home, or unless they get transferred to Weehawken, *you will have to return the invitation.*

You know this, of course. You keep reminding yourself. But it is like telling a small boy to refuse a free ticket to the circus. Too well you remember the golden tranquillity that bathes you, all day, when you know that *somebody else* is going to be doing that fast samba from pantry to sink. In spite of yourself, and with the full knowledge that you're doing wrong, you accept. And there you are, in debt again, and sooner or later, you ask *them* over.

Now, at first it isn't so bad. With the dinner two weeks away, you even feel a bit complacent, thinking of the obligation you're about to clear up. But as the count-down continues, the complacency gives way to grim, clear-eyed appraisal. You realize that no one with even a rudimentary brain would expect anyone to eat what you're going to be setting before them—if, indeed, you can think of anything to set before them. You can't remember a single dinner party dish you ever cooked, and as you look through your recipe books, all the recipes say to add fresh chervil or sauce Noisette or serve on toast points. Not just buttered toast, but *toast points*, mind you, and by now you're hardly up to finding the breadbox.

This chapter should remedy the situation. You can look at the following eight dinner party menus with the comforting awareness that they are stand-bys of other people who hate to cook. If one dish takes a little doing, the others don't, or, at the very least, can be done so far ahead of time that you've forgotten the pain of it.

Actually, eight dinner party menus are quite enough. If you find you are serving the same thing too often to the same people, then invite someone else instead. It is much easier to change your friends than your recipes.

You may note a certain sameness about the suggested dessert in these menus. There are two reasons. For one thing, desserts are something we don't come to real grips with until Chapter 16. For another, my heart leaps down when I behold a hostess coming my way with a Set Piece—a big fat cake or something flaming. I know if I don't eat it, her eyes will start to fill, and if I do eat it, I'll wish I hadn't. It seems to me unfair to place anyone on the sharp horns of this particular dilemma.

In my estimation, those 'Oddments' discussed in the previous chapter have never been surpassed, because the lucky guest can nibble or not, as he prefers, and the lucky hostess didn't have to do any work on that particular department of the dinner. Two desserts are given, both of which can be made well in advance. Or serve a rare, fine, immortal glass of Irish Coffee.

This is a true triple threat: coffee, dessert, and liqueur all in one, and what else can make that statement? To make Irish Coffee, you needn't fuss with dessert, dessert plates, dessert forks, coffeepot, sugar bowl, creamer, demitasse cups, wee spoons, liqueur bottles, and liqueur glasses. You merely need Irish whiskey, instant coffee, hot water, sugar, and whipped cream (which you can whip before dinner, if you like), and, to contain it, Irish whisky glasses. These are stemmed goblets holding seven to eight fluid ounces. (The stems are important, because they'd otherwise be too hot to hold.)

IRISH COFFEE

Put 2 ounces of Irish whiskey into each glass. Add 1½ teaspoons of granulated sugar. Add 1½ teaspoons of instant coffee. Fill to within half an inch of the brim with hot water and stir. Now, on top, float the whipped cream, which should be thick but not stiff. A good ½ cup of cream, before whipping, is about right for 4 Irish Coffees.) And serve.

Obviously, the saving here in money, time, dishwashing, and wear and tear on the leg muscles is phenomenal. And, last but not least, people don't sit around drinking Irish Coffee until the cock crows. Because it is rich, one is enough. It serves as a pleasant punctuation mark to the evening, and, because it also has a slight soporific effect on many people, your guests may eventually go home.

Slainte! Not to mention *bon soir*.

And so to the menus.

Dinner Party Menu No. 1

Chicken-Artichoke Casserole
Plain Baked Potatoes
Fancy Sliced Tomatoes (p. 130)
Irish Coffee

CHICKEN-ARTICHOKE CASSEROLE   *6 Servings*

3 pounds cut-up fryer (or equal weight of chicken pieces)
1 teaspoon salt
½ teaspoon paprika
¼ teaspoon pepper
6 tablespoons butter
3 tablespoons sherry

½ cup mushrooms, cut in large pieces
1 pound artichoke hearts
2 tablespoons flour
½ cup chicken consommé or bouillon

Salt, pepper, and paprika the chicken pieces. Then brown them prettily in some of the butter and put them in a big casserole. Now put the remainder of the butter into the frying pan and sauté the mushrooms in it 5 minutes. Then sprinkle the flour over them and stir in the chicken consommé and the sherry. While this cooks 5 minutes, you may open the can of artichokes and arrange them between the chicken pieces. Then pour the mushroom-sherry sauce over them, cover, and bake at 375°F for 40 minutes.

You can prepare this in the morning, or the day before.

Put your middle-sized baking potatoes in the oven 20 minutes before you put the casserole in, and things will come out even.

That chicken-artichoke arrangement is not only quite good, it's very pretty. But I'd like to mention here that it is unwise to expect your dinner party meals to look *precisely* like the dinner party meals you see in the full-color food spreads everywhere. In this connection, I have news for you: food photographers do not play fair and square. It was once my privilege to watch a beef stew being photographed in the studio of a major food photographer. It was a superb stew—the gravy glistening richly, the beef chunks brown and succulent and in beautiful juxtaposition to the bright carrots and the pearly onions. I can make a respectable beef stew myself, but my gravy is never that gorgeous, and my onions invariably sink as though torpedoed. I inquired about this and discovered that the gravy had been dyed, and the onions propped up on toothpicks! Moreover, that very same morning, they told me, they'd had to lacquer a lobster. There you have it.

Dinner Party Menu No. 2

Vichyssoise—or Leek Soup
(cold, canned, topped with chopped green onions)
Veal Cutlets Victoria
Spinach Surprise (p. 117)
Hot Rolls
Irish Coffee

VEAL CUTLETS VICTORIA   *6 Servings*

6 veal cutlets
½ cup olive oil
salt, pepper
3 cloves garlic, minced
2 large onions, sliced thinly

6 peeled tomatoes, sliced thinly
½ teaspoon salt
¼ teaspoon ground cloves
¼ teaspoon pepper

First, sauté the cutlets in the olive oil until they're light brown, salt and pepper them, and put them in a casserole. Then sauté the garlic and onions in the same oil until they're light brown, too. Now add the tomatoes to this and brutally crush it all to a pulp with a potato masher or a wooden spoon. Add the seasonings (and don't omit the cloves for fear the whole thing will be too highly spiced, because it won't; it will just taste interesting and very good). Simmer the sauce for 5 minutes, pour it over the cutlets, cover, and bake at 350°F for 40 minutes.

A note about rolls and bread. When you hate to cook, you certainly don't ever make your own. If, somewhere in town, you can get the honest, true, genuine, tough-crusted, French bread, your troubles are over. You needn't do a thing to it except put it on the table with a bread knife.

Good bakery rolls are next best, heated in that dampened paper bag for a few minutes, along with whatever else is in the oven.

Next we come to the honest roast-beef dinner.

Never scorn the noble prime rib or the rolled sirloin tip. Remember, most men like plain meat better than a casserole, because most men like a tune they can whistle. Show me the man who doesn't like a juicy pink slab of good roast beef (followed by an Irish Coffee) and I'll show you a vegetarian who's on the wagon.

Dinner Party Menu No. 3

Roast of Beef
High Rise Yorkshire Pudding (optional) (p. 80)
Oven-roasted Potatoes
Horseradish Cream Dressing
Very Edible String Beans (p. 114)
Irish Coffee

ROAST BEEF

Roast the meat, with the potatoes around it, as your big fat cookbook tells you to—probably 22 minutes per pound in a 300°F oven. Be sure the meat is at room temperature, too, when you put it into the oven. If you're feeling like an overachiever and have two ovens, make Yorkshire pudding too.

HORSERADISH CREAM DRESSING

Whip ½ cup heavy cream till it's stiff. Keep on beating while you add ¼ cup of lemon juice, 2 tablespoons prepared horseradish, a dash of salt, and a dash of paprika.

Note: When you hate to cook, it is a good idea to make a habit of looking in the refrigerator *just before you call the people in to eat*. The reason is that since cooking or preparing more than one or two things is alien to your nature and your habits, you're apt to forget that you did. Then when your guests have gone and you find that bowl of Something still inviolate in the refrigerator, you want to shoot yourself.

Dinner Party Menu No. 4
More-or-Less Mediterranean Dinner

Manny's Lamb Stew
Syrian Pecan Salad
Hot Rolls or Scones
Harem Cream

MANNY'S LAMB STEW
6–8 Servings

(This is quite a good lamb stew because it contains no peas of any description, and it's made with lemon juice instead of wine. You could use wine, but you might as well save it to drink with the dinner.)

2½ pounds lean stewing lamb*
    cut in edible-size pieces
4 tablespoons olive oil
1 good-sized onion, peeled and
    chopped
1 clove garlic, crushed
2 tablespoons flour
1½ cups chicken consommé
    (canned or cubes)
1½ teaspoons salt
¼ teaspoon pepper

1 crumbled bay leaf
¼ teaspoon marjoram
2 teaspoons lemon juice
1 pound can small white
    onions
4 carrots, scraped and cut in
    chunks
4 medium potatoes, peeled
    and cut in pieces
1½ tablespoons finely
    chopped parsley

Brown the lamb in the olive oil, using a heavy pan with a lid. Then remove the lamb and pour out most of the oil, leaving only enough to sauté the onion and garlic in. Do that.

Now put the lamb back in, sprinkle it with the flour, and add the consommé, salt, pepper, bay leaf, marjoram, and lemon juice. Stir it thoroughly, then put the lid on the pan and simmer it all for half an hour. (Skim off the fat now, if it seems to need it, though it won't if the butcher did a good job.) 25 minutes before you serve it, add the onions, carrots, and potatoes. Finally, sprinkle the parsley on top.

---

* Lamb shoulder is good. Get the butcher to bone and cut it for you, and make sure he trims the fat off.

SYRIAN PECAN SALAD
8 Servings

Get 2 pounds of fresh spinach and wash it if no one else has done so. Then you'll need:

- 1½ teaspoons salt
- 8 to 10 green onions, using part of the green too
- 4 tablespoons olive oil
- 4 tablespoons lemon juice
- ¼ pound chopped pecan nuts, salted if available

Chop the spinach coarsely, in mouth-size pieces. Sprinkle it with the salt, then toss it with your hands, squeezing the salt into it. This creates some green juice, so squeeze it dry. Then add the sliced onions (and at this point you can let it sit in the refrigerator, several hours if you like). When dinner is ready, add the olive oil, lemon juice, pecans, toss it, and serve.

HOT ROLLS

Get bakery ones.

If you'd rather serve biscuits, roll the dough out twice as thin as usual, butter it all, and fold it over once—then cut. Then they'll split open handily and look quite nice.

HAREM CREAM
*Makes
2 ice-cube trays full:
10–12 Servings*

- 1½ cups whipping cream
- Two 12 oz cans apricot nectar
- 4 tablespoons lemon juice
- ½ cup sugar
- ¼ cup chopped candied ginger
- silvered toasted almonds

Whip the cream till it's stiff, then add everything but the almonds. Remove the dividers from your 2 ice-cube trays, and pour the mixture into the trays, and put them in the freezing compartment.

When it's mushy—you might look in about an hour, and if it isn't mushy then, it won't be long—pour it into a bowl and beat it thoroughly with a tablespoon till it's firm.

When you serve it, scoop it out like ice cream and sprinkle the silvered toasted almonds on top.

Dinner Party Menu No. 5
Amiable Curry Dinner   *6 Servings*

Amiable Chicken Curry
Plain White Rice
Sambals
Green Salad with Oil-and-Vinegar Dressing
Saratoga Torte
Beer

N.B. As beer is good with this dinner, your pre-dinner cocktail might be a Dog's Nose: a jigger of gin added to a tumbler of chilled beer. No ice.

AMIABLE CHICKEN CURRY

(This is a nice cooperative curry which will wait for hours, if it has to, in the top of a double boiler, and it's easy to double. Also, you don't have to stew a whole chicken to get the meat. The 2 tablespoons of curry powder listed here are enough for most people, but if you're exceptionally curry-minded, add another.)

4 whole chicken breasts
2 cans cream of chicken soup
2 tablespoons curry powder
a little milk if you need it, preferably condensed
an onion, chopped
an apple, chopped
4 tablespoons butter

Simmer the chicken in about 1½ cups of water until it's tender. Remove the meat and chunk it, but don't throw out the water.

Now melt the butter, add the curry powder, chopped apple and onion, and sauté 15 minutes. Then stir in the undiluted soup, thinning it with the water you cooked the chicken in, and a little milk if you need it, till it's a good sauce consistency. Add the chicken and keep it all hot in the top of your double boiler.

SAMBALS

Use 3 or 4 of any of these, depending on how much you feel like chopping, and how many little dishes you have:

chopped peanuts
chopped green onions
sliced bananas (*with a bit of lemon juice sprinkled on them to prevent their discoloring*)

chopped crisp bacon
chopped cucumber
raisins
coconut
chutney

SARATOGA TORTE

(This is easy, chewy, and good, and looks as though you'd gone to a lot of trouble. You can make it far in advance, too.)

3 egg whites
1 cup sugar
1 teaspoon vanilla
1 teaspoon baking powder

14 soda crackers (2" × 2"), coarsely crumbled
¾ cup chopped walnuts
½ cup whipping cream

Beat the egg whites till practically stiff and then gradually add the sugar. Combine the crumbled crackers, walnuts, and baking powder, and fold them into the egg mixture along with the vanilla. Spread it in a nine inch pie pan and bake at 350°F for 45 minutes. When it's cool, spread it with slightly sweetened whipped cream and refrigerate it at least 2 hours before you serve it. Grate a little dark chocolate on top, if you like, to give it more expression.

Dinner Party Menu No. 6   6 Servings

Little Crabmeat Casseroles
Crisp Tomatoes (p. 116)
Green Salad with Garlic Croutons (p. 124)
Crisscross Potatoes (p. 133)
Irish Coffee

LITTLE CRABMEAT CASSEROLES

4 tablespoons butter
4 tablespoons flour
2 cups milk
4 unbeaten egg yolks

2 teaspoons lemon juice
2 teaspoons prepared mustard
salt, pepper
dash of Worcestershire sauce

1 lb. fresh or frozen and	additional half lemon
defrosted crabmeat	breadcrumbs
canned or fresh mushrooms,	grated Parmesan
browned-in-butter	

Make a cream sauce out of the butter, flour, and milk, and when it is thick, add the seasonings (the first 4 items) in the right-hand column. Gradually stir in the egg yolks, unbeaten, the crabmeat, and the mushrooms. Then pour it into individual ramekins. Put some buttered crumbs on top, and Parmesan on top of that, and bake at 375°F for 15 minutes. Just before you serve them, squeeze a bit of lemon juice over each one.

The potatoes can cook in the same oven as the crab casseroles and you can be frying the tomatoes simultaneously.

Dinner Party Menu No. 7   *6 Servings*

Very Artistic Salad Plate
French Beef Casserole
Hot Rolls
Irish Coffee

VERY ARTISTIC SALAD PLATE

Get a reasonable-sized can each of:

beets	asparagus
carrots	artichoke hearts
celery hearts	

Cut the beets and carrots into thin julienne strips.

Marinate all the above items *separately* in bowls of oil-and-vinegar dressing (that is so the colors won't run). Then arrange them tidily on a bed of lettuce on a *big* plate: the asparagus and julienne vegetables spotted here and there like stacks of matchwood, the other things in neat clumps.

In the middle of the plate, put a bowl of Roquefort or Blue Cheese dressing.

Either beat mayonnaise, sour cream, and Blue Cheese till it tastes the way you want it to, or you can make this Blue Cheese dressing, which has a slight additional caramba because of the onion salt:

1 cup oil
½ teaspoon salt
2 teaspoons paprika
½ teaspoon onion salt
2 or 3 oz Blue Cheese

½ teaspoon dry mustard
lots of pepper
⅓ cup vinegar (*including a little garlic vinegar*)

FRENCH BEEF CASSEROLE

(This recipe looks pretty disastrous at first, with all those ingredients and instructions. But actually it's only a glorified stew which tastes rather exotic and looks quite beautiful. You can do it all the day before, too. Just be sure you remember to take it out of the refrigerator an hour before you reheat it, so the casserole dish won't crack.)

1½ pounds lean beef shoulder, cut in 1½" cubes
1 pound can tomatoes
bacon dripping and butter
1 pound carrots cut in 2-inch chunks

2 green peppers cut in squares
1½ cups sliced celery
6 oz can big mushrooms
salt, pepper, flour, dried basil and tarragon leaves, minced onion

Brown the meat—which you've sprinkled with salt, pepper, and 1½ tablespoons of flour—in 2 tablespoons of butter and 2 tablespoons of bacon fat. Put it in a big casserole. Put 3 tablespoons of flour in the pan with the remaining fat, and add the juice from the tomatoes and mushrooms. Stir it till it thickens, then pour it over the meat, add the drained tomatoes, and cover it. Bake for an hour at 325°F.

Then take it out and add all the other vegetables, plus 3 tablespoons of minced onion, and 1 teaspoon each of crumbled tarragon and basil leaves. Re-cover it, bake an hour longer at 325°F, cool it, add the mushrooms, and refrigerate.

To serve it, heat the oven to 350°F and bake the casserole covered, for 45 minutes. Put the rolls in to heat as you sit down to your salad, and everything should go along sweet as a May morning.

But don't be unduly upset if it doesn't! If you forget to serve the rolls for a bit, it's actually no great matter, and if your dinner is so dull that your guests have time to wonder where the rolls are, nothing is going to help it much anyway.

The last menu is a mite more work, so consider it only on rare occasions.

Dinner Party Menu No. 8   *6 Servings*

Spiced Tomato Soup
Rich Fish Turnover
Mixed Green Salad with June Dressing (p. 125)
Irish Coffee

SPICED TOMATO SOUP

3 cups tomato juice
a thick onion slice
a celery stalk, cut up
a bay leaf
4 whole cloves

1 cup beef consommé
salt and pepper
¼ cup port wine
juice of half a lemon

Simmer the first 5 ingredients for half an hour. Then strain it, and reheat it with the consommé and salt and pepper added. When it is very hot, add the port and the lemon juice and serve it forth.

RICH FISH TURNOVER

½ cup raw rice
3 eggs
enough pastry for a 1-crust pie
1 can browned-in-butter
    mushrooms, drained
a little butter
    2 cups flaked, cooked fish (any kind, sole to salmon)

½ teaspoon powdered dill
½ teaspoon powdered thyme
chopped parsley, fresh or dried
1½ teaspoon salt
teaspoon pepper

First, cook the rice. It makes about a cup and a half, cooked. Also hardboil the eggs and eventually slice them. Then roll out some pastry into a dinner-plate size circle and about ⅜" thick, to put on a baking sheet.

Next, open the can of mushrooms, drain them, and put them where you won't forget them, because without them the thing isn't as good.

Concentrating hard now, you season the cooked fish with all those seasonings, and then start layering it all on one-half of the circle: rice, mushrooms, egg slices dotted with butter, fish and then repeat it. Finally fold the dough over, crimp the edges, brush with a beaten egg, gash the crust to let the steam out, and bake at 450° for 15–20 minutes.

In the meantime, melt the cube of butter and add some lemon juice to taste, plus some more chopped parsley, for a sauce.

A thing to beware of, when you hate to cook, is the taut, dogged approach when you're faced with cooking for company. Listen: if, by some odd chance, you should put together a perfect little symphony of a dinner, with no slips or absent-minded moments, you might scare some of your female guests to the point where they'll never invite *you* to their house.

I, personally, know a lady whose cooking and coordination are superb, whose menus are inspired, and whose shishkebabs come flaming on the appropriate eighteenth-century rapiers; and I'd never in the world invite this lady to share *my* humble board. I'd hang first.

13. Can't We Take Them Out to Dinner?

NO—NOT ALWAYS

*"The hostess must be like the duck—calm and unruffled
on the surface, and paddling like hell underneath."*
—ANONYMOUS

Unfortunately, as mentioned before, some entertaining at home has to be done from time to time to pay people back or to honor them, or both, as well as to get the silver polished once in a while, and you cannot honor people satisfactorily with a pride of hot dogs. Some work is expected of you, and perhaps something a little unusual.

There is nothing precisely exotic in this chapter. In fact the difference between the what might be loosely termed menus in this chapter and those in the last is that they are for less formal but more specific occasions. If you hate to cook, you don't try to keep up with the Jones; you only hope to stay away from the Browns.

In fact, the following recipes/menus should take care of things for quite some time. You don't entertain that much at home, for one thing. And when you do, your first thought is usually Roast Beef, because it is the easiest and most people like it. If only it weren't so expensive and didn't require accurate timing, and were as easy to serve as a casserole, and no one observed any meatless days, you would probably serve it all the time. But it is, and it does, and it isn't, and they do; so you don't.

Now, just a word, before we get to the menus/recipes. These have been evolved with a buffet service in mind, but with prearranged places where the guests might sit. This is more comfortable, and allows for salad plates too, when it's indicated, instead of having one big sloppy plateful with the salad dressing running into the meat.

It makes no difference what places are prearranged. They can be tables, end tables, kitchen counters, or card tables. If it's card tables, you might have some round composition-board tops made, sometime, to put on top of them for occasions like this. You can then use circular cloths and get rid of that classic card-table look.

About the cooking itself: there's hardly a dish that objects to being interrupted when it's two thirds done cooking. It's usually better to finish the cooking just before serving than to have cooked it completely and then reheat it.

Firstly canapés, although there is a bigger selection in Chapter 4.

It is easy to overlook the canapé, and often advisable. They are bothersome to make. And they have disadvantages for the guest, who stands there growing fuller and often spottier, depending on the consistency of the dip (see a little farther along).

There is a difference between the sexes where canapés are concerned. Women like them pretty, and men usually just don't like them.

The following canapés* and dips are included from a sense of duty, and because they're good to know about when it's cocktails only, not dinner.

THE HANDIEST HOT CANAPÉ

(Good to know about because the ingredients are nearly always on hand, and it tastes far better than it sounds.)

Put a few onion rings, or thinly sliced green onions, on rounds of Melba toast or any good cracker.

Put a dab of mayonnaise on each, and slip them under the broiler till the mayonnaise sizzles.

---

* Plus one more that I'm diffident about putting anywhere but in a footnote: You mix smooth peanut butter with ketchup until each loses its identity—about half and half, but keep tasting. The resultant new flavor is good and hard to analyze. Spread it on crackers or Melba toast.

THE SECOND-HANDIEST HOT CANAPÉ

(One doesn't always have white tuna around, but it's easy to get. You can use dark tuna but it doesn't look as good. This dull-sounding recipe is another proof of a point mentioned earlier, that you can't ever tell.)

1 can white tuna	coarse-ground pepper
4 to 6 chopped green onions	mayonnaise

Put the tuna in a bowl, then add the onions and mayonnaise a little at a time till it's the right consistency. Add more ground pepper than you think you should, tasting as you go.

You can broil this on toast rounds or crackers. Or add more mayonnaise and use it as a dip.

THE DIP

The important thing about The Dip is its consistency. When it is stiff enough to break the chips, it lasts longer, because soon the bowl of solid shards discourages people. Still, the too-liquid type can discourage people, too. You want a sure eye here, and a light touch.

RADISH AND BUTTER SEMIDIP

Mash Roquefort or Blue Cheese with an equal amount of butter. Cream it thoroughly and put it in a bowl.

Put the bowl on a plate and surround it with scrubbed radishes, their green handles left on, and some good crackers (for people who like radishes but radishes don't like them, as they are usually happy to explain). You might also put a knife on the plate, so that the other people can apply a dab of cheese to the radish, which works better than dunking.

SHRIMP CREAM DIP

(Delicate and rather pretty)

Combine these things:

3 oz package cream cheese, mashed	1 teaspoon Worcestershire sauce
can of shrimp soup, thawed but undiluted	chopped ripe olives, as many as you like
	½ teaspoon curry powder

If it needs any thinning, milk is all right. Raw cauliflowerets are good to dip with. So are chips.

And now to the six dinners.

1. The Stretchable Just-a-Fork Dinner

*(It is remarkable how a one-tool plateful seems to simplify
serving and eating, whether it actually does or not.)*

Hearty Beef Goulash
Ready Caesar Salad (p. 127)
Prebuttered Hot Rolls
any Dessert you bought or any dessert
you made yesterday, such as
Immediate Fudge Cake (p. 226)
Wine   Coffee

HEARTY BEEF GOULASH

In a deep casserole with a lid, brown 2 pounds stewing beef in 4 tablespoons of oil. Remove the meat, and in the same oil sauté for about 3 minutes.

½ each onion, thinly sliced   green pepper strips
    celery, thinly sliced   ½ teaspoon garlic powder

Now stir in:

3 teaspoons paprika   1 can beef broth or
1½ teaspoons salt   consommé
1½ teaspoons pepper   ½ cup thinly-sliced carrots
2 tablespoons tomato paste   a crumbled bay leaf

Bring the whole works to a boil, then simmer it, covered, for about 2 hours, till the meat is quite tender. Do it hours ahead or the day before. Just before serving time, heat it through, keeping the heat low, and stir in:

½ cup sour cream

Serve it on buttered noodles.

2. Another Stretchable Just-a-Fork Dinner

Florentine Casserole
Everything else as in No. 1

FLORENTINE CASSEROLE

6 oz noodles (bows or
   elbows)
2 to 3 cups spaghetti sauce
   (canned or foil envelope)
1 pound ground beef

10 oz frozen spinach thawed
   and well drained
2 small containers sour cream
2 oz grated Parmesan cheese

Cook noodles until barely tender, according to directions. If using foil envelope sauce, prepare it according to its directions. Brown the meat in a little fat and crumble it into the sauce.

Mix the sauce with the noodles. Cool it, then layer it with the spinach, sour cream, and cheese (noodles, spinach, sour cream, cheese; noodles, spinach, sour cream, cheese.) Bake for 30 minutes at 375°F. This also freezes well.

These entire dinners, Nos. 1 and 2, are good, by the way, to bring guests home to. Before you go out, set small tables, with a bottle of wine on each. When you return, heat the stew or casserole (or, if you have an oven with an automatic timer and you know how to use it, do so), put the previously buttered rolls in the oven, find the salad dressing and salad greens and dinner will be ready in one or two drinks (depending on the reliability of your oven timer.)

3. The Jolly Family Get-Together

(Of all my husband's relatives, I like myself the best.)

This one—also known as the Out-of-Season Unstuffed Turkey Dinner—has numerous advantages. Turkey tastes much better, for one thing, away from the holiday season. Moreover, an unstuffed turkey couldn't be much easier to cook, and it feeds large numbers.

The important thing is to get away from the Christmas taste, which will then seem fresher when December rolls around. Consider this bird only as pounds of light and dark turkey meat, which you might have bought at the delicatessen for vastly more money.

A frozen Turkey, thawed and roasted unstuffed*
Mushroom Business (p. 166)
Good Spinach Salad (p. 128)
Hot Fruit Compote served cold (p. 198)
Pot-de-Chocolat (p. 192)

One caution: There is nothing spontaneous about a frozen turkey dinner, and the bigger the bird, the less spontaneity you've got to work with. This table of thawing might prevent trouble.

To thaw a frozen turkey on the refrigerator shelf:

4–12 pounds	1 to 2 days
12–20 pounds	2 to 3 days
20–24 pounds	3 to 4 days

You cut the time in half, nearly, by putting it in a pan (it's apt to drip) and leaving it at room temperature. The closed unheated oven is a good place. But be sure to leave enough time so it's thoroughly thawed.

The process is this:

First, decide when you want to serve dinner. Then find a scratch pad and figure out how long you'll have to cook the turkey. The experts say:

20 minutes per pound at 325°F
     for 16 pounds or less
15 minutes per pound at same temperature
     for a larger bird

Then add 20 minutes out of the oven for the turkey's juices to settle before it's carved, and a very handy 20 minutes that can be.

So, at the proper distance from dinner, take the innards out of whatever cavity they're in—at either end or both.

Now tie the legs together neatly, and tie a string around the whole bird to keep the wings close to the chest. (You don't need to sew anything up or skewer anything together.)

Brush the bird generously with melted vegetable shortening or butter. Put it in a roasting pan and cover it with aluminum foil—just bend a piece of it over the turkey, tucking it loosely around.

---

* Of course it needn't be frozen. But fresh or frozen, the cooking rule is the same.

Cook it till 30 minutes short of the time you figured. Then remove the foil permanently, so he'll brown a bit.

This is a good time to test it. Gently pull its leg to see if it's getting loose in the socket. Remember that turkeys are like people, and they can't all be counted on to follow the rules. If the leg comes off in your hand—which is only the remotest of possibilities—the turkey has had it, so get it out of there. It's overdone, though edible.

But the chances are excellent that the time you figured will be right, if you didn't fail third grade arithmetic. So let it roast the remaining 30 minutes. Then let it sit the 20 minutes you allowed for sitting time, outside the oven.

Carve it and serve it. There.

About desserts here: a box of good chocolates would be as good as the Pot-de-Chocolat, come to think of it, and easier.

4. Fat Man's Shrimp Dinner

(Rich and good, easy to double, and handy for Friday night. You needn't have another cooked vegetable, because of the spinach with the shrimp.)

Fat Man's Shrimp
any Salad involving tomatoes and onions
Hot Croissants (bought)
Brown Sugar Apple Pie (p. 189)
or any other dessert you can cope with

FAT MAN'S SHRIMP   6 Servings

Cook 2 packages of frozen chopped spinach according to directions, and let it drain in a colander while you mix a cup of sour cream with 2 cans of undiluted condensed cream of mushroom soup.

Add to it:

8 oz can mushrooms, drained or
½ pound fresh ones (sautéed in butter)
½ cup grated Parmesan
½ teaspoon dry mustard

Heat it through, then add:

2 cups cooked shrimps (fresh, canned, or frozen)

Now put a layer of the spinach in a casserole dish, then a layer of the shrimp mixture, and so on, hopefully ending with the shrimps. Sprinkle some grated coconut on top for a gala note. STOP HERE. It will toast as you bake the dish later, uncovered, at 350°F for half an hour.

If you're out of coconut, you can use very coarse buttered crumbs, though it isn't so gala.

5. *The Very Casual Meatball Dinner*

This is for seemingly random invitations, which are, admittedly, seldom issued by reluctant cooks. And yet, one never knows.

The amount that follows makes enough for 10 servings. Clearly there is no way you will invite 10 people at random but it freezes well for future emergencies.

PARMESAN-WINE MEATBALLS

Mix together:

2 pounds ground beef
1 cup soft breadcrumbs
1 cup milk
2 eggs, slightly beaten
1½ teaspoons salt

⅔ cup Parmesan cheese, grated
3 tablespoons dried minced onions (or ½ cup fresh chopped)
1½ teaspoons pepper

Shape into balls, fry them briefly till they're brown, then take them out of the frying pan and make the sauce. Add a little butter to the hot frying pan, mix it with 3 tablespoons flour, then gradually add:

2 cups consommé or chicken stock
1 cup cream, fresh or sour
juice from an 8 oz can of mushrooms
½ cup dry white wine

Stir till it thickens but don't let it get too hot. Then put the meatballs back in, add the salt and pepper to taste, and the mushrooms. Cover and simmer about 20 minutes.

6. The Interesting Pork Chop Dinner

For any restive Roast Beef Regulars, this could provide a welcome change of pace.

Mrs. Neitzelgrinder's Pork Chops
Mother Bradford's Rice (p. 266)
Asparagus with Crumb Topping (p. 123)
simplest possible Green Salad
Strawberries Mary (p. 194)

MRS. NEITZELGRINDER'S PORK CHOPS   *6 Servings*

6 pork chops, 1–1½" thick
3 tablespoons flour
½ teaspoon garlic salt

½ teaspoon celery salt
½ teaspoon seasoned salt
1 teaspoon paprika

First, put all ingredients except chops in a plastic bag. Bounce the chops around in this, one at a time, then brown them slowly in a couple of tablespoons of fat or oil.

While they brown, slice a *green pepper* into 6 rings, and 3 cored and unpeeled *apples*, the juicier the better, into 6 thick chunks. On each browned chop put a pepper ring and an apple chunk.

Now, in a cup, mix:

½ cup water
1 tablespoon brown sugar
2 tablespoons Worcestershire sauce

and pour it over all the chops. Then put the lid on the pan and simmer it for 40 minutes.

With it you could serve the following cranberry/almond arrangement, which should be made in the morning and left to get cold.

MRS. N'S CRANBERRIES WITH ALMONDS

½ cup almonds, blanched
    and skinned
2 cups sugar
1 cup water

1 pound cranberries
3 good tablespoons orange
    marmalade
juice of 2 lemons

Put the sugar and water in a saucepan and let them boil for 5 minutes, then add the cranberries and let them cook for another 5. When the skins burst, take them off the stove and add the marmalade and lemon juice. When it is cool, add the cold almonds and then chill the whole business.

One more item belongs to this chapter, a kind of mushroom business. It is particularly suggested for the 'Jolly Family Get-Together.' I was given the recipe; my friend said it was to serve with any roasted meat instead of pan-roasted potatoes, and, she continued, you can prepare it the day before. When I asked why one *should* serve anything but good easy pan-roasted potatoes, she looked at me oddly and dropped the subject. Uneasily, I sensed that she knew something I didn't.

When I eventually talked myself into trying it, I found it was extraordinarily handsome. Also it was remarkably good, and it took only 25 minutes to make instead of the hour I'd expected.

Serving it as I did, at an eat-where-you-land buffet, I found, too, that it's simpler for guests—no smashing, buttering, salting, and peppering, which is the accepted attack on an oven-roasted potato in my part of the world.

All in all, the experience was as unsettling as having your horoscope prediction come true. Still, I'm glad it happened.

MUSHROOM BUSINESS   *6–8 Servings*

Sauté ½ to 1 pound of fresh mushrooms, coarsely sliced, in butter, just enough so they start to smell like mushrooms. (Don't peel them or wash them in water before you do this; just wipe them with a damp rag.)

Butter 3 slices of white bread, cut them in 1 inch squares, and put them in a casserole dish.

Combine the mushrooms with:

½ cup each of	mayonnaise
chopped onion	¾ teaspoon salt
chopped celery	¼ teaspoon pepper
chopped green pepper	

and put it on the bread squares.

Now cut 3 more slices of buttered bread the same way. Put them in next, and over it pour 2 eggs slightly beaten in 1½ cups of milk.

It doesn't matter when you do this—the morning before, if you like—just so it's refrigerated at least one hour.

Finally, an hour before you want to serve it, spoon a can of undiluted mushroom soup over it, and 2 more slices of bread, diced smaller. Bake it at 300°F for 60 to 70 minutes, or 325°F for 50 to

60 minutes. About 10 minutes before it's done, sprinkle some grated cheese on top.

This last one doesn't really fit in this section, unless you are forced to entertain right after Easter when the hardboiled eggs are inclined to pile up. If they do, have a:

SHAKEL EGG SUPPER!

Alternate layers of cooked broccoli with sliced hardboiled eggs, pour cheese sauce over it, and bake at 350°F for 30 minutes. (If you have no sauce mix, make your own: Stir 3 tablespoons flour into 3 tablespoons melted butter in a saucepan, then add 1 cup of milk and ½ cup grated sharp cheese, and keep stirring till it's thick.)

COPING IN A CRISIS

Some of the best fiction of our time is written by well-meaning domestic-science experts about how to cope in domestic emergencies. For example, if you bring guests back after the Big Game and find the oven cold and your turkey uncooked. Or similar crises that demand more than merely substituting a tablespoon of vinegar.

Contrary to what you may have read about it, it has been my experience that these seemingly hopeless situations actually are. And when you, as hostess, do something gallant and inventive, the guests will probably wish you hadn't.

They were primed for turkey, you see. All the way from the football ground to your house they could fairly smell it, brown, succulent, bursting with its juices. And even if their taste buds are pickled at that point, as they well may be, they are not going to like that brave baked bean–peanut-butter casserole you created out of what was around. Though it's reasonably good, it will suffer by comparison with what they might have been eating.

In these major crises, then—which are fortunately as few and far between as the nuts in a Bingo-prize fruitcake—one might as well be more gallant still and take the group out to dinner.

14. Potluck Suppers

Do you see that shaft of sunny sunshine cutting across the kitchen murk? This, friends, is the Potluck Supper—quite the best invention since the restaurant.

Potluck, of course, seldom means potluck. Once in a while, Potluck means that your hostess hasn't decided yet what she's going to serve, and, in any case, doesn't intend to knock herself out. Even so, you'll find when you get there that she's done a good bit more than throw another potato into the soup, and you needn't think the family eats that well every day in the week, because they don't.

Often, however, Potluck means a supper to which every lady brings a Covered Dish.

Think of the advantages here!

First, you need to cook *only one thing*.

Second, having cooked and brought your one thing, you don't actually *owe* anyone a dinner, and you needn't invite them to your house unless you feel like it.

The one trouble with Potluck, when you hate to cook, is that you never can think of anything interesting to bring; and so you usually end up bringing a Covered Dish and hoping it stays covered.

It is this situation which the recipes in this chapter are designed to ameliorate. They are a little different from the usual line of groceries, and most of them look and taste like more trouble than they were.

First, however, a word of advice on how to handle yourself when a Potluck is being planned.

Beware of the entrée. The entrée is usually the most trouble, as well as the most expensive. So never volunteer for it. Instead, volunteer somebody else.

"Ethel, *would* you make that marvelous goulash of yours?" you can say. The other ladies will probably join in—it would be rude not to, especially if they've ever tasted Ethel's goulash—and while Ethel is modestly dusting her manicure on her lapel, you can murmur something about bringing a couple of your delectable:

LEFT BANK FRENCH LOAVES

2 loaves French bread
½ lb butter
1 package onion-soup mix

You split the loaves in half, the long way. Then cream the onion-soup mix and butter together. Spread this on the cut side of the 2 bottom halves, put the tops on, wrap the loaves in aluminum foil, and throw them in the back seat of the car. When you get to the party, you can ask your hostess nicely to put them in a 350°F oven for 20 minutes. Open the foil a bit to keep them crisp.

Another good gambit, when a Potluck is under discussion, is to move in fast with the dessert. You say, "Girls, I'll bring my wonderful Hootenholler Whiskey Cake!" (These things must always be done with a good show of enthusiasm.) Suggesting this Whiskey Cake is a shrewd move, too, because you can make it six months ago, it's easy and very good, it's cheap, as good cakes go, and it goes a long way. Also, it has a rakish sound which is rather intriguing.

HOOTENHOLLER WHISKEY CAKE

½ cup butter
1 cup sugar
3 beaten eggs
1 cup flour
½ teaspoon baking powder
¼ teaspoon salt
½ teaspoon nutmeg

¼ cup milk
2 tablespoons molasses
¼ teaspoon baking soda
1 pound seedless raisins
2 cups chopped pecans
   (walnuts will do, but
   pecans are better)
¼ cup whiskey

First, take the whiskey out of the cupboard, and have a small noggin for medicinal purposes. Now, cream the butter with the sugar, and add the beaten egg. Mix together the flour, baking powder, salt, and nutmeg, and add it to the butter mixture. Then add the milk. Now put the baking soda into the molasses and mix it up and add *that*. Then add the raisins, nuts, and whiskey. Pour it into a greased and floured loaf pan and bake it at 300°F for 2 hours.

Your Whiskey Cake keeps practically forever, wrapped in aluminum foil, in your refrigerator. It gets better and better, too, if you buck it up once in a while by stabbing it with an ice pick and injecting a little more whisky with an eye dropper.

Or what about the even easier but almost as good:

Magic Fast

RICH WITCH CAKE

(The magic is in the way the fruit salad disappears.
No one would ever guess.)

In a bowl, mix:

1 cup white sugar
1 cup plain flour
1 teaspoon baking soda
½ teaspoon salt

1 egg
1 can (15 oz) fruit salad

Pour it into a greased cake pan, about 9" × 11" or thereabouts. Sprinkle the top with ¾ cup brown sugar and ½ cup chopped nuts, mixed together, and bake at 350°F for an hour. If you like, serve with ice cream or whipped cream, but think twice.

If you think you can get away with it, propose that you bring the cookies to go with someone else's homemade mousse. Try:

SHUTTEMUP COOKIES

(the fastest chocolate chip cookie)

Cream together:

> 1 cup butter or margarine
> 1 cup brown sugar

Then add:

> 2 cups flour
> 1 cup of chocolate polka dots
> ¾ cup nuts, chopped

Mix it, press it into a 13″ × 9″ rectangular pan, (the sort used for Jelly Roll) and bake for 20 minutes at 350°F. While it's still warm, cut it in bars. If you forget it, just break it up when it's cool.

or even:

I HATE TO COOKIES

(Not a great cookie but a good cookie; a cheap cookie, a fast cookie, an easy cookie. No creaming, sifting, rolling out, cutting out, or pan-greasing.)

Melt:

> ½ cup butter (not margarine)

In it, stir:

> 1 cup brown sugar
> 2 cups quick-cooking rolled oats
> ½ teaspoon baking powder
> 1 teaspoon vanilla

Mix it, press it into a 9″ × 15″ pan with a rim (a little bigger wouldn't hurt) and bake at 400°F for 10 to 12 minutes. It will still be bubbling when you take it out. When it's barely cool, cut in squares.

Another good thing to jump at is the dip and/or canapé bit. This may seem a little odd to the other ladies, but you can say—to the prospective hostess—"Oh, let me bring some odds and ends, and you won't have to go to all that bother." Nor will you, because all you need to do is pick the easiest dip recipe out of Chapter 4—say, for instance, the onion-soup-mix–avocado business on p. 33—and assemble a few boxes of variegated cocktail crackers.

And don't forget about the salad!

"I've got this gorgeous new dressing I think you'll love!" you can cry. You can then collect some varied greenery, arrange it in a bowl, and bring along a jar of:

PRETTY TOMATO DRESSING

Just mix these things together:

3 green onions, minced	1 teaspoon paprika
3 sprigs parsley, chopped fine	1 teaspoon salt
2 large tomatoes, diced	1 tablespoon vinegar
2 tablespoons Parmesan cheese	1 cup sour cream or yogurt

Then there is the matter of the hot vegetable.

To be sure, this isn't apt to come up too often, except when you are about to start over the river and through the woods for a holiday dinner at Mother's. But remember—more often than you may think—Mother hates to cook, too, and she has been doing it even longer. You can add another jewel to your eventual crown by volunteering, no matter how much it hurts, to bring your Festive Onions, though it really doesn't hurt much, because it's quite easy. Also, it is a dish that goes very well with a Christmas turkey or a Sunday prime rib or even an Easter ham.

FESTIVE ONIONS   *6 Servings*

1 lb sliced onions	1 cup cream
6 tablespoons butter	salt, pepper
2 eggs	¼ cup grated Parmesan

First, you sauté the onions in the butter until they're transparent. Then you put them in a baking dish, cover it with aluminum foil, and set it on the floor of the sleigh in which you intend to travel. Now you beat the eggs till they're light, and mix in the cream and a dash of salt and pepper. Pour this into a jar, screw the lid on tight, and before you start out, remember to take along the Parmesan in a little paper bag. When you get to Mother's, you ask her to turn the oven on to 425°F. Then you pour the custard mix over the onions, sprinkle the Parmesan on top, and bake it, uncovered, for 15 minutes.

Well, we have avoided the main issue now for about as long as we gracefully can. There is bound to come a day when none of these little ruses does you any good; a day when the party under consideration is to be held at your own house; a day—in other words—when you are stuck with the entrée for a Potluck Supper.

When this happens, consider first the virtues of:

JOHNNY MARZETTI   *10–14 Servings*

1½ pounds sharp yellow cheese, plus any odds and ends of Blue
    Cheese et cetera that you want to use up. If the yellow cheese
    isn't sharp enough, add a tablespoon of wet yellow mustard
2 pounds lean ground beef
1 pound elbow macaroni
1 large onion
1 can mushrooms—the more the better—
    plus the juice
1 large can (about 23 oz) tomato sauce

Sauté the finely chopped onion till it's tender, add the meat, and cook till the meat stops blushing. Drain the grease. Boil the macaroni as long as the package says to, drain it, then add everything else. Pour this into casserole dishes and heat at 350°F for about 40 minutes, having put a little more grated cheese on top first. This dish freezes very well. Just stop before the reheating bit, cover the casseroles tightly and put in the freezer. Bring to room temperature before reheating.

LUCIENNE'S SPINACH-WITH-CRAB   *6 Servings*

2 packages frozen chopped spinach
½ pound grated sharp Cheddar
1 pound crabmeat, fresh or frozen and thawed
1 tablespoon minced onion
1 tablespoon lemon juice
nutmeg
2 tablespoons butter
2 tablespoons flour
1 can condensed tomato soup
1 cup sour cream

Cook the spinach till it's half done, then drain it well by pressing it with great firmness into a colander. Now put it in the bottom of a greased casserole dish, and sprinkle it with half the cheese, then with the crabmeat, minced onions, lemon juice, a dash of nutmeg—then the rest of the cheese.

Now melt the butter, blend in the flour, add the soup and simmer till slightly thickened. Cool it a little, stir in the sour cream, then pour it over the crab and cheese mixture, dot it with butter, and bake it *uncovered* in a 350°F oven for 30 minutes.

Or:

TIA JUANA TAMALE   *8–10 Servings*

½ cup oil
1 large chopped onion
1 garlic clove, minced
1 pound ground beef
2 teaspoons chili powder
2 teaspoons salt
dash of Tabasco sauce

1 pound tomatoes, canned
   or fresh
1 cup cornmeal
1 cup milk
1 cup cream-style corn
½ cup stoned ripe olives

Sauté the onion and garlic in the oil for 5 minutes, then add your beef and brown it. Next, add the salt, chili powder, tomatoes, and Tabasco, cover it, and cook 15 minutes. Now stir in the cornmeal and milk and cook it another 15 minutes, stirring frequently, then add the corn and the olives. Pack all this into 2 greased loaf pans, brush the tops with oil, and bake them at 325°F for an hour.

You might suggest to the lady who's bringing the salad that she put some avocados in it. Then make sure somebody brings some French bread, or something, and that's all you need.

Lastly, consider the following 3 recipes, all of which are good, easy, somewhat different, and—let's say it—cheap.

ITALIAN TUNA   *6 Servings*

8 oz spaghetti
2 garlic cloves, minced
1 large onion, coarsely
   chopped
4 tablespoons oil, olive or
   corn
2 small cans tomato purée

1½ teaspoons basil
salt, pepper
2 cans tuna, plus the oil it's in
Parmesan or other grated
   cheese
parsley

Start the spaghetti cooking while you fry the garlic and onion in the cooking oil until they're just tender. Then add the tomato purée, basil, salt, and pepper, and bring it to the boil. Turn the heat low, and let it simmer long enough for you to set the table and put on your lipstick. Now add the tuna, let it heat through, and serve all this over the cooked drained spaghetti, garnishing it first with the parsley and the cheese.

Then there is this one, which will never make Escoffier, but which is good, easy, filling, and gets remarkable mileage out of one can of corned beef.

SCOTCH CASSEROLE   *8 Servings*

8 oz elbow macaroni
1 can corned beef, chopped
¼ pound sharp Cheddar
    cheese, diced
1 cup milk

1 can condensed cream of
    mushroom soup, undiluted
½ cup dry breadcrumbs
2 tablespoons chopped onion
dash of garlic salt

Cook the macaroni in 2 quarts of salted water until it's tender. Then blend the milk with the soup and add the beef, cheese, garlic salt, and onion. Grease a large casserole and fill it up with alternating layers of this mélange and the cooked macaroni. Put crumbs on top and dot with butter. Bake it, uncovered, in a 350°F oven for 45 minutes.

Or:

ONE MAN'S BEANS   *6 Servings*

You need:

1½ pounds lean ground beef
1 package onion soup mix
several cans of beans; red kidney beans and
    some butter beans in tomato sauce, to
    total about 1½ pounds
1 cup water
½ cup chili sauce

In a casserole brown the crumbled meat. Then, open the onion soup package and all those bean cans, stir it all into the meat, add water and chili sauce, and let simmer for half an hour (and longer won't hurt). Grate some cheese on top to melt under the broiler.

15. Last-Minute Suppers

OR THIS IS THE STORY OF YOUR LIFE

Dishonesty never got anyone anywhere, or, at the very least, it's apt to trip you up when the last trumpet sounds. So it is just as well to admit, straight out, that few last-minute suppers taste as good as the other kind.

The ones that do are the good broiled steak, the good broiled chop, the superb omelette tossed off by the superb omelette-maker who loves to cook, and a very few other things which I can't think of just now.

The authorities all put immense faith in the Emergency Shelf where the last-minute supper problem is concerned. But actually, when you hate to cook, it doesn't solve very much because it's practically impossible to maintain one. When you have a few choice goodies around, like an all-prepared Whole Canned Pheasant or a complete Mexican Dinner, they burn a hole in your pantry shelf, and you declare an existing State of Emergency until the shelf is empty.

Thus, in one way or another, your goodies disappear and there you are again at quarter to six, with your hat still on, staring at a pound of ground beef or a can of tuna.

This chapter contains a number of ideas on what to do with them, and with other items of their ilk. You *can* have some sort of an emergency shelf, after all; you must merely make sure that none of the items is so exciting in itself that you eat it up willy nilly. No one will go hogwild at the sight of a can of tuna or mushroom soup.

Entrées only are included here, because the vegetables in a last-minute supper are, as we all know, strictly a catch-as-catch-can proposition.

Desserts are not included either, for the same reason. Your big fat cookbook will tell you to "combine two delectable tinned fruits, such as cherries and apricots, add a little sherry, with a puff of ready-whipped cream on top." But when you hate to cook, you wouldn't do that for a last-minute supper, because it's too much work, and you wouldn't have those things on hand anyway. Also, the family might get confused and think it was Sunday.

SIMPLEBURGERS   *4 Servings*

Mix some chopped onion, salt, and pepper with your pound of ground beef and fry some patties. Keep them hot somewhere, and to the fat remaining in the pan add:

½ cup cream
3 tablespoons Worcestershire sauce

Stir it up, simmer a minute, then put the patties on a platter and pour the sauce on top.

SPEED BALLS   *4–5 Servings*

Mix up:

1 pound ground beef
2 tablespoons breadcrumbs, hard or soft
½ cup milk
no seasoning

shape it into small balls and brown them in butter. Next, stir in

1 package onion-soup mix
1 cup water

and mix it around gently so you don't break the meatballs. Then simmer it, while you cook rice to serve it on.

SKINNYBURGERS   *4 Servings*

Make *thin* patties of seasoned ground beef—it's best to roll them between sheets of waxed paper. Between 2 patties place a piece of Cheddar cheese and a thin slice of onion. Pinch the edges together, then fry or broil as usual.

SHERRYBURGERS   *4 Servings*

Make patties from a pound of seasoned ground beef. Brown them in a little butter in a skillet, then put them in a baking dish. Mix and heat in the same skillet

    1 can condensed mushroom soup
    4 tablespoons sherry

and pour it over the patties. Then bake them at 375°F for 15 minutes.

PIERRE'S PATTIES   *4 Servings*

    1 pound ground beef
    1 small can of mushrooms
    1 can prepared onion soup
    toast

Fry beef patties (unseasoned), turning occasionally, till they're half done. Then put the mushrooms on top of them. Open the can of onion soup now, and pour only the liquid into the pan. Then fish out the onion pieces and put them on top of the patties, cover, and simmer till the onion bits start to curl.

This is good served on thick slices of toast over which you've poured the pan juice. Parmesan is good on top, too.

FAST SKILLET SUPPER   *4 Servings*

Cook ½ cup of rice while you fry one pound of crumbled ground beef and 2 chopped onions in 2 tablespoons of butter. Add the rice. Then add:

1½ cups canned tomatoes	½ teaspoon salt
½ teaspoon prepared mustard	⅛ teaspoon pepper
½ teaspoon chili powder	1 package frozen cut green beans

Cover this now and simmer it till the beans are tender but still green—about 15 minutes.

PATTY'S PATTIES   *6 Servings*

With 1½ pounds ground beef, mix:

1 tablespoon parsley, chopped	3 middle-sized tomatoes
1 tablespoon onion, chopped	chopped small, with the
1 teaspoon salt	watery seedy juice
dash of black pepper	drained off.

Now shape all this into small patties and fry them, 2 or 3 minutes per side, in butter. Then take them out, keep them hot somewhere, lower the heat under the pan and add 1 cup of sour cream. Bring it to a boil, season it with salt and pepper, and pour it over the little hot cakes.

Sometimes there isn't much in the house besides bacon and eggs. In that case, you can have Bacon and Eggs. Or you can borrow a potato and an onion from the lady next door and make an:

OLD-FASHIONED FARM FRY   *4 Servings*

4 eggs	1 tablespoon chopped onion
4 strips bacon	2 tablespoons grated cheese
4 boiled potatoes, cubed	salt, pepper

Chop the bacon rather fine and fry it till it's crisp. Now drain off all but a couple of tablespoons of the fat, and add the potatoes, onion, salt, and pepper. Cook it gently till the potatoes are a nice old-ivory color. Then sprinkle the cheese over it all and break the 4 eggs into the pan. Stir it constantly over low heat till the eggs are set, then call the hands.

Just a word here, before we proceed to Fast Fish.

When you arrive home in a dead heat with your family, it's a good idea to set the table *immediately*. Then the children may stop screaming, and even your husband may relax a little, believing things to be further along than they are. It helps, too, to use your best china and serving dishes. A silver bowl gives a certain *je ne sais quoi* to creamed tuna, and plain ice cream tastes better in pretty sundae glasses.

Another thing that helps, if your husband likes wine with his meals, is to keep a few bottles of red wine tucked away somewhere. (Most red wines can be served at room temperature, so this saves chilling time.) You can bring forth a bottle with your last-minute supper, and this may lead him to think he's traveling first class. The sort of wine doesn't matter too much; it's the principle of the thing that counts.

RAGTIME TUNA   *4–5 Servings*

(You won't believe this, but I first tasted this dish at an extremely fancy buffet, knee deep in baby brown orchids. This dish is probably why they could afford the baby brown orchids. Anyway, the hostess told me how she did it, and to keep it to myself which proves you can't trust anybody these days.)

2 cans macaroni cheese
2 cans tuna
grated cheese

Alternate layers of macaroni and tuna in a greased casserole dish till you run out of material. Sprinkle the grated cheese lavishly on top and bake, uncovered, at 300°F for 30 minutes.

CANTON TUNA   *4 Servings*

1 can condensed cream of   celery
   celery soup   1 can chow mein noodles
½ cup milk   1 can tuna
green pepper

Thin the soup with the milk, add the tuna, a bit of chopped green pepper and celery if you have them, heat, and serve over the noodles.

A little soy sauce is good in this, but it isn't essential.

Incidentally, never feel guilty about serving a last-minute supper. Remember, there is certain poetic justice apparent here. Every red-blooded girl gets annoyed once in a while when a dinner that took her 2 hours to prepare gets eaten in 9 minutes. Sometimes it is comforting to reflect that you didn't spend a bit more time making it than it took the family to dispose of it.

BARCELONA BEANS   *4–5 Servings*

In a saucepan mix together:

2 big cans baked beans   ½ pound grated cheese
small can chopped pimentos   small jar stuffed olives, sliced

Stir it over low heat until the cheese is melted and it's hot clear through. Good with sliced tomatoes.

A good thing to remember is soup. In warm weather, jellied consommé is ideal, if your family likes it, because if it's been in the freezer part of the refrigerator, it's totally ready. Open the can, spoon the consommé into cups or glass dishes (which look chillier) with a lemon wedge on the side. Or you can serve cold V-8 juice the same way.

But, hot or cold, soup gives the family something to do while the last-minute supper heats or while you wonder what to do next.

CORNED BEEF DIABLE   *3 Servings*

1 can corned beef
prepared mustard
beaten egg

horseradish
breadcrumbs
butter

Remove the beef from the can and slice it into 6 thick pieces. Mix the mustard and horseradish in equal parts, spread the slices with it, then dip them in the beaten egg (to which you've added 2 tablespoons of water) and in the breadcrumbs, and fry them in butter till they're light brown.

This is good with mashed potatoes.

The next one only works at the last minute if you remember to keep the cream-style corn in the cupboard and nobody gets to it first.

AUNT HENRY'S CORN-AND-CHEESE   *4 Servings*

Mix together:

½ cup bread cubes
2 cans cream-style corn,
    drained
3 teaspoons minced onion
¼ lb. Cheddar cheese, grated

½ teaspoon salt
2 beaten eggs

¼ cup hot milk

Then pour it all into a greased soufflé dish or casserole and put it in a pan of hot water. Bake at 350°F for 45 minutes to an hour or till it's firm.

ANTHONY'S SHRIMP

5–6 Servings

3 tablespoons olive oil
5 tablespoons butter
1 big cut garlic clove
juice of ½ a lemon

1 lb. shrimp, fresh, canned,
or frozen-thawed
½ cup sliced fresh
mushrooms

First, you heat the fat, in a pan with the garlic. Add the shrimp and cook about 7 minutes. While they're cooking, sauté the mushrooms in a little butter in another pan. When the shrimp are browned, add the mushrooms and lemon juice and simmer 5 minutes.

Serve it on toast.

FAST RABBIT

3 Servings

½ pound grated sharp cheese
1 can condensed cream of mushroom soup
¼ cup ripe olives, sliced
a bit of chopped green pepper

Just melt the cheese in with the undiluted soup in the top of the double boiler, and when it's hot, add the olives and pepper. Heat it another minute or two and serve it on toast.

This brings us, logically enough, to Welsh Rabbit, and a mighty handy thing it is, too. You can make it yourself or buy it canned from some of the big supermarkets. You merely heat the canned kind in the top of your double boiler and serve it on whatever is handy—toast, rice, open baked potatoes, et cetera.

And just think of all the things you can add to it if you want to! For instance:

chopped luncheon meat, first fried a bit in butter
sliced hot dogs, first fried a bit in butter
crabmeat, tuna, shrimp, boned chicken
leftover meat of any kind, plus a dash of Worcestershire sauce
sliced hardboiled eggs with any of the above items or by themselves. (Well, your husband had lunch in town, didn't he?)

And you can pour Welsh Rabbit *over* things. Over:

sautéed mushrooms on buttered toast
broiled hamburgers
fried tomatoes on buttered toast

canned or fresh asparagus on buttered toast
buttered toast, then topped with crisp bacon

As you can plainly see, when you hate to cook, you owe it to yourself never to pass the canned Welsh Rabbit shelf in your supermarket without adding a few cans to your collection.

Speaking of this, recipe books are always telling you to get a can of a ready-prepared dish and spike it with something, as though the product isn't quite good enough for you as it is. This is flattering, because it makes you feel like that fairy-tale princess who tossed all night because of the pea beneath the thirteenth mattress. But my own feeling is that you should give the prepared thing the benefit of the doubt and *taste* it before you start spiking. After all, those manufacturers have worked themselves loop-legged in their sunny test kitchens perfecting a formula that a lot of people like. You can spike canned tomato soup with sherry and Worcestershire sauce, for instance, until it's practically unrecognizable, but that doesn't necessarily mean it's any better. Furthermore, if you add seven different herbs and grated cheese to everything that is supposed to be all ready, you might as well have started from scratch in the first place.

Finally, we come to a few random last-minute odds and ends.

FAST SPAGHETTI SAUCE   *4 Servings*

¼ cup olive oil
1 garlic clove, minced
salt, pepper

1 cup fresh mushrooms,
    thinly sliced
¼ teaspoon marjoram
5 tablespoons butter

First, start cooking enough spaghetti for 4—say, an 8 ounce package. Next, warm the oil in a saucepan. Add the butter and simmer till it's melted. Now add the garlic, mushrooms, and salt, and cook till the mushrooms are tender—about 12 minutes—stirring it most of the time. Finally, add the marjoram and pepper, mix everything thoroughly, and serve it over the cooked spaghetti.

CHOPS AND GRAVY   *4 Servings*

4 pork chops
3 whole chopped green
    onions or shallots
⅔ cup rice

1 can condensed cream of
    mushroom soup
5 tablespoons milk

Start cooking the rice. Then fry the pork chops over low heat, browning both sides, about 25 minutes. (Add the chopped onions for the last 2 or 3 minutes of this time.) Thin the soup with the milk, pour it over the chops and onions, and let it simmer till supper is ready. This makes good gravy for the rice.

The following recipe would only be useful at the last minute if someone in the family goes fishing and you have a freezer full of salmon.

SOME HANDSOME SALMON STEAKS   *4 Servings*

Combine in a large heavy casserole:

1 cup each water
white wine vinegar
orange juice
lemon juice

2 teaspoons salt
1 teaspoon peppercorns
¼ teaspoon ground allspice
    (optional)
1 teaspoon dried dill weed
    or tarragon

Bring it to the boil and simmer for 10 minutes. In it put:

4 salmon steaks (about ¾″ thick)

and simmer for 10 more minutes or till the salmon flakes when tested with a fork. Don't overcook it. Take it off the heat and serve immediately with hot melted butter, prettily decorated with whatever you happen to have around.

And finally:

BACK-COUNTRY HAM SLICE   *3 Servings*

1 pound ham slice, ¾ inch
    thick
3 tablespoons fat
2 tablespoons prepared
    mustard

4 tablespoons brown sugar
½ teaspoon salt
1 teaspoon paprika
½ cup water

Fry the ham in the hot fat. Then remove it from the pan and keep it hot—in a 200°F oven. Pour all the other ingredients into the fat, cook 5 minutes, and put the ham back into it for another 5 minutes.

Now take your hat off.

16. End of the Meal

IRISH COFFEE REVISITED

"My! I hope you didn't go to a lot of trouble!"
—CHRISTINE FREDERICK

It is a sorely distressing thing when you are Irish to admit that there is another side to a question. This is particularly true when it is a question of Irish Coffee.* Even though Irish Coffee was invented by an Italian bartender in San Francisco, ancestral honor seems somehow involved.

It is with embarrassed reluctance, therefore, that I revise an original glowing estimate of mine concerning Irish Coffee as a dinner-party dessert. Contrary to my earlier recommendations, it doesn't solve every problem.

Indeed, it can create some. For one, when you bring on the Irish Coffee, an occasional guest will think happily that the cocktail hour is beginning all over again, and he may dig in for the night. For another, some people don't drink.

But its biggest drawback is its extremely last-minute preparation,

---

* See Chapter 12.

186

which is the last thing you need. When you finally get the evening on a downhill pull, you want to keep it that way.

All the recipes in this chapter—with one great awkward exception—enable you to do just that. They can all be made in advance. This chapter will thus contain no STOP HERES.

If you decide to stick with the Irish Coffee rule try serving Elegant Southern/Northern Pralines with it.

ELEGANT SOUTHERN PRALINES

(Known as Elegant Northern Pralines if they are made with walnuts instead of pecans.)

2 cups granulated sugar	2 tablespoons butter
1 cup buttermilk	2 cups nuts, halved or
1 teaspoon baking soda	coarsely chopped
a pinch of salt	1 teaspoon vanilla

Pick a BIG saucepan. (The buttermilk and baking soda will foam with an exuberance that can shortly have you cleaning the whole stove.) In it, put everything except the butter and nuts, and bring it to a boil over medium-high heat. Keep right on stirring till the candy thermometer says 210°F. (And don't be afraid you'll end up with white pralines. Somehow it all turns a beautiful dark gold.) Now add the butter and nuts, lower the heat a little, and keep cooking till the thermometer says 230°F. If you haven't a thermometer, test it: the syrup should form at least a 2-inch thread without breaking, when you tilt the spoon.

Take it off the heat, add the vanilla, and let it sit till it quiets down. Beat it till it loses its gloss, and drop it by spoonfuls on waxed paper. When they've cooled, wrap them individually in waxed paper squares and hide them in an unpleasant-looking used can in the back of the refrigerator.

HOW TO BYPASS PASTRY

Some people, so they tell me, can't make good pastry. I see no reason to doubt them. Some people can't keep their eyes open under water, either. We all have our mental blocks to play with.

But there are several ways around this one.

One is the ready-to-roll frozen variety. Or the packaged pastry mix. Most brands make an adequate piecrust, better than mediocre though not so good as the best. It will be a perfectly all right pie if one's determination holds during the filling.

Then there is the crumb crust with no topping, or with a crumb-sugar topping.

Still another way of side-stepping pastry is the *torte*, which can't technically be considered a pie. Still, it is pie-shaped, and the unwilling pie-maker isn't about to split hairs.

THE CRUMB CRUST

A good basic rule is:

1½ cups gingersnap crumbs
¼ cup confectioner's sugar (not vital, and if
    the filling is to be quite rich, skip it)
6 tablespoons butter, melted

Mix it well and pat it into a pie pan. Don't try to flute it or bring it up over the rim of the pan. It would crumble when you cut into it, because that's the way the gingersnaps.

Then chill it for an hour or so before you fill it. Or bake it at 375°F for 15 minutes.

Instead of gingersnap crumbs you can use vanilla cookie crumbs. Or nearly any sort of crisp plain cookie or graham crackers crumbs. Sometimes the family doesn't eat the last few in a package, and you can put these in the blender or under the rolling pin in waxed paper, then into the jar that houses your sweet-crumb collection. It's rather like the old soup pot on the back of the stove, with something new periodically added. This can make for an interesting pie.

As to what you put in it, there are some packaged mixes that make an okay everyday pie. It won't look too packaged with some lemon rind or chopped ginger sprinkled on a fruit-pudding type, or grated bitter chocolate on a chocolate-pudding type. Or you can save some of the crumbs and sprinkle them on top.

The simplest, quickest filling is:

LEMON PIE FILLING

Mix juice and grated rind of 2 large *lemons* with 1 can of *condensed milk*. Leave to thicken. Whip 1 cup whipping cream and fold in. (Now it's ready to pour onto the crumb base and chill.)

Then there is the matter of TOPPINGS, which bypass a top crust entirely, whatever the bottom one is.

For instance, you can make a very good French-type fruit pie like this:

Have a crumb crust ready. In it, lay 6 sliced apples—and pears work exactly as well, if not better—mixed with:

½ cup sugar
1 teaspoon lemon rind
3 tablespoons lemon juice

Now sprinkle the slices with a mixture of:

½ cup flour	½ teaspoon cinnamon
½ cup sugar	¼ teaspoon mace
½ teaspoon ginger	⅓ cup butter

Bake it at 400°F for 45 minutes.

This is easier and neater than rolling out a piecrust.

Or skip the crumb or pastry shell altogether and make a:

BROWN-SUGAR APPLE PIE

Grease a pie plate, then peel and slice 6 apples. Put a layer of slices in the pie plate, sprinkle with sugar, cinnamon, and dots of butter. Stay with it till the apple slices are all in.

To top it, blend:

½ cup brown sugar
½ cup butter
1 cup flour

and flatten little dabs of this into crude circles (because it's really too sticky to roll out). Arrange these in some casual fashion on top of the apples, then bake at 350°F for about half an hour, or till the apples are soft.

If any is left, you can reheat it next day to serve in pudding dishes, with cream or ice cream.

DAZZLEBERRY TART

(If the dazzleberries aren't ripe yet, use canned cherry pie filling. Actually, canned cherry pie filling is much better in this particular pie, which is more of a cake or pudding anyway, and very good.)

Into a 9-inch pie pan pour a can of cherry pie filling (or apple or any other kind if the birds got all the canned cherries too). Sprinkle a one-layer box of sponge cake mix over it, fairly evenly. Sprinkle a cup of coarsely chopped nuts over that. Now dot the whole thing with plenty of butter—a good ⅓ cupful—and bake it at 350°F for 45 minutes.

Or for those of you who can't face the top *or* bottom crust, this is the pie. It looks like a pie, tastes good, and uses only 2 apples.

NAKED APPLE PIE

Beat 1 egg in a middlesized bowl
Then add:

½ cup brown sugar
½ cup white sugar
1 teaspoon vanilla
½ cup flour sifted with 1
    teaspoon baking powder

½ cup chopped walnuts
2 medium-sized apples—
    peeled then coarsely
    chopped or sliced
pinch of salt

Spread it in a greased 9-inch pie plate and bake it for half an hour at 350°F.

If you have some frozen pastry or a package of mix (or have bought a food processor and made the pastry on p. 253) why not try:

LEMON PUD

(To make into pie or to eat as it is)

6 lemons
½ cup butter
3 cups granulated sugar
6 eggs

Get the juice out of the lemons, some way, and grate up 3 rinds. Mix it. Now melt the butter in the top of a double boiler, stir in the lemon mix and the sugar. When it is all dissolved, stir in the beaten eggs and cook it all over simmering water—don't let the water boil. When it's as thick as thick syrup, cool it and pour it into jars to refrigerate.

This is handy to have on hand. You can eat it from little dishes, as pudding, or spoon it into any unbaked pie-case and bake it 15 minutes at 375°F. If you want to use up spare egg whites, top it with a meringue and shove it for a long minute under the broiler. If not, don't. Or use a squirt of whipped cream.

Or the slightly more taxing:

DRIED APRICOT TART

½ lb. dried apricots
1 cup orange juice
1 tablespoon cornstarch

½ cup light brown sugar
¼ teaspoon salt
butter
pastry for a 2-crust pie

Soak the apricots in the orange juice for 2 hours and line an 8-inch pie plate with pastry at the same time, so it can chill while the apricots soak. After 2 hours, drain the fruit but save ⅔ of the juice. Put it in the top of your double boiler, and blend in the cornstarch, sugar and salt, and let it cook till thick, stirring most of the time. Now spread the apricots around in the pie shell, pour syrup over them, and dot with butter. Cover it with a lattice top or a plain slit top—plenty of slits so the juice can bubble through—and bake for 12 minutes at 400°F. Reduce the heat to 325°F and bake for another 15 or 20 minutes.

And finally, in the pie-shaped department, we come to a:

NICE SIMPLE TORTE

Beat 3 egg whites good and stiff. Gradually add 1 cup of sugar and ½ teaspoon of baking powder.

Now fold in 1 cup of chopped walnuts, hazelnuts, or pecans, and 11 2-inch graham crackers, crushed. Pour it into a well-greased pie dish and bake it at 350°F for half an hour.

When cool, cover it with 1 cup of whipping cream, whipped with ½ teaspoon of vanilla, no sugar. It's a nice touch to spread a little jam on it, any sort, before the whipped cream. Refrigerate for 3 or 4 hours before you need it.

This brings us, as so many things do, to the matter of how to employ the leftover egg yolks.

In the Forgotten Meringue (p. 200) everything comes out even and everyone lives happily ever after. But this is rare. If you don't need Hollandaise—and if you do, look at pages 111–12—the sensible solution is to pretend the yolks were part of the shell and drop them down the sink. When you don't do this and, in a splendid out-of-character moment, you cover the yolks with water to preserve them, and put them in the refrigerator, it only ages them and they don't get used anyway. You made that *torte*, remember, and there is nothing you're about to make for a while that requires 3 egg yolks. Or, to put it another way, there is nothing you're about to make for a while.

Therefore, the pot-de-chocolat egg-yolk recipe we're coming to next doesn't refer to those same egg yolks, less one. These are different eggs, and this time you throw away the whites. Though egg whites are easier to use up than yolks—for meringues, soufflés, chops before crumbing them, and so forth—you never seem to be doing those things when leftover egg whites are around. So it's best to dispose of them, otherwise you've excess baggage on your conscience and in the refrigerator.

POT-DE-CHOCOLAT   *6–7 Servings*

(Most people like chocolate, and this recipe—from a blender booklet I'd gladly acknowledge if I knew which one it was—is a good, velvety affair. It's also much easier than it tastes and has more status than a pie.)

Into the blender bowl put:

   1 cup semi-sweet chocolate bits
   1 cup scalded* light cream
   2 egg yolks
   3 tablespoons brandy (or rum)

Turn the switch to high speed and blend it till the racket stops. Pour it into Japanese teacups or demitasse cups—something small, because it's rich. Chill them about 3 hours.

THE CHEESE PROBLEM The fancy menu-writers like to say, with a casual wave of the hand ". . . And for dessert, bring on the cheese tray, with crackers."

---

* Heat it till just below boiling.

Now, this sounds easy and cheap, but actually it isn't. That one wedge of Cheddar in your refrigerator isn't going to fill up a cheese tray. (Remember the gorgeous illustration that accompanied that little suggestion?) In addition to your Cheddar, you'll need at least an Edam and some good Swiss and Camembert, to make any splash at all; and good cheese is expensive.

Furthermore, the cheese tray doesn't resemble that picture one bit, once you've brought it out and it's been eaten from. You can't very gracefully serve it again, and so there you are, up to your bustle in Cheese Balls, Cheese Sandwiches, Macaroni and Cheese, and cheese-topped casseroles. While these things are quite all right, it's rather a shame to make them from such expensive ingredients.

Then there is another point. Cheese for dessert is rather like *Paradise Lost* in that everyone thinks he *ought* to like it, but still you don't notice too many people actually curling up with it. I like cheese quite well, myself; but I've always remembered one night in a Pullman dining car, while I ate my wedge of Roquefort, noticing that there wasn't another piece of cheese in sight. Chocolate sundaes, chocolate cake, and fruit pie, but no cheese. I felt pretty smug, I can tell you.

In any case, you want to be sure your guests truly like it before you go to all that expense. After all, you hope they'll serve you something you like when you go over to their house.

THE FRUIT BOWL People who have been presented with pretty fruit knives often like to serve a fruit bowl as dessert. Often this serves a double purpose, being merely a centerpiece which may also be eaten, should anyone care to.

This is really quite economical, because usually no one eats much of it. If you've ever noticed, they don't plunge for that pineapple and ask for a paring knife. Usually they settle for a couple of grapes and a cherry, and that's *it*. Whoever thought up the fruit bowl was a canny lassie indeed.

There are, in addition, a number of other uncomplicated things you can do with fruit:

You can remove the seeds from small melon halves and fill the hollows with ice-cream. (This is a good dessert with a curry dinner.)

Or you can fill the hollows with fresh strawberries and diced, slightly sugared fresh pineapple, and over it pour a sauce of vanilla ice cream beaten with a little brandy.

Or you can make:

GRAPE CREAM

6–8 Servings

Mix together:

1½ lb seedless grapes
1 cup sour cream or yogurt

½ cup brown sugar

Refrigerate this at least 2 hours—overnight if you like—and serve it in sundae glasses. Good with cookies.

Here follow some extremely simple things to do with fruit.

STRAWBERRIES MARY

5–6 Servings

(You may have noticed that chefs and other experts like to name dishes after girls, much as the weatherman always used to name his hurricanes: Potatoes Anna, Poires Hélène, Strawberries Susan. These are gourmese for Anna's Potatoes and Helen's Pears and Susan's Strawberries. This recipe is called Strawberries Mary because it is the way Mary adapted Strawberries Susan, a famous fresh fruit recipe, to wintertime use.)

2 or 3 bananas
1 tablespoon lemon juice
1 package frozen strawberries, partially thawed
3 tablespoons strawberry jam

5 macaroons, almond or coconut
1 cup whipping cream
slivered toasted almonds

Slice the bananas into a serving dish. Sprinkle with the lemon juice, then add the strawberries mixed with the jam. Next come the macaroons, crumbled. Cover it all with the cream, whipped and slightly sweetened. Chill it an hour or so before you serve it with the almonds on top.

GINGER PLUMS

6–8 Servings

1 pound can damson plums
1 pound can greengage plums
chopped crystallized ginger

Cool the cans. Then drain the juice from the damson plums and drink it or throw it out. Put *all* the plums into the greengage juice (which you have poured into a pretty glass bowl) and put the bowl in the refrigerator. Several hours before you serve it, sprinkle ⅓ cupful of chopped ginger on top. Don't stir it, just sprinkle it. Then serve it, at the table, in sundae glasses.

APPLE CREAM   *4–5 Servings*

*(A good, easy affair to make when there isn't much fresh
fruit around besides apples.)*

Grate ¾ cupful of raw red apple with skin on, using a medium grater.
Then combine it with:

  1 cup whipping cream, whipped until stiff
  ¼ cup sugar
  2 tablespoons lemon juice
  pinch of salt

Now put it in an ice-cube tray (with divider removed) and freeze it
until it's solid. If you happen to think of it, beat it once, an hour or
so later. Serve it in sundae glasses.

And speaking of fresh fruit, berries and peaches are good topped with
boiled custard (made according to the recipe in your big fat cookbook),
flavored with sherry or vanilla, and kept handy in the refrigerator.
    Or you can use instant vanilla pudding in the same fashion. Add
a little more milk than the package calls for, and flavor it with sherry.
    Then there is sour cream or yogurt. Slightly thinned with sweet
cream or milk, it's a good topping for fresh strawberries, peaches, and
raspberries, as well as for fresh or canned peaches and black cherries.

And in strawberry season there are:

STRAWBERRY FOOL

which is equal parts of crushed berries and whipped cream mixed
together with a little honey. Or just as easy and good, make a:

STRAWBERRY NINCOMPOOP

which is bowls of strawberries, their stems left on, with raw sugar
(light brown will do) and sour cream to dip them in.

Next we come to those smart little fruit-with-wine desserts which
gourmets approve so highly, and which, when you hate to cook, are
hard to beat. These give you maximum effect with minimum pain.
Nor are they expensive, as they may seem at first sight.
    A satisfactory domestic port, sherry, muscatel, or sweet sauterne
costs only a few dollars. If you put the wine where no one else can

find it, it lasts for months, because most of these recipes call for very little.

As for Kirsch and other brandies and liqueurs—which cost more —you might get someone to share the load. Find someone else who hates to cook—this won't be hard—and split a bottle between you. Be sure you pour your half into an ugly preserving jar and label it COOKING BRANDY. Then you won't be so apt to bring it out for company and drink it up.

STRAWBERRIES IN PORT

Pour port wine over slightly sugared ripe strawberries in sundae glasses, chill them, and serve.

STRAWBERRIES IN BRANDY

Put the strawberries in a glass bowl, pour brandy over them, and chill. Just before you serve them, sprinkle well with powdered sugar.

Choose from the following recipes, depending which fruits are in season.

DESERT DESSERT   *6 Servings*

5 oranges, peeled and sliced thin
½ cup toasted almonds chopped

¾ cup dates, shredded
½ cup orange juice
2 tablespoons brandy

Mix these things together in a pretty bowl, chill for at least 2 hours, and serve in sundae glasses.

MELON WINE COMPOTE

cantaloupe balls
honeydew balls
watermelon balls

powdered sugar
sweet Sauterne or Muscatel

Put the balls in a bowl, sprinkle a little powdered sugar on them, and half cover with the wine. Chill for at least 2 hours, stirring occasionally.

PEARS SICILY
8 Servings

4 big pears, halved, with
cores removed
¼ cup chopped almonds
toasted or untoasted

1 tablespoon butter, melted
2 drops almond extract
½ cup sherry

Mix together the almonds, butter, and almond extract, then put this in the pear cavities. Put the pear halves in a baking dish, pour the sherry over them, and bake at 350°F for half an hour. Serve hot or cold.

MEDITERRANEAN MELONS

Cut cantaloupes in half, scoop out the meat, and dice it. Now combine it with whatever other fresh fruits you have around: a few raspberries, strawberries, pineapple chunks, seedless grapes, peaches—any or all. Stir in 2 tablespoons of Kirsch, mix, chill, and serve it in the scooped-out melon shells.

COUPE ROYALE

(Just a fruit cup, but dignified with Kirsch it's a coupe.)

Black Bing cherries, pitted (either fresh or
canned)
½ cup Kirsch
whipped cream, unsweetened
½ teaspoon each nutmeg, powdered ginger,
mace, and 1 teaspoon cinnamon, all
mixed together

Soak the cherries in the Kirsch for at least 1 hour. Then put them in sundae glasses, cover with the whipped cream, and sprinkle the spices on top.

JULY COMPOTE

All together now bring to the boil:

  1 cup water
  1 cup sugar
  1 tablespoon bourbon whiskey or brandy
  grated rind of a big orange

While it's still warm, pour it over:

  3 big peaches, peeled, pitted, and sliced
  5 ripe plums, any kind, quartered and pitted
  ½ lb. seedless grapes

Chill several hours. This looks best in a glass bowl.

Here is a wintertime hot canned fruit dessert that's good and easy to organize. Mix it ahead, then put it in a 300°F oven to heat when you sit down. It needs only heating through.

It's best topped with commercial sour cream, whipped a bit with a fork. Don't use sweet cream soured with vinegar, which is an okay ingredient but a less-than-okay topping.

One other thing about this dessert: it's good as a side dish with an entrée, served hot or cold. If you do serve it cold, heat it through once before you chill it.

HOT WINTER FRUIT

  1 orange and 1 lemon
  2 or 3 tablespoons light
     brown sugar
  8 oz can apricots
  8 oz can pineapple pieces
  8 oz can sliced peaches
  8 oz can pitted cherries (or
     plums)

Grate the orange and lemon rinds in the brown sugar, then cut the orange and lemon pulps into thin slices, removing seeds. Mix these slices with the rest of the fruit, and put a layer of it in a baking dish. Sprinkle it with part of the rind-and-sugar mix, and a spatter of nutmeg. Repeat the layers, then heat it in the 300°F oven.

At the same time, place on top of the stove a ski boot or a pipe wrench or some other object that isn't usually found there, if you can think of one. This may remind you, when you take the dish out, to *turn the oven off.*

Speaking as one who punctually turns off the oven every morning, before I fry the breakfast eggs, I know the importance of this, and the difficulty. The lads who designed our stoves believed they'd solved the problem when they thought up the signal light that's off when the oven is. But for preoccupied cooks, that's only a starter. We need an oven that trumpets and stomps like a mad bull elephant for 10 minutes every night around 10 p.m.

Until they perfect one, keeping the oven on all night is just one of those luxuries that many of us don't especially enjoy but have to put up with.

> *"I sometimes despair of ever meeting my standards."*
> —PETER DE VRIES

And now for 4 clichés.

These are the dogged little recipes that keep appearing through the generations and disappearing and reappearing, like kneecaps in the fashion picture, or dining rooms in houses.

I believe this tenacity indicates certain quiet strengths: that people like them, and that they're easy to make. So I thought it might be comfortable to group the four here, as insurance against the next time they vanish around the bend.

AN EXCELLENT
RAIN-OR-SHINE MOUSSE

4 Servings

6 oz pckge semi-sweet
   chocolate bits
2 tablespoons sherry

¼ teaspoon salt
4 eggs, separated

Find the double boiler, have water simmering in its bottom, and in the top part melt the chocolate. Take off the pan, turn off the burner, beat in the sherry, salt, and egg yolks. Now beat the egg whites till they're stiff and fold them in. Then if you will pour it into 8 little pudding dishes or demitasse cups and refrigerate them for at least 4 hours, the world will be a better place.

FORGOTTEN MERINGUE   *6 Servings*

*(This is that well-adjusted recipe mentioned earlier
that neatly uses up the eggs.)*

First, set the oven at 400°F. Then beat 5 egg whites till they're foamy
(and this time don't throw away the yolks).
Add:

   ¼ teaspoon salt
   ½ teaspoon cream of tartar

and this time keep on beating till they stand in limp peaks. Then, very
gradually, add:

   1½ cups sugar

and keep on beating till they're very stiff indeed.
   Grease and flour a 9-inch pie plate, and spread the meringue in
it, scooping it out of the middle and piling it a bit around the sides
to form a shell. Put it in the 400°F oven, turn the heat off immediately,
and DON'T LOOK IN FOR 5 HOURS. Or overnight.
   It's easiest and very good to fill this with slightly sweetened fresh
fruit topped with sour cream. But to use up the 5 egg yolks, you can
make a:

5-EGG-YOLK LEMON FILLING

Beat the yolks, and gradually add:

   ½ cup sugar

Then blend in:

   4 tablespoons lemon juice
   grated rind of a lemon

Stir this constantly over boiling water (in your double boiler) for 6
or 7 minutes. Now whip:

   1 cup whipping cream

and spread half of it over the meringue. Then pour in the lemon
mixture, top with the rest of the whipped cream, and refrigerate it.
You can do the whole works the day before, because it keeps well.

One of the fast clichés is:

6-MINUTE CHEESECAKE   *4–6 Servings*

*(But I don't believe the optimist who named it allowed for
the crumb crust or the baking time.)*

Have a crumb crust ready and set the oven at 325°F.
  Cream:

2 small packages softened cream cheese	½ teaspoon vanilla 1 slightly beaten egg
½ cup sugar	1 cup sour cream

Put everything except the sour cream in a crumb crust and bake it 20
minutes. Hike the oven up to 450°F, spread the sour cream all over
the top of the pie, sprinkle a tablespoon of sugar on that, and bake
it for 5 minutes. Then chill it.

This is complete as is, but it's good with fresh berries and fruit,
too.

The last of the old faithfuls is:

HOT ORANGE PUFF   *4 Servings*

*(This one seems to surface every 10 years or so wearing a different name.
It's known as Marmalade Soufflé, too, as well as—I'm sorry to say—
Fluffy Duffy. It is, by the way, the one big awkward exception, mentioned earlier, that you can't make well in advance. Worse still,
it needs a sauce. Still, a non-cook I know swears by it.)*

4 egg whites
¼ cup sugar
¼ cup marmalade

Beat the whites till they're stiff, add the sugar, then the marmalade.
Butter the top part of a double boiler. Pour the mixture in, sprinkle
it lightly with sugar, then put on the lid. You're not supposed to sneak
a look or have a feel, though I did once and it didn't make any
difference.

Cook it for an hour, with the water simmering. Presumably you're
at dinner now, and the puff will be ready for you when you're ready
for it.

THE ORANGE PUFF'S VERY OWN SAUCE

(I suppose the other recipe calls it Fluffy Duffy Stuffy.)

Any time before dinner, beat 2 egg yolks thoroughly with ½ cup of sugar. Flavor it with whatever grog you like—a tablespoon of rum, brandy, sherry. Or use vanilla.

Just before serving time, whip ½ cup of cream till it's stiff and fold it into the egg-and-sugar business. This makes a pourable sauce. Don't expect it to stand around in peaks.

I think softened vanilla ice cream blended with brandy would be very good with this, too.

Speaking of which, I know an enthusiastic cook who has relied for years on vanilla ice cream plus a blender for desserts, and she still hasn't worked her way through all the possible combinations.

When I saw her last, she had gone through fresh, canned, and frozen fruits, plus syrups and flavoring extracts. Now, puffing slightly, she was heading for liqueurs—Cointreau, crème de cacao, and so forth. One can acquire a variegated hoard of these things with less pain now that the liqueur people are putting out so many of them in small sizes. Here are some other uncomplicated Things to Do with ICE CREAM:
    You can make:

KAHLUA CREAM   *6 Servings*

1 cup double cream
2 tablespoons Kahlua (or
    Tia Maria)
1 pint vanilla ice cream

⅔ cup finely chopped and
    toasted almonds
paper muffin baking cups

Beat the cream to the stiff peak stage. Then put the ice cream in a bowl and beat it (with the same beaters) to soften it a bit. Then mix in the whipped cream and the Kahlua. Put the paper cups in muffin pans and fill them with the mixture. Sprinkle the almonds on top and freeze till firm.

Or you can mix ¾ cupful of mincemeat and ⅓ cup of brandy or bourbon whiskey with a quart of vanilla ice cream, then spread it in ice cube trays (with dividers removed, of course), and refreeze.

You can do the same thing with almond toffee, coarsely broken, but skip the whiskey.

Ditto with peanut brittle, chopped ginger, coconut, cookie crumbs, chocolate bits.

And next we come to the PARFAITS.

When you hate to cook, one of the best ways to get around the fancy dessert problem is to buy 6 or 8 parfait glasses. Buy 6 or 8 long slender dessert spoons, too, if you haven't any iced-tea spoons. Hours before your guests come, you can fill up the glasses, top them with whipped cream, and put them on the top shelf of your refrigerator. Then there they are and there you are, without a single dessert thing to do at the last minute.

For instance, you might layer:

> strawberry jam with strawberry ice cream
> any nut ice cream with any chopped nuts
> mocha or chocolate ice cream with toasted almonds

and top them all, see above, with whipped cream.

Or you could fill the parfait glass with ice cream, poke a hole in it with a wooden spoon handle, and pour in a liqueur:

> crème de cacao, crème de menthe, or anisette with vanilla ice cream
> crème de menthe with pineapple sherbet
> cointreau with peach ice cream

and top with whipped cream.

(Another good way to serve liqueurs with ice cream is to serve the ice cream, naked in a sundae glass, with the liqueur in a liqueur glass at each plate. You may then pour it over the ice cream or drink it straight or both, as you prefer.)

And don't forget the old-fashioned SUNDAE. People *like* them.

ORANGE SUNDAE

You can pour slightly thawed frozen orange juice over vanilla ice cream and top it with grated orange rind or bitter chocolate shavings.

HONEY ALMOND SUNDAE

Heat the honey and pour it hot over vanilla ice cream. Top it with chopped toasted almonds.

A-1 CHOCOLATE SUNDAE

(A good, easy chocolate sauce that keeps well in the refrigerator.)

2 squares bitter chocolate
2 tablespoons butter
⅔ cup sugar

½ cup evaporated milk
  undiluted
1 teaspoon vanilla
¼ cup sherry

Melt the chocolate and butter over low heat, then stir in the sugar and milk. Cook it, over low heat, until the sugar has dissolved and the sauce has thickened. Then add the vanilla and sherry. (The sherry isn't essential, but it gives it a lovely rich dark taste.)

The next 7 desserts in this chapter are stand-bys in a high wind—good, easy, and nearly foolproof. (I don't know how you could go wrong on the Apple-Nut Pudding if you remembered to shell the nuts.) Also, they're fancy or not, as you like.

For example, this same Apple-Nut Pudding is as homely as great-grandma's kitchen if you serve it in a cereal bowl, plain or with cream. But in a sundae or a champagne glass, with softened vanilla ice cream spiked with rum, it's quite all right for the carriage trade.

NEW HAMPSHIRE APPLE-NUT
PUDDING
4–5 Servings

(Chewy, crisp and fast.)

3 apples, unpeeled but
  chopped
⅔ cup walnuts or pecans
1 teaspoon baking powder

1 cup sugar
2 tablespoons flour
1 well-beaten egg

Mix the dry things together, but don't sift them. Add the apples, the nuts, and the egg, then put it all into a smallish baking dish. Bake at 350°F for 50 minutes.

SHIVERING ELIZABETH
6 Servings

1 package orange gelatine
2 small cans mandarin oranges (drained, but
    save the juice)
2 tablespoons lemon juice, plus enough of the
    mandarin juice you just saved to make half a pint
¾ pint orange sherbet

Heat the juice, then pour it over the gelatine, and stir it till the gelatine is dissolved. Take it off the heat, cool it, and keep an eye on it, because it sets *fast*. Maybe 10 minutes. When it starts to, add the sherbet and orange sections, stir it, pour it into a well-oiled 6-to-8 cup mold and put it away in the refrigerator. Serve with whipped cream.

A PUFFY PRUNE WHIP   *5–6 Servings*

about 22 pitted cooked prunes (you can buy
     them in cans) or enough cooked dried
     apricots to make about 1½ cupfuls
½ cup orange marmalade
1 tablespoon lemon juice
¾ cup broken pecans or walnuts, for prunes;
     chopped toasted almonds, for apricots
3 egg whites, beaten stiff with 2 tablespoons
     sugar

Put the prunes, marmalade, and lemon juice into the blender and blend till smooth—about 6 to 8 seconds. Put it in a bowl, then fold in most of the nuts and the egg whites. Pile it into sundae glasses and top with the rest of the nuts.

SHERRY CHOCOLATE PUDDING   *4 Servings*

1 package chocolate-pudding mix
1¾ cup milk
2 tablespoons sherry

Combine the mix and milk according to directions on the box. When you take it off the heat, stir in the sherry, and pour it all into sundae glasses. It's good topped with whipped cream lightly dusted with cinnamon.

Also, you might make:

COFFEE PUDDING

Melt 12 marshmallows in 2 cups of strong black coffee. Then add enough unwhipped whipping cream to make it a pretty *café au lait* color, and pour it into a freezing tray. Leave it for 8 hours. Serve it in sundae glasses with whipped cream on top, and some chopped nuts if you have them.

Then we come to:

CAFE CHANTILLY

Add 1 tablespoon of cognac to a cup of really strong hot black coffee. Top it with a teaspoon of unsweetened whipped cream.

To strike a high note, that's only 50 calories per cup.

SWIFT FUDGE SAUCE

In the top of a double boiler heat 1 can *condensed milk*, 3 tablespoons *water*, 3 squares bitter *chocolate*.

Keep a jar in the refrigerator and serve over vanilla or coffee ice cream in an emergency. Or even if it's not an emergency . . .

And finally perhaps the best way of all to end a meal:

PORT WINE WITH WALNUTS

The British discovered this centuries ago, and no one has improved on it since. Put a bowl of semicracked walnuts on the table. Put a bottle of tawny port or ruby port on the table. Put wine glasses and small individual plates on the table. Pour the port and pass the walnuts.

17. Going on a Picnic

WHAT EVER HAPPENED TO POTATO SALAD?

*"Some things are of that nature as to make
One's fancy chuckle, while his heart doth ache...."*
—JOHN BUNYAN

Ever since someone discovered that it is possible to make a picnic as complicated as a six-course dinner, the picnic picture has been as cloudy as the probable weather on picnic day.

You used to know where you stood or sat at a picnic, besides right in the poison oak, because picnics came in four standard stanzas, like "The Star-Spangled Banner":

the fried chicken
the potato salad
the stuffed eggs and relishes
the cake and the fruit

But now the whole thing seems to have been upgraded while many of us weren't looking. The fire you see in yonder dell isn't for toasting marshmallows; it's the Cherries Jubilee, flaming nicely. You're apt to find almost anything on picnics these days, from Sole Amandine to

Dutch Curry, if you can believe what you read in the papers, and sometimes you can.

Well, then, it might logically be asked: "If the picnic has escalated on us like this, why bother with it?"

The answer is twofold.

For one thing, giving a picnic is still easier than giving a dinner party, because it bypasses several big problems: house cleaning, table setting, timing. Remember, this is a *picnic* we're talking about, out of reach of the house, not a backyard barbecue or a patio party, either of which usually means about as much work as you'd have done otherwise, including hot-and-cold-running canapés, with you doing most of the running. The legwork for the hostess at these things can be tremendous.

Also, your guests are quite as indebted to you, if you did the whole picnic, as though you'd entertained them at home. We'll presently come to a couple of points worth observing if this is a hearty group endeavor, with you as the organizer.

Therefore, let's spread out the blanket in this nice little patch of clover and take a look at the view, which includes some picnics and some picnic situations in which you might find yourself.

There are several ways to upgrade your own picnics, if you think it's indicated. Depending on the folk in the group, one way is to start thinking in terms of wine instead of beer. And to bring wine glasses. Wine in a paper cup is a shame (although, as in Picnic 5, it's better than none).

Too, it's good to keep in mind the words of M. Raymond Oliver, official ambassador of the cuisine Française, and owner of the historic Paris restaurant Le Grand Vefour. In San Francisco, after ordering a seafood salad for lunch, he said, "Bring us a red California wine, a Cabernet Sauvignon, and be sure to chill it."

And, he continued, to the party at large, "I don't see why we should let our tastes be dictated by some code. I like red wine, even with fish, and prefer it chilled. Who is going to tell me what I must or must not drink with such a dish?"

So let's not fret about these things. Run your own ship.

The next step in upgrading your picnic is to upgrade the Standard Picnic Menu we just passed. So let's do that.

1. THE UPGRADED CHICKNIC

If you can buy good whole rotisseried or otherwise barbecued chickens where you live, do so, allowing one for two people—split, so that each gets half.

If you can't, make Bastard Barbecue, on p. 104, which is a swift, satisfactory way to cook a lot of chicken. Allow 2 or 3 pieces per customer.

The upgraded salad could be:

NON-POTATO SALAD   *6 Servings*

(This turns out to be a bulgur salad, with considerable class. Some other time you could add fresh crab, lobster, or shrimp, and serve it as an entrée.)

Pour 2 cups of boiling water over 1 cup of bulgur wheat. Let it stand for about 10 minutes, or till the wheat has absorbed the water. Add:

¼ cup garlic wine vinegar
¼ cup olive oil

and chill it. Then add:

1 small jar sliced green stuffed olives
½ cup chopped green onions and stems
½ cup chopped parsley
2 or 3 chopped tomatoes, peeled
2 cups finely chopped raw spinach
salt, pepper, celery salt

Put it all in a salad bowl, and lay some green pepper and onion rings on top. Chill.

As a dressing, bring along in a separate jar mayonnaise mixed with a little curry and vinegar.

Bread could be breadsticks.

You'll need no stuffed eggs and relishes. They'd taste a little repetitious.

For the upgraded dessert, fresh fruit is good, anything but bananas.*

Or you could bring a frozen sponge-cake from the luxury-frozen-food department. Or your Hootenholler Whiskey Cake (p. 170), which, being unexpected, has more appeal at picnic time than at Christmas time.

Another version of the upgraded picnic is:

---

* Raw bananas haven't made it socially. I think that's because they don't begin with a p. But take pears, now, or pineapple or peaches or papayas or plums. . . . Prunes are a moot fruit of course, except in situations like the fruit whip on p. 205.

2. THE CHAMPAGNE TURKNIC

Take a boned rolled turkey out of its can, wrap it in foil or plastic wrap, and bring it, along with a sharp knife. And bring some chilled domestic champagne in a tub of ice, one bottle per 4 people.

Also, bring a loaf each of good brown bread and good white bread, the type small bakeries pride themselves on, plus some butter, mayonnaise, salt and pepper. People may want to make their own sandwiches. Even if they don't, you needn't. As the madam of the picnic, you have other things on your mind, and they can eat their turkey sliced.

Bring a salad bowl, too, with salad greenery in a plastic bag. (Have it crisp, torn, and ready when you put it into the plastic bag, then put the bag in an ice chest or insulated picnic bag.) Bring croutons (p. 124) and a jar of Ready Caesar Salad Dressing (p. 127).

For relish, the classic uncooked cranberry-and-orange is good, and certainly easy. The day before the picnic, grind together, in the blender or otherwise, 1 quart of raw cranberries and 1 whole orange (chunked first, if you use the blender). Mix in 1½ cups of sugar and store it in covered jars in the refrigerator till picnic time.

With the bread, plus the croutons in the salad, you needn't bother with rolls or potatoes.

A painless dessert here would be a big box of chocolates, to keep passing around.

The highest-graded picnic of the lot is a:

3. July 4 Picnic

Firecrackers
Baked Fried Chicken
Crumpacker's Cucumber Coleslaw—Whole fruit
French bread
Soccatumi Cake
Wine

FIRECRACKERS

½ cup butter
¼ lb. sharp Cheddar, grated
1 cup flour
several drops Tabasco

¾ teaspoon salt
¼ teaspoon cayenne pepper
1¼ cups Rice Krispies

Cream the butter with the cheese, add the seasonings, then the flour and cereal. Shape into marble-size balls on a lightly-greased baking sheet, flatten with a fork, and bake at 350°F about 12 minutes. These are crisp, short, and hot. To cool them off, omit the Tabasco.

Betty's Good
BAKED FRIED CHICKEN

Sprinkle some chicken parts with garlic salt. Coat them with mayonnaise, roll them in Ritz cracker crumbs, and spread them out on a baking-sheet. Bake them at 300°F for as long as it takes the New Ashmolean Marching Society followed by the Tri-County All-Girl Brass Band to get from one end of Main Street down to the town square, or, say, an hour and a half, though another half hour won't do a bit of harm.

Crumpacker's
CUCUMBER COLESLAW

(Coleslaw is to the vegetable compartment as meatloaf is to the whole refrigerator. Any raw vegetable sliced fine can go into it . . . radishes, turnips, zucchini, carrot . . . This is a good basic rule.)

Shred a head of cabbage fine, then mix in a chopped cucumber and ¼ cup sliced green onions. Chill it while you mix the dressing:

2 eggs	1 tablespoon sugar
½ cup vinegar	2 teaspoons dry mustard
1 tablespoon salt	¼ teaspoon white pepper

Cook this until it's thick, and cool it. Then add 2 cups of SOUR CREAM, mix it, and keep it cold till you eventually put the coleslaw together. Add as much as you like to the shredded vegetables, then keep the rest handy for potato salad sometime later. Or for more coleslaw.

THE AMAZING SOCCATUMI CAKE

(Invariably rich, moist, and delicious. Actually, Soccatumi is the name of the American Indian princess who often made it for the larger tribal functions. "Wow! Soccatumi!" the braves would yell as they waited for a piece, and a passing anthropologist thought it was the name of the cake.)

1 box yellow cake mix	4 eggs—add them one at a
½ cup sugar	time, unbeaten
¾ cup butter, melted	1 cup sour cream

Mix it all together with a big spoon, then beat it for 5 minutes with an electric beater. Pour it into a round cake pan or a mold with a hole in the middle. Bake it for an hour at 350°F . . . doesn't need icing. Good all alone. Or with somebody else.

The final upgraded picnic is:

4. THE ROAST SIRLOIN TIPNIC

Roast the meat slightly pinker than you ordinarily would. Bring along a jam jar of sour-cream-and-horse-radish dressing. (Add horseradish and lemon juice to sour cream, tasting as you go.)

Bring a cooked artichoke per person, and mayonnaise.

Bring a loaf of prebuttered French bread.

If men are involved in this picnic, as they so often are, you might want something hearty. For instance:

FAR-OUT POTATO SALAD   *6 Servings*

Cook, peel, and drain 5 good-sized potatoes, then slice them into a bowl. Pour ½ cup dry white wine over them, and leave them alone for a couple of hours, till the potatoes drink the wine. While they're living it up, mix together:

⅓ cup Italian Dressing
4 green onions, chopped
⅔ cup sliced cauliflowers
2 coarsely chopped pimentos
½ teaspoon salt
1 tablespoon bottled capers, drained*

---

* You don't usually have capers around, and they seem expensive. But a jarful lasts and lasts—mine's in its second year now—and they add a festive little kick in the pants to certain fish things and salads.

Put this in the refrigerator, in a covered jar.

Bring the bowl of spuds and the dressing separately to the picnic, and mix the two thoroughly just before you serve it. Parsley on top is nice but not vital.

A big thing about picnics, by the way, is to make sure there are plenty of napkins.

Not long ago I was invited to a picnic that proved educational. When we'd finished eating, the hostess handed around small, steamy-hot scented towels, as they do on the daintier airlines. It was an impressive piece of business, I can tell you, and refreshing, too.

I asked her how she did it. She said she adds a good dash of her husband's cologne (the poor fellow always gets some for Christmas) to hot water. Then, wearing lined rubber gloves, she wrings them out and drops them into a preheated wide-mouthed gallon thermos jug.

I wouldn't go to that trouble myself, but I like to go to her picnics.

Another good thing to remember to bring is several big plastic bags, which are so handy at cleaning-up time.

Next, we come to a picnic that's tailor-made for the unwilling cook. I refer to the:

5. A AND P-ICNIC

This type can simply happen, or—with a little forethought and artistry—you can make it happen. It fits nicely into an en route situation on a beautiful day when restaurants seem stuffy. Properly promoted, it goes down well with people who have happy memories of *la piquenique* in France or roadside lunches outside Lisbon.

In the car's glove compartment, keep salt, pepper, and a knife, just in case. Then, when you come to a likely looking grocery or market, pick up:

salami*

pumpernickel or French bread

cheese

butter

whatever fresh fruit looks good

a bottle of wine and some paper cups

For plates you may use the paper the food came wrapped in, and the knife can be enjoyed by all.

To add a touch of class, bring some of your own:

* Or liver sausage. Or Polish sausage. . . . Not luncheon meat though, or the strange jellied affairs you sometimes see. One slice of jellied Cheddar-and-veal loaf and you've lost your Continental accent.

BETTER BUTTER FOR COLD MEAT SANDWICHES

1 stick of butter creamed with a teaspoon each of minced onion, prepared mustard, horseradish, and a dash of garlic powder.

Finally, we come to the Potluck (or Everyone-Bring-Something) Picnic, which is popular in many circles. But it has caused unnecessary misery through lack of planning. As the third bowl of the same thing turns up, you begin to think you're celebrating National Eat-More-Baked-Beans Week, or Macaroni, as the case may be.

Definitely, the Potluck Picnic should be masterminded by someone. If you find you're It, as a result of an off-guard moment, you could do it this way:

You state that you're bringing the entrée—say, Bastard Barbecue—and the wine. You'll also be responsible for:

plates	napkins	cups
ice	glasses	salt and pepper
cutlery		

Announce with equal clarity that Couple-2 will bring:

baked beans or a hearty salad (her choice)	breads or rolls, and butter relishes

and Couple-3 will bring:

fresh fruit	coffee
cheese	cake or cookies

If someone is left over, he might be given the janitorial details: going back to the car for the ice and the insect repellent, unloading, and, finally, loading up again.

On the other hand, if you're an organizee rather than the organizer, you will probably find your own morale holds up better when you bring something a bit different, even though it's not necessarily better: Gorgonzola instead of Swiss cheese, lychees instead of peaches, spiced kumquats instead of pickles. Something, that is, with a modicum of flair.

Not that everyone has to.

Once upon a summertime I went to a potluck picnic (I brought that Non-Potato Salad) to which a gourmet cook of considerable local standing was invited, too. Her assignment had been dessert. So, at dessert time, she brought out big plastic bags of old-fashioned plump chocolate-marshmallow cookies.

"I adore these, don't you?" she beamed, handing them around. And everyone did, thinking, moreover, *How original, how posh!* But if someone else had done this, they'd have thought, *Poor child, how naïve!*

Mrs. Tiffany can wear paste beads, and J. Paul Getty can wear out-at-the-elbow sweaters, too. That's the way the world wags, and no one has yet discovered what to do about it.

18. Little Kids' Parties

OR THEY ONLY CAME FOR THE BALLOONS

It is a lucky thing that little children can't just decide, bang, they're going to have a party, the way grownups do, and then have it. This is one area where what Mama says still goes. What little kids have is *birthday* parties, and that's *it*. And actually they're not quite so horrible close up as they are at a distance. The only thing to fear is fear itself.

In the first place, the decorations are easy. Little children are endearingly uncritical of such trivia. If it's bright, it's fine.

Always tie your Birthday Party to the nearest festival—St. Valentine's Day in February; St. Patrick's Day in March; April Fool's Day in April (and Easter, too, when it isn't in March); May Day in May. And then there's Hallowe'en in October, Thanksgiving in November, Christmas and New Year's Eve in December. Thus you won't need to spend time devising dreadful things like Pirate Parties or Rodeo Parties. January can be a Snowball Party, whether there's any snow or not: white balloons, marshmallow-men place-card holders, coconut-icing-dipped cupcakes, white play dough for a snowman contest, et cetera, et cetera. And in June, July, August, and September you can always make it a Hobo Party—see a little later on.

216

Now an important thing to remember is this: You are giving this party for the children, not for their mamas. That's why you needn't clean the house before they come, merely afterwards. It also means that you mustn't let a mother in, when she brings her little charge up to the door. Give her a harried mother-to-mother look and say, "I know you'd rather not set foot in this chaos, and we'll bring Angela home in about two hours, when the party's over."

(Volunteering to bring the children home is the shrewdest move of your life, even though it means chauffeuring, because it enables *you* to end the party. When the little ones start throwing their birthday cake instead of eating it, and before the little Bates boy has time to wreck any more of the birthday gifts, you clap your hands merrily and call out, "Party's over!" Then you hustle them into their coats and home.)

The second big point to remember is this: Be wary of anything Amusing or Different! I know a fond mother who knocked herself out once to give her little boy a gala Mexican Christmas birthday party. Striped tissue serapes, Mexican hats, and big tissue-paper balloons hung around—one of them full of small surprises. The children took turns with a broom handle trying to knock the balloons down. But, as my friend reported to me, there was a certain grimness about the proceedings; and one small guest finally announced to the group that this was a rotten old party, not a bit like Christmas.

Never forget that children are hidebound traditionalists, and never more so than in the matter of food. Just try to get Johnny to taste the chestnut stuffing if this is his first sight of a chestnut, and if that deep pure wisdom of childhood has informed him that chestnuts are icky.

The first birthday party my daughter ever had, at the age of three, is a case in point. I wanted it to be a nice party, a special party. So I served the three- to six-year-olds chicken à la king minus pimentos, but they still didn't trust it. They didn't eat the hot toast either, because toast is for *breakfast*. The carrot strips were a howling success, comparatively speaking, because they each gnawed one. But the milk was a dead loss because they were all too excited about the oncoming birthday cake. If bakers would perfect a delicious birthday cake containing spinach, carrots, lean meat, and whole milk, they'd have a hit on their hands.

This chapter, therefore, contains 6 birthday lunch or supper menus which the little ones are apt to eat some of.

The questions might well be asked, If you hate to cook, why invite the kids for a meal at all? Why not cleave to good old-fashioned ice cream and birthday cake and that's *that*?

The answer is two-fold: When your little child knows it is going to have a birthday party that afternoon, it gets all excited and won't eat its lunch (and neither will its little prospective guests, once they've learned that they're going to a birthday party). Then, if it gets a lot of ice cream and cake in the middle of the afternoon, it certainly won't eat its dinner, and you are apt to be coping with collywobbles that night. Furthermore, you may be indebted to other mamas who have lunched or supped *your* child. *Noblesse oblige.*

Menu No. 1

(Until someone perfects a bubblegum and peanut-butter casserole that really sings, the old tuna-mushroom standby does remarkably well.)

Tuna-Mushroom Casserole
Tiny Fruit Salad
Milk
Ice Cream
Birthday Cake

TUNA-MUSHROOM CASSEROLE   *6 Small Servings*

Mix together

7 oz. can tuna
2 to 3 cups cooked noodles
1 can condensed mushroom soup diluted with ½ can milk
½ cup frozen or canned peas
salt, pepper
grated cheese

Put it in a greased casserole dish, sprinkle the cheese on top, and bake at 325°F for half an hour.

Menu No. 2

(The younger they are, the better here.)

Scrambled Eggs
Green Peas
Potato Chips
Ice Cream
Birthday Cake

Menu No. 3

Broiled or Barbecued Hamburgers
in Buns
Celery Stalks stuffed with Cheddar Cheese
or Peanut Butter
A few Cherry Tomatoes
Ice Cream
Birthday Cake

Menu No. 4

Grilled Hot Dogs
in Buttered Buns
(let them apply their own mustard)
Orange-carrot Salad
Ice Cream
Birthday Cake

ORANGE-CARROT SALAD   6 Small Servings

Prepare one package of orange Jell-o, using 1½ cups of liquid. Pare
and shred a large carrot. When the Jell-o is semi-firm, avert your eyes
and stir in the carrot shreds—also a small can of pineapple chunks, if
you have some. Let it jell the rest of the way in the refrigerator.

Menu No. 5

Fried Chicken Drumsticks
Celery Stalks stuffed with Peanut
Butter
Bread-and-Butter Sandwiches
Ice Cream
Birthday Cake

(Note: Cut the crusts off the sandwiches, and cut the sandwiches
into triangles.)

Menu No. 6

Cream of Chicken Soup
Sandwich Plate
(3 triangles: 1 peanut butter, 1 egg
salad, 1 tuna)
Carrot Sticks
Ice Cream
Birthday Cake

THE HOBO PARTY

This is the best way out of the summer birthday party situation. You advise the mothers to send the children dressed in old clothes. Then you buy a spotted handkerchief for each little guest, put his lunch in it, and tie it to the end of a stick. His lunch could be: 3 different sandwich triangles, wrapped separately, an apple or a banana, a small chocolate bar, a sealed container of milk, and 2 straws. You then lead the little bums, each carrying his bundle, to the park or the zoo for a picnic. (If there's no park or zoo handy, or no car to ferry them in, let them parade around the block with their bundles and some noise-makers, then have the picnic in the back yard or on the porch.) Bring them into the house last, for the ice cream and cake.

WEE WISDOMS AND INCIDENTAL INTELLIGENCE

A big bed sheet makes an excellent tablecloth.

Any drink tastes better with a straw in it.

When you bake birthday cake cupcakes, bake them in flat-bottomed ice cream cones. The cones don't overbake, as you'd think they would, and little children find them quite exciting and easy to eat.

When you ice the cupcakes, don't use a spatula. You save time by dipping the top of each cupcake into the icing bowl.

If you're serving individual cupcakes instead of a big birthday cake, put a candle on each one, so everybody can wish and blow.

When you write names on balloons for chair markers or favors, do it after you've blown the balloons up, and use a felt-tipped pen, or nail polish.

If you're ever stuck with having to *make* a children's party cake, you make a ready-mix cake, of course, and decorate it like this: Make some uncooked sugar icing (p. 227), color half of it pink, the other half green, ice animal crackers with it, and march the animals in a parade around the edge of the cake.

A child's sand pail makes a good centerpiece. Put a small wrapped gift for each child in it, then run paper streamers from the gifts to the children's plates.

Two shiny red apples, cored, make good candlestick holders.

Most children will eat peanut butter *on* anything or *in* anything. Should you ever fear your child will grow up without ever becoming intimate with a green vegetable, spread some peanut butter on a lettuce leaf and roll it up and give it to him. He will probably eat it. Equally successful, usually, is the celery stick–peanut-butter maneuver, as in Menus No. 3 and No. 5.

You can also, if you feel up to it, spread peanut butter on rolled-out biscuit dough, spread jam on top of it, then roll it up like a jelly roll, slice one inch thick, and bake as usual.

In the summertime, you can freeze maraschino cherries inside ice cubes, for the lemonade.

And speaking of lemonade, you can serve it in clear plastic glasses with a drop of different-colored food coloring in each, which looks mighty gay, and furthermore the little children can then tell whose is which.

Little children will often arrive at a birthday party ahead of time. They just can't wait, that's all. So it's a good idea to have a card table set up somewhere, with crayons and coloring books on it, to occupy them till the party starts. If you get desperate, you can also improvise a ring-toss game out of empty pop bottles and rubber jar rings.

You needn't set a party table at all if you'll round up a bunch of shoe boxes and do this: In each box put wrapped-up sandwiches, a paper cup of Orange-Carrot Salad (see Menu No. 4), cookies, a small carton of chocolate milk, a straw, a paper napkin, and a spoon. Then wrap each box like a present, in bright paper, with a name tag for each, and let the guests open and eat their lunch on the playroom floor.

The little ones think it's lots of fun to write secret messages with invisible ink; and on rainy afternoons, there are worse things they could be doing. So you give them a cup of milk and let them write with it, on plain white bond paper. (The brush from their set of paints works fine.) Then you stick around, for safety purposes, while they hold the paper close to the fire, or over a hot stove burner, and see the message appear.

Also, if they are out of modeling clay and need some desperately, you can mix:

1 cup salt
1 cup flour
1 cup water

plus a drop of food coloring. Then cook it over low heat till it thickens, and let it cool.

When little children are eating frozen popsicles indoors, it is a good idea to punch a hole in a small paper plate and slip it up the stick so it's just under the popsicle proper, to catch the drips.

Also, it is nice to know that you can keep the little ones out of your hair for a bit while you're arranging a birthday party by letting them stick balloons on wood or plaster surfaces, like walls and doors. They rub the blown-up balloons briskly on the wool carpet (or anything else that's wool), and it will then stick to the wall, more or less, by static electricity.

You can turn it into a party game, too, by having a contest to see whose balloon sticks the longest, though I doubt that this will ever replace pro football.

19. Cakes, Cookies, etc . . .

OR PEOPLE ARE TOO FAT ANYWAY

It is truly an awe-inspiring experience to gaze down the opulent ready-mix aisle of the supermarket, its shelves brilliant and bulging with nearly everything you ever heard of, all ready for you to add water to, mix, and bake.

At moments like this, you see clearly how far science has come. Now if they will only hustle along with a cure for the common cold and the Bomb, we may yet have our season in the sun.

I understand that the ready-mix people, through exhaustive surveys, learned that most women prefer not to have the entire job done for them. The theory is that if women realize they haven't done a thing besides add water, mix, and set the dish in the oven, they miss the creative kick they would otherwise get from baking that cake or tray of biscuits. The ready-mix people accordingly revised many of their recipes, and now you often add an egg, too.

But so far as we are concerned—we ladies who hate to cook—they needn't have bothered. We don't get our creative kicks from adding an egg, we get them from painting pictures or bathrooms, or potting geraniums or babies, or writing stories or amendments, or, possibly, engaging in some interesting type of psycho-neuro-chemical research like seeing if, perhaps, we can replace colloids with sulphates. And we simply love ready-mixes.

This chapter, therefore, contains no pastries, no fabulous meringue-chocolate-chip-cashew-nut tortes. Should you ever want to make one, your big fat overweight cookbook contains all kinds. But don't ever feel guilty about *not* wanting to make one. As the sage has said, these things remain for a moment or two in your mouth and for the rest of your life on your hips. And you know what the doctors say.

What this chapter does contain is one cockeyed cake recipe, several slightly less cockeyed recipes, a recipe for that Famous Old Scripture Cake, a few icing recipes, and a few cookie recipes—for those occasions when your ready-mix shelf is bare.

COCKEYED CAKE

(This is a famous recipe, I believe, but I haven't the faintest idea who invented it. I saw it in a newspaper years ago, meant to cut it out, didn't, and finally bumped into the cake itself in the home of a friend of mine. It was dark, rich, moist, and chocolatey, and she said it took no more than 5 minutes to mix it up. So I tried it, and, oddly enough, mine, too, was dark, rich, moist, and chocolatey. My own timing was 5½ minutes, but that includes hunting for the vinegar.)

1½ cups sifted flour	½ teaspoon salt
3 tablespoons cocoa	5 tablespoons cooking oil
1 teaspoon baking soda	1 tablespoon vinegar
1 cup sugar	1 teaspoon vanilla
	1 cup cold water

Put your sifted flour back in the sifter, add to it the cocoa, soda, sugar, and salt, and sift this right into a greased square cake pan, about 9 × 9 × 2 inches. Now you make 3 grooves, or holes, in this dry mixture. Into one, pour the oil; into the next, the vinegar; into the next, the vanilla. Now pour the cold water over it all. You'll feel like you're making mud pies now, but beat it with a spoon until it's nearly smooth and you can't see the flour. Bake it at 350°F for half an hour.

HONEST SHEEPWAGON CARROT CAKE

(Remember to start it the day before you want it)

In a middle-size saucepan put:

1⅓ cups sugar
1⅓ cups water
1 cup raisins (or chopped
    candied fruit if you like)
1 tablespoon butter

2 large carrots, finely grated
1 teaspoon each:
    cinnamon
    cloves
    nutmeg

Simmer it all together for 5 minutes, then cover and rest it for 12 hours. Why it gets so tired is one of those little mysteries. But do it. Then add:

1 cup chopped walnuts
2½ cups sifted flour
½ teaspoon salt

1 teaspoon baking soda
2 teaspoons baking powder

and mix it all up. Bake it in 2 oiled loaf pans at 275°F for 2 hours. Cool, then wrap it in foil. A good-tasting, rich-looking, moist, sturdy pioneer cake, this is, and good for every meal including breakfast.

A War Cake usually means an eggless cake, for reasons that escape the present scribe. Perhaps the hens get nervous and forget to lay, or maybe the chicken farmers get nervous and drop the eggs. No matter, here's how to make one:

AUNT HENRY'S EGGLESS RAISINFUL WAR CAKE

(Fast, easy, and easy to double in the event of a larger war.)

1 cup raisins
2 cups water
½ cup margarine
1¾ cups flour
1 cup sugar

½ teaspoon salt
1 teaspoon baking soda
½ teaspoon cinnamon
½ teaspoon nutmeg

First find a big saucepan because it's the mixing bowl too, and boil the raisins in the water for 10 minutes. Then add the margarine and let it cool. Then, without sifting, add everything else, mix it up, and bake it in a greased 10″ × 10″ pan for 35 minutes in a 350°F oven. If you'd rather use a loaf pan, bake it for 55 minutes to an hour, same temperature, and test it with a broom straw. (Chopped nuts are good in this cake too, she says, but they're not at all essential.)

The next is a rich, elegant and foolproof (once you've coped with the chestnuts) party cake.

THE ENGSTEAD CAKE

¾ cup butter
1 cup sugar
4 eggs
1 tablespoon rum
1 cup whipping cream

2 cups chestnuts (shelled, cooked till tender, then ground fine)
¼ cup grated almonds
more almonds for decoration

Cream the butter, gradually beat in the sugar, then add the well-beaten eggyolks and the rum. Now add the mashed chestnuts and grated almonds, beating thoroughly, and fold in the stiffly-beaten eggwhites. Pour it into 2 cake pans greased with shortening and sprinkled lightly with graham cracker crumbs. Bake 45 minutes at 350°F and cool.

Put the 2 layers together with whipped cream: Whip the cream, and the merest minimum of sugar—let's say, a teaspoon or two—and spread it on one layer. Set the other layer neatly on top.

Now cover with chocolate butter icing: Melt ½ pound Swiss plain chocolate with ½ cup butter, in the top of a double boiler. Beat it till it's thick enough to spread. Then do so.

IMMEDIATE FUDGE CAKE

(As the name strongly suggests, this is rather fast. And you use only a saucepan for the mixing—no bowls. It's a firm-textured, rather chewy cake, and the pan is good to lick.)

Melt ⅓ cup butter in a saucepan, and into it melt 2 squares plain chocolate. Stir it, then add:

1 cup sugar
2 eggs
½ teaspoon vanilla
¾ cup flour

¼ teaspoon salt
½ or ¾ cup coarsely chopped pecans or walnuts

Pour it into a greased brownie-type cake pan—that's about 8 inches square and bake it at 375°F for 25 minutes.

A SHORTBREAD TART

(Although not exactly a cake, this can serve the same purpose, cheaply too if strawberries are in season.)

THE CRUST
Mix 1 cup flour with 2 tablespoons confectioner's sugar, then cut in 1 stick butter till it rather resembles oatmeal. Chill it half an hour, then press into a 9″ pie or tart pan and bake for 10 minutes at 450°F. Cool it.

THE FILLING:
Rinse and dry plenty of red strawberries, pinch off the stems, and arrange them, points up, in the pie crust. Melt a 10 oz jar of red currant jam over low heat and pour it carefully over, to glaze each berry. Chill it. Just before serving sprinkle a few nuts around . . . almonds, walnuts, pistachios.

Just a word, by the way, about icings.

In a sudden rush of inventiveness, some years ago, a home economist placed some chocolate-mint creams (or plain chocolate bars) on a hot fresh cake, reheated it 2 or 3 minutes, then spread them around. The idea spread like chocolate-mint creams (or chocolate bars) on a hot cake.

It is a good thing to know, although when the cake gets cold, the sweets are going to revert to their original solid consistency. So it's best to eat the cake quickly. Good packaged icing is better. You could just dust the cake with icing sugar, too. Or leave it alone.

Here are some easy ICINGS:

GOOD OLD SUGAR ICING

Sift 2 cups confectioner's sugar with a dash of salt. Then add a teaspoon of vanilla and beat in enough cream to make it the right consistency to spread.

FRUIT ICING

In the top of your double boiler over boiling water, put:

½ cup any kind of jelly   dash of salt
1 unbeaten egg white

and beat this with a rotary beater for about 5 minutes, or until the jam has disappeared. Now take it off the heat and keep beating until it stands in stiff peaks, then spread it on the cake.

MAGGIE'S SUGAR TOPPING

Bake your cake 5 minutes less than the recipe says. Take it out of the oven, but don't turn the oven off. Let the cake cool just a bit. Then on it spread this mixture:

4 tablespoons softened butter   chopped nuts or coconut (as
⅔ cup brown sugar   much as you want, or
2 tablespoons cream   have)

Put the cake back in the oven for 5 minutes, or until the frosting bubbles.

Easier still, you can put marshmallows on top of hot, just-baked cupcakes and put them back in the oven or under the broiler until the marshmallows brown.

Now to cookies.
    When you hate to cook, you ask a lot of a cookie recipe. It must call for *no exotic ingredients*. It must be *easy*. It must not, above all, call for any *rolling out and cutting*. It must produce *extremely good cookies*. And quite a lot of them.
    The following cookie recipes meet these stern requirements.

MELTAWAY SHORTBREAD

You cream together:

1 stick butter   2 scant cups flour
½ cup vegetable shortening   1 cup flaked coconut
                                  3 tablespoons sugar

Roll it into 2 rolls, wrap them in waxed paper, and chill until you can slice them neatly—say, an hour and a half in the freezer compartment.

Bake on an ungreased baking sheet at 375°F for 20 minutes—until they're a *very* light brown—then dip in powdered sugar.

ELEVATOR LADY SPICE COOKIES

(Once, in an elevator, I was eating some spice cookies which I had made from a recipe in my big fat cookbook. I gave one to the Elevator Lady, who tasted it and said reflectively, "I can sure make a better spice cooky than that." So she brought me her recipe, and she was quite right. This is a short, rich, ginger-snap sort of cooky, and the recipe makes plenty.)

Mix together:

¾ cup shortening
1 cup sugar

1 egg, unbeaten
¼ cup molasses

Then sift together and stir in:

2 cups flour
2 teaspoons baking soda
¼ teaspoon salt

1 teaspoon cinnamon
¾ teaspoon powdered cloves
¾ teaspoon powdered ginger

Now mix it all together, and form it into walnut-sized balls. Put them 2 inches apart on a greased baking sheet and bake at 375°F for 10 to 12 minutes.

LITTLE THIMBLE CAKES

(Not quite cookies but they meet all other requirements.)

1 cup butter
⅓ cup powdered sugar,
    preferably sifted
1 egg, separated
½ teaspoon vanilla

1 cup unsifted flour
¼ teaspoon salt
¾ cup finely chopped pecans
jams, marmalade

Cream the butter and sugar, add the egg yolk and vanilla, then the flour and salt. (Put the eggwhite in a little dish for dipping, later.) Mix it well; if it's hard to handle, chill it. Then shape it into ¾" balls, dip them in the eggwhite, and roll them in the chopped nuts.

Now we come to the thimble part: Put the balls on an ungreased baking sheet and with a thimble, poke a little crater in each. Bake for 5 minutes at 350°F. Then take them out and re-poke them—the craters tend to level out—and bake for about 6 minutes longer, till they're set. After they've cooled on racks, fill the centers with the jams/marmalade. (If you're storing these, store them unfilled, or things will get pretty sticky.)

PEANUT BUTTER POKIES

Liberate 2 eggwhites from 2 eggs and slip them into a bowl. Mix with 1½ cups of peanut butter and 1 cup of white sugar. Drop by the teaspoonful onto a greased baking sheet, press gently with the tines of a fork, and bake for 8 to 10 minutes at 350°F.

SELMA'S BEST OATMEAL COOKIES

(These bear the same relationship to the ordinary oatmeal cooky that the Rolls-Royce does to the bicycle.)

Cream together:

> 1 cup shortening
> 1 cup white sugar
> ½ cup brown sugar

and add one beaten egg. Now sift together:

> 1½ cups flour
> 1 teaspoon baking soda
> 1 teaspoon cinnamon

and add it to the first mixture. Then add:

> 1½ cups quick rolled oats
> ¾ cup finely crushed walnuts or pecans
> 1 teaspoon vanilla

Chill it for an hour. Then put walnut-sized pieces on a greased baking sheet. Butter the bottom of a small glass, dip it in granulated sugar, and flatten out the little pieces. Just keep doing this—you don't need to rebutter the glass bottom, just resugar it each time. Then bake at 350°F for 10 minutes.

Note: This system of chilling the cooky dough and then flattening bits of it with a buttered, sugared glass bottom will work for nearly any sort of cooky that originally called for rolling out and cutting with a cooky cutter; and it's a lot easier.

Knowing this you can make the following without breaking your rule of no rolling.

MERRY CRISPNESS COOKIES

(Very crisp with a smooth semi-shortbread texture)

1 cup butter
1 cup sugar
3 cups flour
½ teaspoon salt

1½ teaspoons baking powder
1 egg
2 teaspoons cream or
    evaporated milk
1 teaspoon vanilla

Cream the butter and sugar, and add the sifted dry ingredients.

Then beat the egg, cream and vanilla together and add them.

Maybe you'll need to chill it before you roll it. Then roll it thin, about ⅛″ thick, cut into shapes, put a walnut-half on each if you like, sprinkle them with sugar, and bake on a greased baking sheet for about 10 minutes till they're gilt-edged. They'll stay crisp a good while in a closed pan.

OVERNIGHT MACAROONS

(These are mighty speedy cookies if you remember to mix the oil and oatmeal and sugar together the night before. They have a chewy texture and an almond-macaroon taste.)

The night before, mix together:

    4 cups quick-cooking oatmeal
    2 cups brown sugar
    1 cup vegetable oil

Next morning, mix in:

    2 beaten eggs
    1 teaspoon salt
    1 teaspoon almond extract

Drop them from a teaspoon onto a greased baking sheet, bake at 325°F for 15 minutes, and remove them promptly when they're done.

MANILA WAFERS

(A great little cooky which stays crisp in a tin with a good tight lid.)

1 stick butter
1⅛ cups sugar
1 egg
¼ teaspoon salt

¼ teaspoon baking powder
1¼ cups flour
1 teaspoon vanilla

Cream the butter with the sugar till they're well-acquainted, add the unbeaten egg, then the sifted dry things and the vanilla. Then drop them by the teaspoonful onto a greased baking sheet and put it on the middle rack in a 400°F oven, to bake for 7 or 8 minutes. And watch them. When they start to brown, they *brown*.

THE WOOKY COOKY

(Singularly crisp and buttery.)

1 cup butter
1 cup sugar
1½ cups flour
½ teaspoon baking soda
½ teaspoon baking powder

½ cup chopped nuts
½ cup Rice Krispies (not crushed)
1 teaspoon vanilla

Cream the first two ingredients together. Then without sifting anything, add all the rest and mix it well. After cooling it in the refrigerator for say, 45 minutes, shape it into balls, press them firmly with a fork on a greased baking sheet, and bake them at 325°F for 10 to 15 minutes.

McGUFFEY BISCUITS

4 cups flour
¾ cup dry milk powder
2 tablespoons baking
    powder
⅓ cup sugar
½ teaspoon salt
1¼ sticks butter

1¼ sticks margarine
1¼ cups water (or a bit more)
5 drops of yellow coloring
    makes them look lovely
    and rich

First mix the dry ingredients together, then cut in the butter and marge with a pastry cutter (or a fork) till it's all tiny lumps, like small peas. Put the yellow coloring into the water, then add it to the first mixture, stirring just enough to moisten all the flour. Drop them by the tablespoonful (or the icecream scoopful) on a greased baking sheet and bake at 425°F for 20 minutes.

This makes a lot of nice big biscuits that freeze well. Reheat them at 425°F for 10 to 12 minutes.

CHEWY FUDGE-CAKE COOKIES

(They are good plain, or iced with Good Old Sugar Icing,
p. 227, or ready-mix fudge icing.)

Find your saucepan and melt in it:

2 squares cooking chocolate
¼ cup cooking oil (not olive)

Then stir in:

1 cup sugar
2 eggs, unbeaten
1 teaspoon vanilla

Then sift together and add:

1 scant cup flour
1 teaspoon baking powder
¼ teaspoon salt

Chill it for an hour. Then, after dampening your hands, form it into little balls, roll them in powdered sugar, and bake at 400°F for 10 minutes.

And finally in the People Are Too Fat Anyway department here is that:

FAMOUS OLD SCRIPTURE CAKE

(If you know your Bible well, this will pose no problems. If you don't know it quite that well, the translation is on p. 270.)

¾ cup Genesis 18:8
1½ cup Jeremiah 6:20
5 Isaiah 10:14 (separated)
3 cups sifted Leviticus 24:5
3 teaspoons II Kings 2:20
3 teaspoons Amos 4:5
1 teaspoon Exodus 3:23
¼ teaspoon each II Chronicles 9:9
½ cup Judges 4:19
¾ cup chopped Genesis 43:11
¾ cup finely cut Jeremiah 24:5
¾ cup II Samuel 16:1
Whole Genesis 43:11

Cream Genesis 18 with Jeremiah 6. Beat in yolks of Isaiah 10, one at a time. Sift together Leviticus 24, II Kings 2, Amos 4, Exodus 30, and II Chronicles 9.

Blend into creamed mixture alternately with Judges 4. Beat whites of Isaiah 10 till stiff; fold in. Fold in chopped Genesis 43, Jeremiah 24, and II Samuel 16. Turn into 10-inch tube pan that has been greased and dusted with Leviticus 24.

Bake at 325°F till it is golden brown or Gabriel blows his trumpet, whichever happens first. Usually it takes 1 hour and 10 minutes. After 15 minutes, remove it from the pan and have it completely cooled when you drizzle over it some Burnt Jeremiah Syrup.

BURNT JEREMIAH SYRUP

1½ cups Jeremiah 6:20
½ cup Genesis 24:45
¼ cup Genesis 18:8

Melt Jeremiah 6 in heavy frying pan over low heat. Keep cooling it till it is a deep gold, then add the Genesis 24. Cook till smooth and remove from the heat. Add Genesis 18 and stir till it melts, then cool. After drizzling this on the cake, you can decorate it with whole Genesis 43.

20. Some of My Best Friends Are Fat

AND WHAT THE OTHER ONES DO

*"The huge Brontosaurus of the Jurassic Period
stayed in the shallow water to take the weight off his feet."*
—BRYAN PATTERSON

Cooking—if you ever noticed—involves you with food to an alarming
extent: shopping for it, driving it about, carrying it in, washing it,
wiping it, putting it away, hunting for it. . . .

When you're dieting, you should have as little to do with all this
as possible, for it only makes dieting harder. The delicious-sounding
recipes and earnest menus in low-calorie cookbooks make sense only
if you have a cook who cooks them for you. Otherwise, like the driver
who crashed his car while fastening his seat belt, overconscientiousness
can do you in.

I once spent an 800-calorie-per-day week at a so-called beauty
farm, from which one emerges hungry if not beautiful. The food, what
there was of it, was certainly good, and the cook was certainly fat.

Often, as I munched the celery root that passed for canapés, I pondered the immortal words of Maxim's Louis Vaudable: "Dieticians are the worst enemy of the great cuisine; it is impossible to have low calories in excellent food."

Clearly, then, if a dieter cooks much of anything, in this ready-packaged diet-food day, she has pixies at the bottom of her pea patch. Or a family to feed.

Then there's another situation that can develop: perhaps it is her husband who goes on a diet. Not that the reluctant cook gives up early here. At first, she stocks the refrigerator with fruit and cans of liquid diet for her husband. As the days go by, she watches him uneasily, taking his pulse now and then.

But if he's shooting at a ten- or fifteen-pound target, she may eventually heave a sigh that blows the Sunday papers out the window, then go dig out the non-stick frying pan.

Nor is her reaction wholly unselfish, especially if she's noticed lately that she's been asking a good deal of her stretch pants. She may get wholeheartedly into the act then, and feed him fascinating tidbits along with the yogurt, like the fact that you lose weight when you eat a hard-boiled egg* but take on some plus calories with a soft-boiled one, not even counting the piece of toast you generally eat with it.

This chapter will contain a few recipes for easy low-calorie goodies, or Not-So-Goodies, which I consider a better name. Mainly, though, it will contain more important things, like how to start a stretch of dieting, and the fastest way to get your waistline back, and a rule of thumb for finding how much you can eat to stay the size you'd like to be, and a rule of belly button, for determining whether you're absolutely enormous, in case you haven't looked in the looking glass lately.

Or at least I think it will contain all these little things. Sometimes it's hard to see around the bend. Or over the belly button.

Now more women diet needlessly than men, who usually wait for

---

* For the reason that your body has to work so hard to digest the hard-boiled egg that it actually uses up more calories than the egg contributes (whereas a soft-boiled egg digests easily and leaves you with a plus). According to Dr. Heinz Humplik, a Viennese specialist in these matters, a hard-boiled egg represents 80 calories. Yet it requires 92 calories to digest it. Therefore, you've lost weight just in the process of eating it. If you eat 4 hard-boiled eggs, you will lose 48 calories just because you ate them. (And just think, if you'd eat 100 hard-boiled eggs every day, you'd be minus 1200 calories each day and presently fade away to nothing! Perhaps it doesn't pay to examine these things too thoroughly.)

However, the same thing holds true of a whole orange compared with a glass of orange juice. And liquor—in spite of the Drinking Man's Diet furore—is a cinch to digest. Alcohol converts more easily to fat, say the experts, than most things. So it seems, at this writing, that though all calories are equal, some are more equal than others.

word from a doctor or until something won't fasten. But sometimes a big-boned woman will expect herself to weigh the same as a small-boned woman of the same height.

However, bone size has a good deal to do with it. The rule for everyone is 100 lbs for the first five feet in height. Then medium-framed people are allowed five pounds each for the additional inches, while small-framed people get fewer and big-framed people get more. (The best clue to the size of the frame is the size of the hands and the feet.)

More often though, people diet unnecessarily because everything from television to fashion ads has made it seem wicked to cast a shadow.

It's easy to figure out how many calories you can eat and maintain your proper weight (though you'd have to eat fewer than that, of course, to get down to it). You multiply your proper weight (in pounds) by 15 calories. If you want to stay 116 lbs that's 15 × 116 lbs, or 1,740 calories you have as a daily allowance.

To learn if you're truly obese, pinch yourself just below the belly button. If the distance between your fingers is over 1½ inches for a woman or 1 inch for a man, you sure are. This is up to you and the doctor then, if you want to try to do something about it, though some people don't.

The approaching diet suggestions assume that no one is going to change food habits very much, for hardly anyone ever does. Even jockeys and models, who must weigh in skinny in order to work, usually eat themselves bowlegged, once they retire.

What we'll consider here is what some wag has termed the Rhythm Method of Girth Control. It involves the 5-to-15 pound overweight* that you keep dropping and picking up again like a familiar suitcase. The Rhythm Method has the clear merit of letting people feel virtuous while they are being Spartan, and sinful while they are living it up, both very pleasant feelings.

Some RM people are more organized about it than others. I know a couple who live a mainly watercress-and-skim-milk life every January and February, then shift to whipped cream and lobster for the rest of the year. And I know a woman who doesn't eat on Mondays, just the other days. And I know a man who diets every afternoon between lunch and dinnertime.

The rest diet somewhat spasmodically, often in the late spring when the buds and the buttons start to pop. They don't see their

---

* About the distance between manufacturers' clothes sizes.

doctors, either; they just see the new bathing suits. And they usually depend, for a start, on the Fad Diet.

Though greatly maligned, the Fad Diet has its virtues. There is one for everybody, regardless of race, creed, or color, and it's something to get up in the morning for, just to see what today's is going to be: booze it up, eat it up, live high on the fat, low on the sugar, or heavy on the egg noodles.

Every Fad Diet roars in like a lion and sneaks out like a lamb chop with a slice of pineapple, which was the start of the whole thing, some decades ago. And at each and every Fad Diet the experts wag their whiskers and say, "No, you've simply got to stop eating so much."

But I can't believe Fad Diets are all bad. No one in his right mind could stay on one for longer than three days,* and if you're healthy you can stand anything for three days, even no food at all.

Moreover, fad dieting for three days gives you a great psychological start. When your digestive system is insulted like this, it quickly gets the message that things are rough and apt to get no better for a while. Then it settles down to the longer low-calorie pull.

The most interesting Fad Diet I've heard about lately, by the way, is the Wolf-all-you-like-of-whatever-you-like-for-two-minutes-three-times-a-day Diet. Depending on what you chose to wolf, I think you could also charge admission at feeding time.

The big thing is to choose your Fad Diet carefully, as you do your television repair man, and get the one that's right for *you*. Generally speaking, it should emphasize the foods you like best.

Each of these diets will lose 3 to 5 pounds for you in three days, a little less in two.

1. *Steak, prunes, and coffee.*
   BREAKFAST: 5 stewed prunes, 1 cup of coffee
   LUNCH: a big steak, fat and all, 1 cup of coffee
   DINNER: same as lunch.

2. *Nothing but fruit juice*—any kind—and tea.

3. *Milk and bananas.*
   FOR EACH MEAL, 1 glass of milk, 2 bananas.

---

* Though I did know one girl in her wrong mind who lived on pears and cottage cheese for 10 months and lost 40 pounds that included her gall bladder. She gained the 40 pounds back but not the gall bladder.

4. *Pear, cottage cheese, and lettuce salad,* with 1 tablespoon of French dressing, three times a day.

5. *Only liquids till dinner* (nonalcoholic, and not more than a cup of milk, with artificial sweeteners in drinks).
   FOR DINNER: lean meat, 2 vegetables (not potato), fresh fruit.

6. *The mainly protein pattern.*
   BREAKFAST: 3 hard-boiled eggs, coffee
   LUNCH: 3 oz each of raisins and shelled nuts
   DINNER: lean meat, 2 vegetables (not potato), and coffee.

7. *Painless Plasma,* to make yourself.
   Mix together every morning:

   1½ cups skim-milk powder
   1¾ pints water
   3 tablespoons honey
   2 tablespoons corn oil
   Whatever flavoring you like—instant coffee, brandy, vanilla, nutmeg.

Drink it all in one day, spacing it as you prefer.

8. *Health Juice,* to make yourself.
   Mix, chill, and drink as above:

   1 cup pineapple juice
   1 can, large size, evaporated milk
   6 tablespoons dextrose
   2 tablespoons corn oil
   ½ cup brewer's yeast.

After this three- or two-day start comes a few hours of nearly unbearable virtue. All orange juice looks evil because it's 50 calories more than the same amount of tomato juice. You regard from a tall skinny summit the people who eat the buns surrounding their hamburgers (at a good 150 calories per bun).

You must get over this promptly, for pride now is the devil's own pitfall. Before you know it you'll be right back in the soup, a good calorie-loaded cream of chicken, for instance, at 260 per cupful. So you decide quickly on the system you're going to follow for the next few weeks. This, too, is an individual matter, though mainly you think back to what you did last spring and do it again.

Easiest of all is to cut out a few lardy habits that total around 500 calories a day. For instance, just omitting:

a Danish pastry	150
cream and sugar in 3 cups of coffee	100
one 2½ ounce dry Martini*	180
one slice of buttered toast	100

would lose a pound a week for the person who does it.

More impatient types, who want to lose two pounds a week, also omit all desserts, breads, potatoes, or whatever formerly made a meal satisfying. Or they cleave to the liquid diet for breakfast and lunch, then have a 600-calorie dinner of lean meat and vegetables.

One of the neatest diets I've heard about was given to a friend of mine by his doctor, who wanted him to shake off 15 pounds. "No fat, no wheat," said the doctor briskly. Which my friend obediently omitted, and he lost the 15 pounds in five weeks.

It is wise, by the way, to stop at the bookstall and buy another calorie-counting booklet to replace the one that probably got lost after last spring-cleaning.

This can prevent mistakes, like baking powder biscuits, one of which—with enough butter to make it worth the powder that blew it up—costs about 75 calories. That's expensive, unless you're truly devoted to those biscuits. For the same calorie price, you could buy an ounce of brandy, or 20 asparagus spears with a little butter and lemon, which might do more for your psyche. And only 5 fried grass-hoppers cost 225 calories. So that's something else to beware of.

Another booklet almost essential for getting somewhere quickly, like back into your clothes, is *How to Exercise without Moving a Muscle* by Victor Obeck, Professor of Physical Education and Director of Athletics at New York University.

These are isometric exercises. They lose you no pounds, only inches. But because clothes sizes are geared to waist rather than weight, Mr. Obeck's six-second waist exercise alone is worth the price of the book.

(In modified form, it is holding your stomach in hard, trying to press it through your backbone, for a slow count of six. Done 10 times a day, it pares you over an inch a month. Until there's nothing extra to pare, of course.)

These exercises are especially nice because they can be done almost anywhere, including in bed.

* If you prefer to hang on to the Martini and will take a brisk half-hour's walk, the walk will burn up 150 calories and you'll come out about the same, though merrier.

Now for some words to post on the refrigerator door:

"... *Dr. W. J. Bryan (founder of the American Institute of Hypnosis) concludes that obesity in the U.S. is a result of good food, cooked too well, and eaten in too pleasant an atmosphere. He suggests that autosuggestion should begin at home with worse food, bad atmosphere, and maybe a little willful carelessness thrown in which can do as much as medicine in weight control.*"

And so to the scatter of recipes predicted earlier.

1. HOW TO SPOIL THE APPETITE BEFORE DINNER

You can eat large amounts of these vegetables (previously crisped in ice water):

celery sticks	turnip sticks
carrot strips	radishes
cucumber strips	zucchini strips

They all taste livelier if you sprinkle them with seasoning salt.

50-CALORIE DEVILED HALF-EGG

Mix the yolk with prepared mustard and a little skim milk. Stuff it back into the egg halves and put the merest squiggle of an anchovy or a sardine on the top.

Or you could serve a:

30-CALORIE PER SERVING WINE CONSOMMÉ

6 Servings

3 cups chicken bouillon
2 tablespoons gelatine
1 cup dry white wine

Use a little of the cold bouillon to soften the gelatine. Then dissolve it over hot water and add the rest of the bouillon and the wine. Chill it till it's firm, then chop it up, more or less, with a fork, spoon it into bowls, and garnish it with something green—parsley, watercress—plus a lemon slice.

Or you could have as a first course:

YOGURT SALAD

Be sure it's the low fat yogurt. Mix it sparingly with sliced cucumbers, chopped fresh mint if you have it (but dried will do), lemon juice, and a suspicion of salt.

Or you could simply eat half a head of lettuce before dinner. It tires the jaws and fills the stomach and annoys other people and is a pretty good way to derail a meal.

2. FISH—EXCELLENT SLIMMER'S FARE

SKINNY FISH FOR ALL SEASONS

Dip fresh or thawed fish fillets—almost any kind—in slightly salted milk.* Roll them in fine crumbs mixed with paprika. Lay them out companionably side by side in a well-greased shallow baking pan. Drizzle just a little melted butter on top. Bake from 8 to 10 minutes in a 500°F oven.

GIGI'S FILLETS DE FISH

(A lovely French fish dish. This one serves 4 at 109 calories per serving, or possibly, 110, depending on the amount of beurre.)

    un pound de fillets de fish blanc
    demi-oignon dans les slices
    un quartier pound des mushrooms (aussi slicé)
    un quartier coup de lait (skimmé)
    la juice de demi-lemon
    un demi teaspoon de la sauce du Worcestershire

Maintenant! Puttez les fillets dans un pan greasé, et couvrez les avec les oignons et les mushrooms. Mixer les autres thingés tout ensemble et pourez les sur la fish. Appliez les dots de beurre, aussi du salt et poivre. Bakez le decouvert 15–20 minuits a 400°F. Servez votre guest et dites-lui, Fermez la bouche.

FANCY FISHWICHES

Thaw 4 frozen fillets of sole or plaice and cut each one in half. Spread 4 of the halves with this filling:

4 tablespoons chopped mushrooms sautéed briefly in butter
2 tablespoons finely-chopped onion
a little salt, pepper, tarragon

Top each one of the remaining fish halves and put the resultant fish-wiches in a lightly buttered dish. Salt and pepper them, and brush them with a little melted butter OR heavy cream. Finally sprinkle them with fine toasted breadcrumbs and bake at 500°F about 10 minutes—no need to turn them over. Garnish them with plenty of parsley and quartered lemons.

3. THE OLD STANDBY IN NEW SLIMLINE FORM

SKINNY MEATLOAF

Mix together:

2 pounds lean ground beef   2 tablespoons minced onion
3 tablespoons melted butter   ½ teaspoon white pepper
2 eggs, slightly beaten   2 teaspoons salt substitute
1 cup skimmed milk

Pack this into a greased loaf pan and bake it for about an hour at 350°F.

4. SOME HOT VEGETABLES

With a lean plain entrée, these can help dispel the underprivileged feeling. (When the calorie count is mentioned, it means per serving.)

HOT DILL BEANS

Use canned heated string beans, or frozen or fresh, cooked till barely tender. Then season, while they steam, with a good teaspoon of chopped dill, preferably fresh, plus a little corn oil and dry sherry. Serve quickly.

60-CALORIE BAKED HALF-SPUD   *4 Servings*

Bake 2 big potatoes. Cut them in half, scoop out and mash the innards, then mix with:

3 tablespoons skimmed milk   pepper
½ cup cottage cheese   2 tablespoons green onions
1 teaspoon salt   or chives

Pile this back into the potato shells and heat for 10 minutes at around 400°F.

50-CALORIE EGGPLANT   *4 Servings*

Grease a baking dish with olive oil. In it layer these vegetables till you run out:

1 eggplant, sliced thinly
2 onions, sliced thinly
2 chopped tomatoes

Sprinkle it all with a little salt, pepper, and a good pinch of oregano. Bake for 45 minutes at 350°F.

60-CALORIE CHEESE BROCCOLI   *4 Servings*

Cook a package of frozen broccoli according to directions. Then, in a saucepan, mix:

⅓ cup buttermilk
⅓ cup Parmesan cheese

Simmer it over low heat for 5 minutes, and pour it over the broccoli.

5. THE DESSERT SITUATION

Rich desserts are a problem best solved by leaving occasional calorie room for a decent one. The low-calorie gelatine soufflés and so forth are seldom good enough to be worth the work, and the artificially sweetened ones so often taste bitter.

But you can choose what you like from the calorie booklet and allow for it—say, a scoop of vanilla ice cream with a tablespoon of chocolate sauce for 250.

Otherwise, whole fresh fruit or a small can of the dietetic variety does fine. By the way, a sauce that's good on most fruits and berries is:

22-CALORIE BANANA WHIP

(Several generous tablespoons per serving.)

Beat an egg white till it's stiff. Then add:

½ cup ripe mashed bananas
1 tablespoon sugar
slight dash of salt

and beat some more. Serve it chilled, over fresh peaches, strawberries, raspberries. . . .

LONDON TRIFLE   6 *Servings*

1 cup of marmalade among 6 people is not many calories!

1 cup yogurt
1 cup marmalade

Mix them up. Then taste. Maybe you'll want more yogurt. Or marmalade. Spoon it into sundae glasses, grate some orange rind on top, and chill it a bit.

And finally to a few Small Comforts:

Dry wine before dinner—about 3½ fluid ounces—contains only 70 calories. That's 110 less than a 2½ fl oz dry Martini.

You can be generous with dry wines in your cooking, because it's the alcohol that contains the calories, and it cooks away.

More lemon juice and less butter makes most hot vegetables better anyway.

You can make most sour-cream recipes you like—if you like any—with low-fat yogurt (115 calories per cupful) instead of sour cream (400 per cupful).

In cooked foods you can't detect the taste of dried skimmed milk, and it's far more thinning than the whole.

When something needs sweetening, a little vanilla often does it, with no cost in calories.

If you don't like fake whipped cream (though some of them are all right), you can extend true whipped cream with beaten egg white, thus lowering the calories, too.

And—as mentioned earlier—non-stick cookingware makes cooking fat unnecessary unless you specifically want the taste of fat.

6. A HEALTHY SKINNY BREAKFAST

(240 calories)

1 cup tomato juice
2 oz high-protein non-sugar cereal
1 teaspoon sugar
½ cup skimmed milk
Black coffee or tea

All these things are good to adopt as habits, for they can lengthen the span between diet times—from lilac-time to daffodil-time, perhaps, and maybe right on up to roses. Not that you would want to dispense with the random diet altogether. There is always that good victorious feeling when you lick the situation again, which you certainly wouldn't want to be without.

* Remember that salt makes your body retain water, so use as little as possible.

21. Assorted Newish Discoveries

"On the Runway of Life You Never Know What's Coming Off Next."
—ARTHUR KOPIT

Once upon a time, a lady was given a piece of electrical equipment that could have been a Chinese noodle machine or a 120-volt pretzel-bender or an electroplated futuristic sock dryer, she couldn't tell which. As she was making glad cries and wondering, her little boy said, with resoluteness, "It'll be a good place to hide Easter eggs."

He showed the proper attitude here. It is important to think positively when we can.

But sometimes there isn't a positive side. Only the other day, I saw that they have perfected an electric paper-towel-snatcher, designed to save us all from the arduous work of tearing off the paper towels by hand, which makes you wonder whither we're drifting, besides in the direction of a fat-wristed society.

Clearly, new kitchen equipment poses a problem for people who

247

hate to cook. We're either reluctant to spend anything on that end of the house or we're subject to short-lived but expensive spasms of buying a new gadget in the wistful hope that it will solve everything.

But we've learned that nothing does. We've learned that so many things don't work for us the way they work for the demonstrator.* We've learned, too, that some things are designed with a certain malevolence to take ten seconds off the preparation time and add ten minutes to the wash-up time, which is no bargain.

And yet, some things there be—gadgets, habits, food products, even attitudes—that can take some of the pain out of the kitchen.

First, there is the matter of equipment.

THE IMPORTANCE OF PAIRS AND TRIOS
AND EVEN SEXTUPLETS

It didn't take me long in my kitchen career—say, five minutes—to realize that I needed another oven or roaster or *something*.

Indeed, as Eve discovered when she made her first applesauce cake, it required a temperature different from the ass's-jawbone casserole she wanted to bake at the same time. All right, she should have thought of this earlier and baked her cake in the morning. But she didn't.

When you hate to cook but have to, an additional baking and/or roasting appliance is almost essential, because it helps to compensate for inferior planning and forgetful shopping. When you have one and you've forgotten to buy the rice that was supposed to thicken up the chicken casserole, you're in a position to shift gears—cook the chicken in one oven, and bake the ready-mix orange muffins or whatever you have in the other.

An appallingly large variety of ovens is available, ranging from expensive ones that include rotisseries to simple camp styles. Whichever kind you get doesn't matter, so long as it is easy to clean. And operate. With most of us, in the kitchen a little science goes a long way.

"My attitude towards the news that a body falling freely in a vacuum accelerates at the rate of thirty-two feet per second, or whatever the hell it is, has since childhood been 'Who cares?'"

—NORMAN WARD

Another thing: you owe it to yourself to buy enough frozen pies and somehow dispose of the contents so that you have a tidy collection of aluminum-foil pie pans. These, besides stacking neatly, have a cu-

---

* Did you ever get involved with a bean Frencher?

rious psychological value. If you're heating food, or if you sometimes feel compelled to toss some crumbs around in melted butter (see p. 123 for why you might be), an aluminum-foil pie pan is a good thing to do it in. It feels so here-today-gone-tomorrow that you've no hesitation about throwing it out instead of washing it. Even if you don't throw it out, it was nice knowing that you could have.

Another item of kitchen equipment that can make life pleasanter back there is a mirror and a vanity shelf. Kitchen designers put miles of shelves inside cupboard doors for you to fill with spice jars. There is no reason you can't use one for a mirror and make-up. Then when you're feeling warm and ragged around the edges like a bride's poached egg, you can do something about it on the premises.

A POINT ABOUT POTS

Unfortunately, a pot—stew pot, saucepan, double boiler, whatever it is—had better be a good pot if it is in the kitchen of someone who hates to cook. Otherwise it won't last very long. Its bottom will burn out as it sits empty on the red-hot burner. Heavy cast-iron frying pans are usually preferable.

They're even better for you. As Dr. Carl V. Moore, authority on anemia, told a medical-association meeting, "Food cooked in this type of utensil has a much higher iron content, and the gradual substitution of aluminum and stainless steel for iron in the manufacturing of cooking utensils may have a most unfortunate effect on dietary iron intake."*

He noted further that studies of the iron intake of populations all over the world show that the large amount of iron consumed by the Bantus of Africa is due to their custom of cooking food and fermenting beverages in iron pots.

It might be said, of course, that all that iron hasn't got the Bantus very far. But be that as it may. What mainly concerns us is the fact that when your whole attention isn't on your cooking, you need all the help you can get. A flimsy pot gives you very little, and it increases, immeasurably, your chances of disaster.

Additionally, when you specialize in interrupted cooking, observing some of the STOP HERES in the recipes throughout this book, the cast-iron things plus porcelain-coated pots or casseroles make considerable sense. You can reheat the food on the top of the stove to the point where it was when you left it, then finish it in the oven.

As to smaller gadgets, anyone who doesn't have a separate minute-

* As quoted in *The Woman's Medical News Service*, 1965.

minder yet will produce fewer charred cookies after she gets one. It's always the last batch that is cremated.

Another thing: I found that my poached-egg performance improved immeasurably when I got a poacher. But my English muffin slicer hasn't changed my life any, though I know a lady who would rescue hers if her house caught fire.

As to the little gourmet gadgets, they, too, are a highly individual matter. One girl's Mouli* is another girl's mistake. Though it is a great little garnisher, it takes an interminable time to grate or mince sizable quantities of anything. If you are nicely adjusted to a grater for cheese and kitchen shears for parsley, you probably won't acquire the Mouli habit. Habit has a great deal to do with these things.

The French garlic press has its fan club. But I find it almost magically hard to clean. Moreover, if it isn't cleaned immediately, the whole kitchen smells like a low-grade pizza parlor. More and more often I use garlic powder. Not garlic salt. Garlic powder. (When it's a matter of only peeling a garlic clove, swat it hard with the flat side of a heavy knife.)

My brief encounter with the French salad basket was also unrewarding. I mean the collapsible kind you swing around at arm's length to dry the greens without bruising them. It was raining that night, so I used it in the kitchen, and a couple of guests thought it was raining indoors, too. And I didn't think it really dried the greenery.

(When I feel like doing it right, I wash the greenery in a sinkful of cold water, separate it, lay it on a fresh tea towel, wrap it up like a tramp's bundle, and pat it or swing it dry. Then I wrap it in paper towels and put it in a plastic bag. Most of the time, I just wash it, drain it, and put it in the hydrator, and five minutes later it's sitting in a puddle of water.)

And so it goes; each to her own. Good pots and good knives, well sharpened, seem the main essentials for the person who hates to cook—and oddly enough, for the person who likes to. The best cooks I know go on cooking with whatever they have, unless something comes along that makes truly revolutionary sense. They don't upgrade their equipment from year to year, as the merchants of discontent would have us do.

Indeed, one sometimes wonders. Last year's whatever-it-is was heralded as The Ultimate. But this year's brand-new Ultimate makes last year's look sick. You get the impression that the manufacturers

---

* I mean the little French rotary mincers for fresh herbs, and rotary grater for crumbs, cheese, and so forth.

and ad men are backing away from it, daintily holding up their trouser legs and scraping their boots, the way a city slicker leaves the barnyard.

Still, that old Ultimate has served you all right, even though it doesn't have a Contour Handle. So take a deep breath and relax. There will be another Ultimate next year.

As for electrical appliances, they should be studied carefully before they're bought. One must try to visualize how they'll fit into one's own system—to use the word loosely—of running a kitchen.

Should you decide on an electrical gadget as fundamental as a can opener, do not—in an excess of enthusiasm—throw the old hand-operated variety away. In out-of-the-way places such as Bolinas (pop. 320) and in-the-way places like New York City (pop. 7,086,096), the power sometimes goes off.

And now, before we move on to some possibly helpful habits and some new groceries, let's stop for a short visit with

THE BLENDER

For years I thought—foolishly, as it turned out—that a blender was something that liquefied turnips and was hard to clean. Then I was given a blender, by a lady who owned two. It is probably one of the earlier models. Undoubtedly some refinements have been added, though my basic lethargy in the field has prevented me from finding out. Anyway, I wouldn't look a gift blender in the bowl except when I'm washing it, which couldn't be easier,* and it hasn't liquefied a turnip yet.

What it *has* done, among other things, is improve the weekend lunch situation. Little children like to make their own milk shakes, which I consider a superb idea if they'll clean up after themselves. Even a man who isn't especially milk shake prone often likes one made with a shot of whiskey, and he usually won't mind fixing it himself. You can suggest that he might drop an egg into it, too.

As for recipes, a blender doesn't exactly fix you up pronto with a "dazzling array of epicurean delights," as the box around mine said. Indeed, one must beware of enthusiasts who call something "Blender Beef Stew" when it contains 18 ingredients, only 2 of which ever see the blender. Thus you can be hoodwinked into trying a recipe that— like a built-in set of bunk beds—sounds like a practical idea but is a real pain in the neck to make.

But it does greatly simplify some recipes you wouldn't ordinarily bother with. Some of these are scattered throughout this book.

* Certain situations like fruit pulp may call for a bottle brush, but it's nothing serious.

One final word before we sail away from the blender and into something else. It is fact, sterling and indisputable, that a blender swiftly:

grinds coffee beans

makes bread crumbs, both fresh and dry. (A leftover dinner roll or French bread—even buttered and garlicked—makes good crumbs, too, though if the bread's been buttered, be sure you keep the crumbs in either the fridge or the freezer.)

de-lumps hardened brown sugar

makes remarkably good soups from quite ordinary ingredients—just check the blender booklet

crushes cookies for piecrusts or casserole toppings (and it will similarly take care of the last third of a box of cereal the family lost interest in. To that, you can add the last six soda crackers or tired cheese crackers or whatever you have, and keep your pantry shelf clearer and your crumb jar fuller simultaneously)

chops or grinds nuts

blends things with ice cream for good desserts (see p. 203)

TWO IMPORTANT ADDITIONS

Since this book appeared, two important new products have too; and I think they were specifically designed for reluctant cooks.

First, the microwave oven. Way back in Chapter 3 we passed the girl who bought and froze 2 lb of chopped steak for future meatloaf but could never remember to thaw it in time to make the meatloaf. This, among many other problems, is what the microwave oven solves so well. So long as you've a number of items in the freezer, you can wait till well into the cocktail hour before deciding what to cook for dinner, because your microwave will thaw it for you with such remarkable speed. Thus, you needn't live with the dreary knowledge of Meatloaf Ahead all day. Or, at the last minute, you can switch to sole or lambchops, with no one the wiser. Moreover, the microwave oven actually improves leftovers; and as previously mentioned we reluctant cooks need all the help we can get.

I must admit that I resisted The Microwave for years, on the theory that I didn't want to have to learn to cook all over again at this late date. But that is not what it entails; and sometimes when I think of those wasted years when I could have had one and didn't, I cry a little.

The second invaluable item is the Food Processor, the magical, magnificent Food Processor. No one who hates to cook but has to should be without one. Not only does it do all the things a blender does (but more efficiently), it also makes pastry—for which an infallible recipe appears below—and it chops or slices or grates, all in one phenomenal instant—besides being a cinch to wash. The only thing it can't do—but neither can your blender—is whip an eggwhite. So go buy a Food Processor right now.

INFALLIBLE HATE-TO-COOK PASTRY

1¼ cups plain flour   ¼ teaspoon salt
½ cup butter   3 tablespoons iced water
3 tablespoons shortening

Put first 4 ingredients in Processor and add water with the motor running. It will instantly become a ball of perfect pastry. Let it rest for half-an-hour in the refrigerator before rolling it out. That's it.

Now for some good habits.

In a spirit of idle inquiry once, I asked a couple of friends if there were one thing they wished they'd had the good sense to do when they got married. One said, Marry somebody else. The other said she wished, very much, that she had done what her sister had done.

Early on, it seems, her sister had established a tradition: on one day of the week (she chose Sunday) she didn't cook. It was simply a fact of life in that household. Mother didn't cook on Sundays, any more than the mail came on Sundays. The members of the family simply coped for themselves, using Saturday night's leftovers and whatever else was around. This strengthened their characters, the sister felt, as well as giving her a refreshing oasis to look forward to every weekend.

But my friend ruefully admitted that she's finding it hard to start a tradition after 10 years.

There are some other good habits, however, which you can start at any time.

If your grocery load includes tomatoes, you can start water boiling in a saucepan as you put things away. Drop the tomatoes in it, leave them about 45 seconds, and *then* put them in refrigerator. The skins will slip off easily when you get around to using the tomatoes, and a skinless ato always adds a nice touch. That's a good time to process the greenery, too, according to your fashion.

Another good habit, for the preoccupied cook, concerns baking or mixing anything that requires a number of ingredients. If you set them all forth on the kitchen counter and remove the top, and then *replace* each top the moment you add the ingredient, you're less apt to add something twice or omit it altogether.

Take pantry shelves. They can become so cluttered that finding anything is more trouble than it's worth. This is especially likely if you have high shelves that don't make efficient use of the cubic space. If you can find a two-by-four board that will fit into the cupboard, you can set it on 2 tall empty baked bean* cans, one at each end. That makes an additional shelf for short cans, like tuna and salmon. (You can't call this a habit, exactly, but it is a good idea.)

And so we come to the matter of new food products.

First off, a thing to beware of, if it costs extra, is the new food product that solves problems you didn't know you had. Advertisers like to invent food problems the way they invent diseases.

For instance, salad dressing that's "homogenized to cling to greens." If you haven't noticed that yours has been sliding off, there is no clear advantage for you here.

Or round spaghetti. If the long kind is a challenge to you, and cheaper, keep on buying it; and if the children have trouble with theirs, chop it up for them.

Indeed, the flood of new food preparations can be confusing in many ways. You read, for instance, a recipe calling for, say, marinated peach halves.

Marinated in what? you wonder, crossly. Soy sauce? Maple syrup? Do they come in a can? You never saw them at *your* grocer's, and by the time you finish wondering, you don't care if you never do.

Accomplished home-economics people sometimes assume at their audience knows more than it does; and for this, as Socrates said in another context, we may gently blame them.

Still, we mustn't blame them too much. Many of us lead ltered lives where new groceries are concerned. Because our busy little minds are elsewhere, we tend to trundle down the same old isles at the grocer's, buying the same old products. This can go on for years, and the home economists, meanwhile, grow tired of explaining that you an find canned green chilies in most well-stocked ry stores, just as you do cake mix.

All this is a shame, because so many of the new or products ight down our culinary alley.

But it is fruitless to do more than touch upon the swiftly shifting food picture. I doubt if anyone is wholly up with it, including the biggest frozen, canned, or ready-mixed people. Truly, we live in a food-minded age, as well as a scientific one, and the result is a marvel

---

* Or pineapple juice or tomato juice. That part doesn't matter.

a minute—some major, some minor, and some even bad-tasting marvels you wouldn't want to keep up with anyway.

Still, there are two things it is wise to do.

One is to make an eagle-eyed exploratory expedition to a good supermarket every month or so when one is in a lively, eagle-eyed mood, solely to see what's new.

The other is to allow, consciously, a fair margin in the budget for basic research: buying and trying new products to see if they're worth buying again, as many certainly are.

Also, these experimental monies (one says monies when speaking of funds devoted to serious purposes) can be employed to compare various brands of the same thing to see which is best. Or which, though all right, is wildly extravagant for what it is, unless you want to end up a fiscal mess. (One says fiscal instead of financial for grave situations like this.)

Then jot it on the blackboard, so you don't get fooled again. There are several pie fillings on the market, for instance, including one that makes a remarkably vile pie. For quite a while that's the one I kept buying, till I finally wrote it large on the kitchen wall with a skull and crossbones underneath.

22. Stealing From Knowledgeable People

I SEEN HER WHEN SHE DONE IT BUT I NEVER LET ON

"He ought to be good, he's using my act."
—FRED ALLEN

I believe that the truly dedicated cook has food in her mind, or at least on the periphery of it, at all times. As a poet unconsciously earmarks a word that rhymes handily with another, or as a painter mentally notes a tint of a shade of a color that spells Dawn, so the food-minded person sniffs an out-of-the-way herb, like costmary, and thinks in a flash, *Braised moose hocks!*

But the rest of us are not similarly talented. While our reflexes are dependable—if you say Fried Chicken, we think Mashed Potatoes; say Baked Beans, we think Brown Bread—they're hardly inspired. If we get a sniff of costmary, we'll only think, with mild surprise, *For goodness' sake*.

For this reason it is important to observe the little ways of these knowledgeable cooks. It is equally important, sometimes, not to let them know you're observing them for some are absolute stinkers when it comes to sharing the wealth. Ask one for that soufflé recipe she's so proud of, and the chances are you'll get it without the eggs. But perhaps this recipe is the brightest jewel in her crown, and you wouldn't want to take it away from her, especially since you'd end up with a mess.

Not that all of them are this way, by any means. Indeed, some are almost too generous with their inspirations. Should you be shopping with one and you pause at the halibut, she's apt to explode with something like, "I make the most marvelous whipped-cream-cucumber sauce for my baked halibut!"

That's a cue to ask for the recipe. But you're not *obliged* to. You may answer "Do you?" and hang onto your original notion of serving it fried and plain as the good Lord grew it.

One thing, though: Should a knowledgeable cook ever erupt like this with a recipe you happen to want, it is important to *write it down*. Unwilling cooks have the attention span of a four-year-old and should never trust to memory.

This happened to me once with a salad—a devastatingly delicious *new* kind (my friend said) and a real break-through on the green salad front. She gave me the recipe, which I didn't write down, and accordingly I forgot the brown sugar and the tarragon. It didn't amount to much.

However, when I ate it at her house, I discovered that it definitely does, when you make it right. So I include it here.

BREAK-THROUGH SALAD   *6 Servings*

2 medium green peppers, thinly sliced in strips
1 very large bunch coarsely chopped parsley
2 cups coarsely chopped chicory or endive
3 medium tomatoes cut in eighths
2 tablespoons chopped chives
2 tablespoons minced black olives (not strictly necessary)

Then mix together

¼ cup water
½ cup tarragon vinegar
½ teaspoon salt

1½ tablespoons lemon juice
1 tablespoon brown sugar

Pour this over the vegetables and let it wait in the refrigerator till serving time. Then put a good tablespoon of sour cream on each serving.

---

* I customarily use a thumb-and-two-finger pinch. A one-finger pinch retrieves slightly less.

Of course, it isn't merely recipes that these people contribute. They have all sorts of wee wisdoms, like the fact that if you keep Brazil nuts in the freezer overnight, they'll crack beautifully and with ease. They also know efficient ways of doing things. Take, for example, the Rule of Thumb and Forefinger.

A knowledgeable French-schooled cook stresses the convenience of knowing how much salt (and so forth) you can take in a pinch. Then you needn't mess up measuring spoons.

I've found my own capacity to be a scant one-eighth teaspoon.* To get a teaspoonful, doing that eight times is more trouble then measuring. But it's handy for small quantities.

Also, it helps in casual recipes to be able to gauge, by eye, four tablespoons of chopped or grated cheese or celery and so on. Once you've shaped this amount of it into a small funeral mound and stared at it hard, you can gauge it from then on, at least well enough for stews, salads, toppings, casseroles . . . though of course you wouldn't do this for mousses or other precision affairs, or you would find yourself up the old creek.

Then consider the matter of leftover chicken. Recipes that begin with "1½ lb of leftover chicken" have little allure, because there's seldom any left over except for a wing and a neck, and you're not about to roast or fry one. The tendency is to skip it.

I won't easily forget that day I saw a friend of mine matter-of-factly start simmering some frozen chicken thighs in a little water with a chicken bouillon cube, and then, for about 25 minutes, go and do something else. She was going to use them that night in a casserole; and being the foresighted little thing that she is, she probably saved the broth to use later for diluting a can of soup.

This is the sort of beautiful, simple thing that natural cooks do naturally, but unnatural cooks don't think of. Even when they hear about it, their strong tendency is to skip it. Still, it is a good thing to know.

At a dinner party once, I ate a small broiled *filet mignon* on a slice of broiled eggplant that had been dipped in egg and oregano-spiked crumbs. It was quite good and made the steak seem bigger.

I asked my hostess, a real swinger, if she'd thought it up. She said No, that it was her habit to keep her little red eyes open, and that's what *her* hostess had served the previous Saturday night. Thus does information get around.

---

* This is largely true of the Cocktail Party as well, except that there is sometimes more *veritas* in the *vino.*

And once I saw a weekend hostess spread prepared mustard-horseradish and plenty of pepper all over a pork roast before she cooked it. This impressed me considerably, and so did the way it tasted later. The treatment seemed to cut the richness.

Then there was the time I saw a lady pour off the juice from a brand-new bottle of olives and cover them with olive oil. That way, she said, they don't get moldy. I thought this was shrewd of her, because it also provided a small reserve of olive oil, like a penny in your pants pocket.

As a matter of fact, a cook needn't be expert to be worth stealing from. Once, I saw the worst cook I ever met (her husband is philosophic about it, and they dine out a great deal) use a cheese grater to remove the charred part from the burned toast. This could be a handy technique for burned cooky-bottoms too.

However, the two main areas in which observation, or stealing has been of most value to me are those of The Tea and The Lunch.

The Tea

As James Thurber has put it so nicely, "There are rules and rites and rituals, older than the sound of bells and snow on mountains."

These three R's underline the social tea, consisting mainly—as it does—of women standing about and saying things they don't mean* while eating things they don't want.

Most of these rules, rites, and rituals are in any big fat cookbook. The main thing to remember is that if you have a number of small pale objects around on pretty plates, you probably have a good tea going. The fact that they look a little anemic and unnecessary doesn't mean that you're unimaginative; only correct.

When you don't like to cook you're undoubtedly talented and energetic in other ways, one of which is probably avoiding teas, either going to them or giving them. The one possible peril is a committee you might find yourself on—a committee of an organization given to good works and large teas, to which each member is expected to bring something rather devastating in the line of sandwiches.

Someone has already volunteered, probably, her marvelous homemade thin-brown-bread-and-butter sandwiches. Or her marvelous homemade thin-orange-bread-and-butter sandwiches. You can't say she's fibbing, because she's going to make the sandwiches, all right—spread and trim them. But the chances are she'll buy the bread from a good bakery or small gourmet shop. These places often have specialty bread that's better than most amateurs can make.

As a general thing, you can volunteer whichever kind she didn't.

Therefore, these three sandwich rules are offered only as one would offer a bottle of Kaopectate, in the hope that it won't be necessary.

(Cakes or cookies are no problem, because you can usually buy good ones. And if you can't, find something in Chapter 19.)

For all these sandwiches, cream the butter first.

CUCUMBER DILLWICHES

Flatten thin-sliced white bread with a rolling pin (which is a good idea for any thin sandwich) and cut it in rounds with a cookie cutter. Unless you have square cucumbers.

On each, spread butter. Put a thin slice of peeled cucumber on the butter, sprinkle fresh chopped dill or the dried kind on the cucumber. Then put another buttered bread round on the top. That's all, but they have a very nice ladylike look.

ALMOND CHICKWICHES

Spread bread slices with softened butter. (You cut and trim these later.)

For the filling, mix:

1½ cups minced chicken
1 small jar pimento pieces drained and chopped
⅔ cup chopped salted almonds
4 tablespoons mayonnaise

1 teaspoon minced chives (or chopped green onion tops)
1 tablespoon parsley
2 or 3 drops angostura bitters, if you like

Spread it on half the bread slices, put the other buttered bread slices on top, trim the crusts, and cut each sandwich into 4 small squares or 4 small triangles.

OPEN FACEWICHES

Butter flattened bread slices. Spread each with:

a mixture of 8 oz cream cheese, softened and well blended with
3 tablespoons finely chopped chutney
2 tablespoons finely chopped preserved ginger
2 tablespoons grated coconut
½ teaspoon curry powder

Now—a messy operation, this—trim the crusts off and cut each slice into 3 strips. Wash hands when done.

The Lunch

This is a more rewarding area of research, because most ideas you pilfer can be used for other occasions, too.

The best lunch I've been to in years was basically ham and eggs and champagne. It had two big advantages: It was a cinch for the hostess, and the men liked it as well as the women. The menu was:

Melon Balls
Ham and Eggs in Individual Baking Dishes
Biscuits
Champagne

THE HAM AND EGGS   *4 Servings*

Put a slice of boiled or baked ham in each of 4 shallow baking dishes. Break 2 eggs—rather carefully—over it in each. Then make a sauce:

Melt 4 tablespoons of butter, stir in 4 tablespoons flour, add ½ cup each of milk and chicken stock. (Bouillon-cube stock does fine.) Cook till it's thickened, then salt and pepper it, and add ⅓ cup of vermouth.

Pour the sauce over the eggs and sprinkle it with grated Cheddar cheese or Parmesan. STOP HERE (and if you've done this early, you'd better refrigerate it because of the eggs).

Bake the little dishes at 400°F for 10 to 15 minutes.

THE BISCUITS

Use a biscuit mix and add chopped walnuts. These can bake along with the ham and eggs.

THE MELON BALLS

They needn't be balls; they could be chunks. Or strips. Or just plain melon.

Our hostess told me later that she had everything ready to put in the oven or take out of the refrigerator by 11 a.m. And indeed, I noticed that she was relaxed enough to enjoy the champagne quite as much as the rest of us.

One other sort of lunch, I've noticed, seems equally easy on the person who is giving it. This is the Soup-with-Something Lunch. The soup is ready on the back of the stove; and the Something (dessert, or French loaf, or sandwiches) needs only putting in the oven or on the table, as the case may be.

It is best to have a hard-to-analyze soup. I've noticed that the knowledgeable hostess seldom serves anything you have a pantry full of yourself, or, at least if she does, you don't recognize it. (And in any case, the knowledgeable guest would never beam and say, "I simply *adore* Murgatroyd's Chowder; we have it all the time at home!" for this would say volumes about her upbringing, or downbringing.)

This is why you combine soups, or doctor them conscientiously. However, this must be tempered with sense. If you're going to take half an hour out of your life to make Picayune Pecan Pie (p. 84), your guests could get along nicely with plain vegetable soup, which is excellent as is. You could add some fresh chopped cucumber to it at the last minute if you wanted to, but you certainly wouldn't have to.

The next 4 recipes include 2 easy and almost unrecognizable soups and a moderately interesting sandwich.

SUDDEN SOUP
4 Servings

(*Light, somewhat exotic, and good with the Voodoo Sandwiches.*)

Boil together till it's reduced about half:

    4 cans chicken broth
    1 cup tomato juice
    salt and pepper

Then add a dash of sugar, the grated rind of half an orange, and ¼ cup dry vermouth. STOP HERE. Heat it again and serve.

PHILOSOPHER'S CHOWDER
4–6 Servings

(*Rather pretty, and good with a fruit dessert.*)

Cook a box of frozen chopped spinach in the least possible water. Drain it.* Then put it in the blender with 2 cans of minced clams, including the juice, for 7 to 8 seconds, till it's thoroughly puréed.

    Then pour it into a saucepan and add 1½ cups of light cream (or

---

* Another thing I've noticed is that expert cooks seem to drain their spinach very hard, especially when it's going into a casserole. They practically stamp on it to get all the water out. It isn't all that important in soup though.

1½ cups of whole milk with a walnut-size chunk of butter) and bring it to just below the boil. Season it with salt, pepper, and a spatter of nutmeg. Good cold, too.

VOODOO SANDWICHES   *8–10 Servings*

(A two-stage operation—the onions need fixing the day before.
It all adds up to a rather subtle-tasting sandwich that's good with the
Philosopher's Chowder, say, or 2 canned soups combined: cream of
tomato with cream of celery, or cream of mushroom with cream of
oyster. They're good hearty canapés, too.)

The day before, slice 2 mild medium white onions into a deep bowl. Bring 1 cup water and ½ cup sugar to a boil and pour it over them. Now apply a layer of ice cubes and put the bowl in the refrigerator.

Next day, drain the onion slices and dry them between paper towels. Then mix:

1 cup mayonnaise
½ teaspoon dry mustard
1 teaspoon lemon juice

Spread good white bread with it, using the onion slices for filling, with a good sprinkle of salt and coarse-ground pepper. Trim the crusts, then cut into 4 triangles. Spread the edges with mayonnaise and dip the edges in chopped parsley (you'll need a large bunch). Then refrigerate them till lunchtime.

A good thing to know about onions, by the way, is how to make a strong harsh onion more presentable. You slice it thinly and pour boiling water on the slices. Then drain and chill them, and they'll emerge sweeter as well as crisper.

One other point: Knowledgeable cooks are often comforting as well as informative.

For example, I once saw one become annoyed at the way her eggs poached, or didn't—the whites disintegrating into ectoplasmic wisps. She was annoyed not at herself but at her grocer, for selling her stale eggs, which, she said, was the reason for their poor performance. I was glad to learn this. Knowing something isn't your fault can improve the morale if not the meal.

Or take Hollandaise. As indicated earlier, preoccupied cooks find Hollandaise about as dependable as false eyelashes in a wind tunnel, and the blender type (p. 112) is no help if you haven't a blender. I was delighted to learn from a good-cooking friend of mine about an absent-minded sour-cream dressing, affectionately known as:

CHANNEL TWO HOLLANDAISE

(To make before settling down with a noggin before dinner to watch the news.)

See to it that the water in the bottom of the double boiler is definitely below boiling. Just good and hot. In the top mix:

4 egg yolks
1 cup dairy sour cream
1 tablespoon lemon juice
dash of hot pepper sauce
½ teaspoon salt

Then go away. It doesn't much matter when you come back . . . 1 hour, 2 hours. Stir it thoroughly then, and it will be lovely on the fish. Or the broccoli. Or the asparagus . . .

Clearly, then, these knowledgeable cooks can be of assistance. They do know some tidy little ways of doing things, as well as some tidy little things to do.

But all this can be deceptive. You find yourself beginning to trust them. Until they come up, one day, with something like, "It's no trouble at all to poach a bit of sole in wine, then garnish it with cooked prawns to serve as a first course and show off your pretty fish forks!"

Statements like this make you realize that some of these people have a great respect for the truth—in fact, too much respect to use it just any old time.

23. Shutting the Garden Gate

NOW WHAT DID I FORGET THIS TIME?

"Farther along we'll know all about it . . .
Farther along we'll understand why. . . ."
—GOSPEL SONG

Like a love affair, a cookbook is probably easier to get into than out of. At the end of both, sins of commission and omission loom large. What was said that had better been left unsaid? Is the chocolate sauce really that good?* And what was not said that might have been? Shouldn't there have been some mention of brunches?†

In writing a cookbook, it is the possible omissions that are especially worrisome. The trouble is, a paragraph or a chapter can unexpectedly close its doors, leaving a perfectly good item outside. There stands the Mustard Sauce, looking for the ham.

* Yes.
† No.

265

That Mustard Sauce, by the way, runs into other things, as so many sauces do. Therefore, we may as well get into it now.

Here is the situation: many a devout non-cook depends heavily on a canned cooked ham for emergencies, like those times when she doesn't feel like cooking. This ham stays in the refrigerator, diminishing steadily once it is opened (for these emergency periods can last several days). But it doesn't quite disappear, because it's replaced by another, just before the shortage becomes critical. This is known as the ham-in-residence.

But on the third or fourth day, a simple sauce can provide a nice change of pace. This one has the additional advantage of tasting good on the neighboring vegetables, if they happen to be broccoli, asparagus, Brussels sprouts, or string beans.

GOLD SAUCE

In the top of a double boiler mix ½ cup sugar with 4 teaspoons of dry mustard and 1 teaspoon of salt.

In a bowl beat 2 eggs in ½ cup milk, pour this into the dry mixture, then add ½ cup vinegar and 4 tablespoons of melted butter. Cook it over gently boiling water for 15 minutes.

Now, something fast to go *with* the ham, if you're out of potato chips and time, is:

MOTHER BRADFORD'S RICE   *6–8 Servings*

*(Since Mother Bradford discovered this one, her family
hasn't tasted a baked potato.)*

In a saucepan put:

  1 can onion soup
  1 cup raw rice, any kind
  1 cup water

Cook it covered over medium heat until the rice is tender—about 25 minutes.

Another good thing to do with the h-in-r is the informal:

EGGS BENEDICT

Toast a soft roll half, butter it, lay a slice of warm ham on it, and a poached egg on top of that. Cover it with the Channel Two Hollandaise on p. 264. Asparagus goes very nicely with this.

Then, one other ploy I know of will sometimes distract attention from Ham Again.

FAST CHEESE BISCUITS

Mix together:

> 1 packet biscuit mix
> ½ cup grated Cheddar cheese
> 2 tablespoons dried onion

Add a beaten egg to it and milk as specified on the box. Stir till just moistened, then spread it out on a greased cake pan, and on the top sprinkle another ½ cup of cheese and a lot of poppy seeds. Bake it for 20 minutes or so at 400°F, till it's a lovely brown, like a freckled palomino.

And now your ham probably looks like an ha'penny's worth of soap after a hard week's wash, and you'd love to give it to the dog. But with just 2 cupfuls left you can still make a darned good:

END-OF-THE-LINE HAM CASSEROLE

1 can condensed cream of celery soup	3 medium potatoes, peeled and sliced
½ cup milk	1 medium onion, ditto
pepper	2 cups chopped ham

Mix the soup and milk, add a good grind of pepper, then layer things like this, in a casserole dish: potatoes, meat, onion, celery-soup-sauce. Cover and bake for an hour at 375°F. Then take the lid off, which makes it easier to sprinkle some grated cheese on top, and bake it uncovered for another 20 minutes.

Two good hearty dishes to go with a slice of that Ham (or any other cold meat):

1. JETTY SPAGHETTI

Into the blender put:

2 cups parsley, stripped from the stems	½ teaspoon pepper
1 teaspoon each: basil, oregano, marjoram, salt	½ teaspoon garlic powder
	½ cup olive oil

Blend it at a high speed; occasionally you'll have to push it down the sides with a spatula. Ten minutes before dinner time, cook and drain a pound of spaghetti (this will serve 8 to 10, so cut it in half for 4 or 5; no need to make less sauce, though, because it keeps) and mix it well with 3 tablespoons of butter. To it add ¼ cup chopped pecans or walnuts, and 2 tablespoons grated Parmesan cheese. Add the parsley sauce, see that it's all hot through, and serve.

2. WINE SPOON BREAD

3¼ cups milk	3 tablespoons butter
1 cup yellow cornmeal	4 eggs
1½ teaspoons salt	½ cup dry white wine

Scald the milk and stir in the cornmeal and salt. Put an oven mitt on your hand, because the stuff spatters, while you stir it for 3 or 4 minutes. When it's a good thick mush, take it off the heat and add the butter. Beat the eggs, and to them add the wine. Stir the mixture slowly into the hot mush, then pour it into a well-buttered casserole dish. Put the oven rack just a notch below the center of the oven and bake the spoon bread at 375°F for about an hour. When its top is a pretty puffy light brown, it's done. Serve.

So much for the ham then. It's a relief to get it cleared up.

Right here might be the place for a minor point that wouldn't fit in anywhere else, and it has been troubling me. I refer to the occasional value of television at the family meal.

It isn't all bad, though a delicate snobbery prevails in some groups which hold that televiewing at the table ranks with putting the ketchup bottle on it. Still, many people do that, too.*

---

* They probably wouldn't if the ketchup people would pack it in squat wide-mouthed pots, so it could be served in something pretty and then replaced. But nearly everyone has better things to do with her time than trying to reinsert ketchup into a ketchup bottle.

The fact is, the family's evening meal isn't always the lightsome, stimulating occasion it is in the picture books. Families are sometimes cross, as a result of too much togetherness—possibly a hangover from a long day *en famille* or simply the daily stresses that come from living around the clock.

Many fathers seem to feel put upon 32% of their dinnertimes. And mothers feel especially so when Dick and Jane are snooty about the food she thinks they ought to eat, and which she reluctantly but dutifully cooked.

Dr. William Kalb, consultant to the U.S. Food and Drug Administration in 1966 said: "There's no reason for a child to eat a particular food unless he wants to. If he doesn't want fish when he's 6, he may want it when he's 16—if you don't force the issue. There is no one food such as fish or spinach that is vital. If a child doesn't get his nutrients one way, he can get them another. Let the child eat what he wants providing he has enough protein, vitamins, and carbohydrates."

This could be of some small comfort. But I'm afraid I disagree that there's no reason for a child to eat a particular food unless he wants to. No one should grow up with a totally unadventurous palate, or he'll miss a lot of fun. Also, some tastes are acquired, and he might as well start acquiring them. Moreover, he should learn that an untouched plateful can hurt people's feelings, even his mother's.

However, when the atmosphere becomes sticky, for these and other reasons, a good television news program can keep everyone from brooding over how unpleasant everyone else is.

The children will learn more from it than they do from their father's "Butter, please." And the lady who cooked the dinner can get her mind off the whole thing and on to Southeast Asia or Off Broadway, or wherever the action is.

One more note belongs here—a few words for the family, not the cook.

As good audiences make good theater, good eaters make good— and happier—cooks. Though the reluctant cook will never really enjoy her kitchen work, punctuality, kind words, and clean plates are the carrots that will keep the donkey going.

Bouquets get better results than spitballs; and families had best keep this in mind if for no other reason than survival.

But space runs out, and we're on page 269 now, with things still left over, like the unwashed saucepan you usually find the minute you've cleaned the sink.

I had hoped to be able to mention the semi-recipe which a gentle-woman of my acquaintance says has saved her hide at many a lunch and supper time. She heats a can of tuna mixed with a can of undiluted condensed cream of mushroom soup, then fills avocado halves with it, covers them with crumbs, and bakes them for 20 minutes at 350°F.

Then, somehow, the sesame seeds got lost. I wanted to explain that if you toast one side of bread then butter the other, spread it thickly with sesame seeds, and brown *that* under the grill, it's good for breakfast. Cut in strips, it's good with salads, too.

But clearly there isn't space left to mention these things, or another helpful tidbit I had, something to do to fresh corn on the cob. Still, there's not much reason to do anything to fresh corn on the cob. Because it's really very good the way it is. . . .

There isn't room because I promised you that translation for The Famous Old Scripture Cake on p. 234. So here it is:

THE SCRIPTURE CAKE

GENESIS 18:8—"And he took *butter*, and milk, and the calf which he had dressed, and set it before them."

JEREMIAH 6:20—"To what purpose cometh there to me frankincense from Sheban, and the *sweet cane* from a far country?"

ISAIAH 10:14—"And my hand hath found as a nest the riches of the peoples; and as one gathereth *eggs* that are forsaken, have I gathered all the earth."

LEVITICUS 24:5—"And thou shalt take *fine flour*, and bake 12 cakes thereof."

II KINGS 2:20—"And he said, Bring me a new cruse, and put *salt* therein."

AMOS 4:5—"And offer a sacrifice of thanksgiving of that which is *leavened*, and proclaim free will offerings and publish them."

EXODUS 30:23—"Take thou also, unto these the chief spices: of flowering myrrh 500 shekels, and of *sweet cinnamon* half so much."

II CHRONICLES 9:9—"And she gave the king a hundred and twenty talents of gold, and *spices* in great abundance."

JUDGES 4:19—"And he said unto her, Give me, I pray thee, a little water to drink; for I am thirsty. And she opened a bottle of *milk* and gave him drink."

GENESIS 43:11—"Carry down the man a present, a little balm, and a little honey, spicery and myrrh, nuts and *almonds*."

JEREMIAH 24:5—"Thus saith Jehovah, God of Israel: Like these good *figs*, so will I regard the captives of Judah, whom I have sent out of this place into the land of the Chaldeans, for good."

II SAMUEL 16:1—"And when David was a little past the top of the ascent, behold, Ziba, the servant of Mephiboseth met him, with a couple of asses saddled, and upon them 200 loaves of bread, and a hundred clusters of *raisins*."

GENESIS 24:25—"And before I had done speaking in my heart, behold Rebekah came forth with her pitcher on her shoulder; and she went down to the *fountain*, and drew: and I said unto her, Let me drink, I pray thee."

I was finishing this book on the front porch, glancing out occasionally at the long march of eucalyptus trees lining the beach, and the green-grey reach of the Pacific beyond. And suddenly the eucalyptus trees, with their strong trunks and forked branches and blossomy tops, looked like broccoli, and the ocean was turtle soup.

This is what can happen. Cooking can become intrusive, the kitchen itself looming larger than life-size. But there's no need to let it. We'll just shut the garden gate quietly now, for it's time we all took off for wider horizons.

INDEX